Walter F. Adeney

The Song of Solomon, and the Lamentations of Jeremiah

Walter F. Adeney

The Song of Solomon, and the Lamentations of Jeremiah

ISBN/EAN: 9783337318253

Printed in Europe, USA, Canada, Australia, Japan

Cover: Foto ©Thomas Meinert / pixelio.de

More available books at **www.hansebooks.com**

THE EXPOSITOR'S BIBLE

EDITED BY THE REV.
W. ROBERTSON NICOLL, M.A., LL.D.
Editor of "The Expositor"

THE SONG OF SOLOMON

AND

THE LAMENTATIONS OF JEREMIAH

BY

WALTER F. ADENEY, M.A.

NEW YORK
A. C. ARMSTRONG AND SON
51 EAST TENTH STREET
1895

First Series, 1887-8.

Colossians.
By A. MACLAREN, D.D.
St. Mark.
By Very Rev. the Dean of Armagh.
Genesis.
By Prof. MARCUS DODS, D.D.
1 Samuel.
By Prof. W. G. BLAIKIE, D.D.
2 Samuel.
By the same Author.
Hebrews.
By Principal T. C. EDWARDS, D.D.

Second Series, 1888-9.

Galatians.
By Prof. G. G. FINDLAY, B.A.
The Pastoral Epistles.
By Rev. A. PLUMMER, D.D.
Isaiah I.—XXXIX.
By Prof. G. A. SMITH, D.D. Vol. I.
The Book of Revelation.
By Prof. W. MILLIGAN, D.D.
1 Corinthians.
By Prof. MARCUS DODS, D.D.
The Epistles of St. John.
By Rt. Rev. W. ALEXANDER, D.D.

Third Series, 1889-90.

Judges and Ruth.
By R. A. WATSON, M.A., D.D.
Jeremiah.
By Rev. C. J. BALL, M.A.
Isaiah XL.—LXVI.
By Prof. G. A. SMITH, D.D. Vol. II.
St. Matthew.
By Rev. J. MONRO GIBSON, D.D.
Exodus.
By Very Rev. the Dean of Armagh.
St. Luke.
By Rev. H. BURTON, M.A.

Fourth Series, 1890-1.

Ecclesiastes.
By Rev. SAMUEL COX, D.D.
St. James and St. Jude.
By Rev. A. PLUMMER, D.D.
Proverbs.
By Rev. R. F. HORTON, D.D.
Leviticus.
By Rev. S. H. KELLOGG, D.D.
The Gospel of St. John.
By Prof. M. DODS, D.D. Vol. I.
The Acts of the Apostles.
By Prof. STOKES, D.D. Vol. I.

Fifth Series, 1891-2.

The Psalms.
By A. MACLAREN, D.D. Vol. I.
1 and 2 Thessalonians.
By JAMES DENNEY, D.D.
The Book of Job.
By R. A. WATSON, M.A., D.D.
Ephesians.
By Prof. G. G. FINDLAY, B.A.
The Gospel of St. John.
By Prof. M. DODS, D.D. Vol. II.
The Acts of the Apostles.
By Prof. STOKES, D.D. Vol. II.

Sixth Series, 1892-3.

1 Kings.
By Ven. Archdeacon FARRAR.
Philippians.
By Principal RAINY, D.D.
Ezra, Nehemiah, Esther.
By Prof. W. F. ADENEY, M.A.
Joshua.
By Prof. W. G. BLAIKIE, D.D.
The Psalms.
By A. MACLAREN, D.D. Vol. II.
The Epistles of St. Peter.
By Prof. RAWSON LUMBY, D.D.

Seventh Series, 1893-4.

2 Kings.
By Ven. Archdeacon FARRAR.
Romans.
By H. C. G. MOULE, M.A.
The Books of Chronicles.
By Prof. W. H. BENNETT, M.A.
2 Corinthians.
By JAMES DENNEY, D.D.
Numbers.
By R. A. WATSON, M.A., D.D.
The Psalms.
By A. MACLAREN, D.D. Vol. III.

Eighth Series, 1895-6.

Daniel.
By Ven. Archdeacon FARRAR.
The Book of Jeremiah.
By Prof. W. H. BENNETT, M.A.
Deuteronomy.
By Prof. ANDREW HARPER, B.D.
The Song of Solomon and Lamentations.
By Prof. W. F. ADENEY, M.A.
Ezekiel.
By Prof. JOHN SKINNER, M.A.
The Minor Prophets.
By Prof. G. A. SMITH, D.D. Two Vols.

THE SONG OF SOLOMON

AND THE

LAMENTATIONS OF JEREMIAH

BY

WALTER F. ADENEY, M.A.

PROFESSOR OF NEW TESTAMENT EXEGESIS, AND CHURCH HISTORY,
NEW COLLEGE LONDON

NEW YORK
A. C. ARMSTRONG AND SON
51 EAST TENTH STREET
1895

CONTENTS

THE SONG OF SOLOMON

CHAPTER I

	PAGE
THE STRUCTURE OF THE BOOK .	3

CHAPTER II

| TRUE LOVE TESTED | 15 |
| i.–v. 1. | |

CHAPTER III

| LOVE UNQUENCHABLE . . | 28 |
| v. 1–viii. | |

CHAPTER IV

| MYSTICAL INTERPRETATIONS . | 41 |

CHAPTER V

| CANONICITY . , . . . | 53 |

THE LAMENTATIONS OF JEREMIAH

CHAPTER I
HEBREW ELEGIES . . . 63

CHAPTER II
THE ORIGIN OF THE POEMS . 75

CHAPTER III
THE THEME . . . 87

CHAPTER IV
DESOLATION 97
i. 1-7.

CHAPTER V
SIN AND SUFFERING 108
i. 8-11.

CHAPTER VI
ZION'S APPEAL 120
i. 12-22.

CHAPTER VII
GOD AS AN ENEMY . . . 132
ii. 1-9.

CHAPTER VIII
THE CRY OF THE CHILDREN . 144
ii. 10-17.

CHAPTER IX

PROPHETS WITHOUT A VISION . . 156
ii. 9, 14.

CHAPTER X

THE CALL TO PRAYER . . 168
ii. 18-22.

CHAPTER XI

THE MAN THAT HATH SEEN AFFLICTION 180
iii. 1-21.

CHAPTER XII

THE UNFAILING GOODNESS OF GOD . . 194
iii. 22-24.

CHAPTER XIII

QUIET WAITING 206
iii. 25-36.

CHAPTER XIV

GOD AND EVIL . . . 218
iii. 37-39.

CHAPTER XV

THE RETURN . . . 230
iii. 40-42.

CHAPTER XVI

GRIEVING BEFORE GOD . . . 242
iii. 43-54.

CHAPTER XVII

DE PROFUNDIS 253
iii. 55-66.

CHAPTER XVIII

CONTRASTS 265
iv. 1-12.

CHAPTER XIX

LEPERS 277
iv. 13-16.

CHAPTER XX

VAIN HOPES . . . 288
iv. 17-20.

CHAPTER XXI

THE DEBT OF GUILT EXTINGUISHED . . 300
iv. 21, 22.

CHAPTER XXII

AN APPEAL FOR GOD'S COMPASSION . . 311
v. 1-10.

CHAPTER XXIII

SIN AND SHAME 324
v. 11-18.

CHAPTER XXIV

THE EVERLASTING THRONE 335
v. 19-22.

THE SONG OF SOLOMON

CHAPTER I

THE STRUCTURE OF THE BOOK

THE Song of Solomon is a puzzle to the commentator. Quite apart from the wilderness of mystical interpretations with which it has been overgrown in the course of the ages,[1] its literary form and motive are subjects of endless controversy. There are indications that it is a continuous poem; and yet it is characterised by startling kaleidoscopic changes that seem to break it up into incongruous fragments. If it is a single work the various sections of it succeed one another in the most abrupt manner, without any connecting links or explanatory clauses.

The simplest way out of the difficulty presented by the many curious turns and changes of the poem is to deny it any structural unity, and treat it as a string of independent lyrics. That is to cut the knot in a rather disappointing fashion. Nevertheless the suggestion to do so met with some favour when it was put forth at the close of the last century by Herder, a writer who seemed better able to enter into the spirit of Hebrew poetry than any of his contemporaries. While accepting the traditional view of the authorship of the book, this critic described its contents as " Solomon's songs of love, the oldest and sweetest of the East;" and

---

[1] To be considered later. See chap. iv.

Goethe in the world of letters, as well as biblical students, endorsed his judgment. Subsequently it fell into disfavour, and scholars who differed among themselves with respect to their own theories, agreed in rejecting this particular hypothesis. But quite recently it has reappeared in an altered form. The book, it is now suggested, is just a chance collection of folk songs from northern Palestine, an anthology of rustic love-poems. These songs are denied any connection with Solomon or the court. The references to royalty are accounted for by a custom said to be kept up among the Syrian peasants in the present day, according to which the week of wedding festivities is called "The king's week," because the newly-married pair then play the part of king and queen, and are playfully treated by their friends with the honours of a court. The bridegroom is supposed to be named Solomon in acknowledgment of his regal splendour—as an English villager might be so named for his conspicuous wisdom; while perhaps the bride is called the Shulammite, with an allusion to the famous beauty Abishag, the Shunammite of David's time.[1]

Such a theory as this is only admissible on condition that the unity of the poem has been disproved. But whether we can unravel it or not, there is much that goes to show that one thread runs through the whole book. The style is the same throughout, and it has no parallel in the whole of Hebrew literature. Everywhere we meet with the same rich, luxurious language, the same abundance of imagery, the same picturesque habit of alluding to a number of plants and animals by name, the same vivacity of movement, the same plead-

---

[1] 1 Kings i. 3.

ing tone, the same suffused glow as of the light of morning. Then there are more peculiar features that continually recur, such as the form of the dialogue, certain recognisable characters, the part of chorus taken by the daughters of Jerusalem, in particular the gentle, graceful portrait of the Shulammite, the consistency of which is well preserved. But the principal reason for believing in the unity of the work is to be found in an examination of its plot. The difficulty of making this out has encouraged the temptation to discredit its existence. But while there are various ideas about the details, there is enough in common to all the proposed schemes of the story to indicate the fact that the book is one composition.

The question whether the work is a drama or an idyl has been discussed with much critical acumen. But is it not rather pedantic? The sharply divided orders of European poetry were not observed or even known in Israel. It was natural, therefore, that Hebrew imaginative work should partake of the characteristics of several orders, while too naïve to trouble itself with the rules of any one. The drama designed for acting was not cultivated by the ancient Jews. It was introduced as an exotic only as late as the Roman period, when Herod built the first theatre known to have existed in the Holy Land. Previous to his time we have no mention of the art of play-acting among the Jews. Nevertheless the dialogues in the Song of Solomon are certainly dramatic in character; and we cannot call the poem an idyl when it is rendered entirely in the form of speeches by different persons without any connecting narrative. The Book of Job is also dramatic in form, though, like Browning's dramatic poetry, not designed for acting; but in that work each of the several speakers is introduced by a sentence that indicates who he is, while in our poem no such indication is given. Here we only get evidence of a change of speakers in the form and contents of the utterances, and the transition from the masculine to the feminine gender and from the singular number to the plural. Even the chorus takes an active part in the movement of the dialogue, instead of simply commenting on the proceedings of the principal characters as in a Greek play. We seem to want a key to the story, and the absence of anything of the kind is the occasion of the bewildering variety of conjectures that confronts the reader. But the difficulty thus occasioned is no reason for denying that there is any continuity in the book, especially in view of numerous signs of unity that cannot be evaded.

Among those who accept the dramatic integrity of the poem there are two distinct lines of interpretation, each of them admitting some differences in the treatment of detail. According to one scheme Solomon is the only lover; according to the other, while the king is seeking to win the affections of the country maiden, he has been forestalled by a shepherd, fidelity to whom is shewn by the Shulammite in spite of the fascinations of the court.

There is no denying the rural simplicity of much of the scenery; evidently this is designed to be in contrast to the sensuous luxury and splendour of the court. Those who take Solomon to be the one lover throughout, not only admit this fact; they bring it into their version of the story so as to heighten the effect. The king is out holiday-making, perhaps on a hunting expedition, when he first meets the country maiden. In her childlike simplicity she takes him for a rustic swain; or perhaps, though she knows who he is, she sportively addresses him as she would address one of her village companions. Subsequently she shews no liking for the pomp of royalty. She cannot make herself at home with the women of the harem. She longs to be back in her mother's cottage among the woods and fields where she spent her child days. But she loves the king and he dotes on her. So she would ake him with her away from the follies and temptations of the court down to her quiet country retreat. Under the influence of the Shulammite Solomon is induced to give up his unworthy habits and live a healthier, purer life. Her love is strong enough to retain the king wholly to herself. Thus the poem is said to describe a reformation in the character of Solomon. In particular it is thought to celebrate the triumph of true love over the degradation of polygamy.

It is impossible to find any time in the life of David's successor when this great conversion might have taken place; and the occurrence itself is highly improbable. Those however are not fatal objections to the proposed scheme, because the poem may be entirely ideal; it may even be written *at* the king. Historical considerations need not trouble us in dealing with an imaginative work such as this. It must be judged entirely on internal grounds. But when it is so judged it refuses to come into line with the interpretation suggested. Regarding the matter only from a literary point of view, we must confess that it is most improbable that Solomon would be introduced as a simple peasant without any hint of the reason of his appearing in this novel guise. Then we may detect a difference between the manner in which the king addresses the Shulammite and that in which, on the second hypothesis, the shepherd speaks to her. Solomon's compliments are frigid and stilted; they describe the object of his admiration in the most extravagant terms, but they exhibit no trace of feeling. The heart of the voluptuary is withered, the fires of passion have burnt themselves out and only the cold ashes remain, the sacred word "love" has been so long desecrated that it has ceased to convey any meaning. On the other hand, frequent practice has outstripped the clumsy wooing of inexperienced lovers and developed the art of courtship to a high degree. The royal bird-catcher knows how to lay his lines, though fortunately for once even his consummate skill fails. How different is the bearing of the true lover, a village lad who has won the maiden's heart! He has no need to resort to the vocabulary of flattery, because his own heart speaks. The English translations give an unwarrantable appearance of warmth to the king's language where he is represented as calling the Shulammite "My love."[1] The word in the Hebrew means no more than *my friend*. When Solomon first appears he addresses the Shulammite with this title, and then immediately tries to tempt her by promising her presents of jewelry. Take another instance. In the beginning of the fourth chapter Solomon enters on an elaborate series of compliments describing the beauty of the Shulammite, without a single word of affection. As she persists in withstanding his advances her persecutor becomes abashed. He shrinks from her pure, cold gaze, calls her terrible as an army with banners, prays her to turn away her eyes from him. On the theory that Solomon is the accepted lover, the beloved bridegroom,

---

[1] i. 9.

this position is quite unintelligible. Now turn to the language of the true lover: "Thou hast ravished my heart, my sister, my bride; thou hast ravished my heart with one look of thine eyes."[1]

A corresponding difference is to be detected in the bearing of the maiden towards the rivals. Towards the king she is cool and repellent; but no dream of poetry can equal the tenderness and sweetness of her musing on her absent lover or the warmth of love with which she speaks to him. These distinctions will be more apparent in detail as we proceed with the story of the poem. It may be noticed here, that this story is not at all consistent with the theory that Solomon is the only lover. According to that hypothesis we have the highly improbable situation of a separation of the newly married couple on their wedding day. Besides, as the climax is supposed to be reached at the middle of the book, there is no apparent motive for the second half. The modern novel, which has its wedding at the middle of its plot, or even at the very beginning, and then sets itself to develop the comedy or perhaps the tragedy of married life, is not at all parallel to this old love story. Time must be allowed for the development of matrimonial complications; but here the scenes are all in close connection.

If we are thus led to accept what has been called "the shepherd hypothesis" the value of the book will be considerably enhanced. This is more than a mere love poem; it is not to be classed with erotics, although a careless reading of some of its passages might incline us to place it in the same category with a purely sensuous style of poetry. We have here

---

[1] iv. 9.

something more than Sappho's fire. If we are tempted to compare it with Herrick's *Hesperides* or Shakespeare's *Sonnets*, we must recognise an element that lifts it above the sighs of love-sick youths and maidens. Even on the "Solomon theory" pure love and simple living are exalted in opposition to the luxury and vices of the royal seraglio. A poem that sets forth the beauty of a simple country life as the scene of the true love of husband and wife in contrast to the degradation of a corrupt court is distinctly elevating in tone and influence, and the more so for the fact that it is not didactic in form. It is not only in kings' palaces and amid scenes of oriental voluptuousness that the influence of such ideas as are here presented is needed. Christian civilisation has not progressed beyond the condition in which the consideration of them may be resorted to as a wholesome corrective. But if we are to agree to the "shepherd hypothesis" as on the whole the more probable, another idea of highest importance emerges. It is not love, now, but fidelity, that claims our attention. The simple girl, protected only by her virtue, who is proof against all the fascinations of the most splendid court, and who prefers to be the wife of the poor man whom she loves, and to whom she has plighted troth, to accepting a queen's crown at the cost of deserting her humble lover, is the type and example of a loyalty which is the more admirable because it appears where we should little expect to find it. It has been said that such a story as is here depicted would be impossible in real life; that a girl once enticed into the harem of an oriental despot would never have a chance of escape. The eunuchs who guarded the doors would lose their heads if they allowed her to run away; the king would never give up the prey that had fallen into his trap; the shepherd lover who was mad enough to pursue his lost sweetheart. into her captor's palace would never come out alive. Are we so sure of all these points? Most improbable things do happen. It is at least conceivable that even a cruel tyrant might be seized with a fit of generosity, and why should we regard Solomon as a cruel tyrant? His fame implies that there were noble traits in his character. But these questions are beside the mark. The situation is wholly ideal. Then the more improbable the events described would be in real life, the more impressive do the lessons they suggest become.

Who wrote the book? The only answer that can be given to this question is negative. Assuredly, Solomon could not have been the author of this lovely poem in praise of the love and fidelity of a country lass and her swain, and the simplicity of their rustic life. It would be difficult to find a man in all history who more conspicuously illustrated the exact opposites of these ideas. The exquisite eulogy of love—perhaps the finest in any literature—which occurs towards the end of the book, the passage beginning, "Set me as a seal upon thine heart," etc.,[1] is not the work of this master of a huge seraglio, with his "seven hundred wives" and his "three hundred concubines."[2] It is impossible to find the source of this poetry in the palace of the Israelite "Grand Monarch"; we might as soon light on a bank of wild flowers in a Paris dancing saloon. There is quite a library of Solomon literature, a very small part of which can be traced to the king whose name it bears, the greatness of this name having

---

[1] viii. 6, 7.   [2] 1 Kings xi. 3.

attracted attention and led to the ascription of various works to the royal author, whose wisdom was as proverbial as his splendour. It is difficult to resist the impression that in the present case there is some irony in the singular inappropriateness of the title.

The date of the poem can be conjectured with some degree of assurance, although the language does not help us much in the determination of this point. There are archaisms, and there are also terms that seem to indicate a late date—Aramaic words and possibly even words of Greek extraction. The few foreign terms may have crept in under the influence of revisers. On the other hand the style and contents of the book speak for the days of the Augustan age of Hebrew history. The notoriety of Solomon's court and memories of its magnificence and luxury seem to be fresh in the minds of people. These things are treated in detail and with an amount of freedom that supposes knowledge on the part of the readers as well as the writer. There is one expression that helps to fix the date with more definiteness. Tirzah is associated with Jerusalem as though the two cities were of equal importance. The king says:—

> "Thou art beautiful, O my love, as Tirzah,
> Comely as Jerusalem."[1]

Now this city was the northern capital for about fifty years after the death of Solomon—from the time of Jeroboam, who made it his royal residence,[2] till the reign of Omri, who abandoned the ill-omened place six years after his vanquished predecessor Zimri had burnt the palace over his own head.[3] The way in

---

[1] vi. 4.   [2] 1 Kings xiv. 17.   [3] 1 Kings xvi. 18, 23, 24.

which the old capital is mentioned here implies that it is still to the north what Jerusalem is to the south. Thus we are brought to the half century after the death of the king whose name the book bears.

The mention of Tirzah as the equal of Jerusalem is also an evidence of the northern origin of the poem; for it is not at all probable that a subject of the mutilated nation of the south would describe the beauty of the rebel headquarters by the side of that of his own idolised city, as something typical and perfect. But the poem throughout gives indications of its origin in the country parts of the north. Shunem, famous as the scene of Elisha's great miracle, seems to be the home of the heroine.[1] The poet turns to all points of the compass for images with which to enrich his pictures— Sharon on the western coast,[2] Gilead across the Jordan to the east,[3] Engedi by the wilderness of the Dead Sea,[4] as well as the northern districts. But the north is most frequently mentioned. Lebanon is named over and over again,[5] and Hermon is referred to as in the neighbourhood of the shepherd's home.[6] In fact the poem is saturated with the fragrant atmosphere of the northern mountains.

Now this has suggested a striking inference. Here we have a picture of Solomon and his court from the not too friendly hand of a citizen of the revolted provinces. The history in the Books of Kings is written from the standpoint of Judah; it is curious to learn how the people of the north thought of Solomon in all his glory. Thus considered the book acquires a secondary and political meaning. It appears as a

---

[1] vi. 13.   [3] iv. 1.   [5] iii. 9; iv. 8, 15; vii. 4.
[2] ii. 1.   [4] i. 14.   [6] iv. 8.

scornful condemnation of the court at Jerusalem on the part of the poorer and more simple inhabitants of the kingdom of Jeroboam and his successors.[1] But it also stands for all time as a protest against luxury and vice, and as a testimony to the beauty and dignity of pure love, stanch fidelity, and quiet, wholesome, primitive country manners. It breathes the spirit that reappears in Goldsmith's *Deserted Village*, and inspires the muse of Wordsworth, as in the poem which contrasts the dove's simple notes with the nightingale's tumultuous song, saying of the homely bird,

> "He sang of love with quiet blending;
> Slow to begin, and never ending;
> Of serious faith and inward glee;
> That was the song—the song for me."

---

[1] See *Ency. Brit.*, Art. "Canticles," by Robertson Smith.

CHAPTER II

TRUE LOVE TESTED

CHAPTER i.—v. 1

THE poem opens with a scene in Solomon's palace. A country maiden has just been introduced to the royal harem. The situation is painful enough in itself, for the poor, shy girl is experiencing the miserable loneliness of finding herself in an unsympathetic crowd. But that is not all. She is at once the object of general observation; every eye is turned towards her; and curiosity is only succeeded by ill-concealed disgust. Still the slavish women, presumably acting on command, set themselves to excite the new comer's admiration for their lord and master. First one speaks some bold amorous words,[1] and then the whole chorus follows.[2] All this is distressing and alarming to the captive, who calls on her absent lover to fetch her away from such an uncongenial scene; she longs to run after him; for it is the king who has brought her into his chambers, not her own will.[3] The women of the harem take no notice of this interruption, but finish their ode on the charms of Solomon. All the while they are staring at the rustic maiden, and she now becomes conscious of a growing contempt in their looks. What is she that the attractions of the king before which the dainty

---

[1] i. 2.   [2] i. 3.   [3] i. 4.

ladies of the court prostrate themselves should have no fascination for her? She notices the contrast between the swarthy hue of her sun-burnt countenance and the pale complexion of these pampered products of palace seclusion. She is so dark in comparison with them that she likens herself to the black goats-hair tents of the Arabs.[1] The explanation is that her brothers have made her work in their vineyards. Meanwhile she has not kept her own vineyard.[2] She has not guarded her beauty as these idle women, who have nothing else to do, have guarded theirs; but perhaps she has a sadder thought—she could not protect herself when out alone at her task in the country or she would never have been captured and carried off to the prison where she now sits disconsolate. Possibly the vineyard she has not kept is the lover whom she has lost.[3] Still she is a woman, and with a touch of piqued pride she reminds her critics that if she is dark—black compared with them—she is comely. They cannot deny that. It is the cause of all her misery; she owes her imprisonment to her beauty. She knows that their secret feeling is one of envy of her, the latest favourite. Then their affected contempt is groundless. But, indeed, she has no desire to stand as their rival. She would gladly make her escape. She speaks in a half soliloquy. Will not somebody tell her where he is whom her soul loveth? Where is her lost shepherd lad? Where is he feeding his flock? Where is he resting it at noon? Such questions only provoke mockery. Addressing the simple girl as the "fairest among women," the court ladies bid her find her lover for herself. Let her go back to her

---

[1] i. 5.   [2] i. 6.   [3] See viii. 12.

country life and feed her kids by the shepherds' tents. Doubtless if she is bold enough to court her swain in that way she will not miss seeing him.

Hitherto Solomon has not appeared. Now he comes on the scene, and proceeds to accost his new acquisition in highly complimentary language, with the ease of an expert in the art of courtship. At this point we encounter the most serious difficulty for the theory of a shepherd lover. To all appearances a dialogue between the king and the Shulammite here ensues.[1] But if this were the case, the country girl would be addressing Solomon in terms of the utmost endearment —conduct utterly incompatible with the "shepherd hypothesis." The only alternative is to suppose that the hard-pressed girl takes refuge from the importunity of her royal flatterer by turning aside to an imaginary, half dream-like conversation with her absent lover. This is not by any means a probable position, it must be allowed; it seems to put a strained interpretation on the text. Undoubtedly if the passage before us stood by itself, there would not be any difference of opinion about it; everybody would take it in its obvious meaning as a conversation between two lovers. But it does not stand by itself—unless, indeed, we are to give up the unity of the book. Therefore it must be interpreted so as not to contradict the whole course of the poem, which shews that another than Solomon is the true lover of the disconsolate maiden.

The king begins with the familiar device by which rich men all the world over try to win the confidence of poor girls when there is no love on either side,—a device which has been only too successful in the case

---

[1] i. 9—ii. 6.

of many a weak Marguerite though her tempter has not always been a handsome Faust; but in the present case innocence is fortified by true love, and the trick is a failure. The king notices that this peasant girl has but simple plaited hair and homely ornaments. She shall have plaits of gold and studs of silver! Splendid as one of Pharaoh's chariot horses, she shall be decorated as magnificently as they are decorated! What is this to our stanch heroine? She treats it with absolute indifference, and begins to soliloquise, with a touch of scorn in her language. She has been loaded with scent after the manner of the luxurious court, and the king while seated feasting at his table has caught the odour of the rich perfumes. That is why he is now by her side. Does he think that she will serve as a new dainty for the great banquet, as a fresh fillip for the jaded appetite of the royal voluptuary? If so he is much mistaken. The king's promises have no attraction for her, and she turns for relief to dear memories of her true love. The thought of him is fragrant as the bundle of myrrh she carries in her bosom, as the henna-flowers that bloom in the vineyards of far-off Engedi.

Clearly Solomon has made a clumsy move. This shy bird is not of the common species with which he is familiar. He must aim higher if he would bring down his quarry. She is not to be classed with the wares of the matrimonial market that are only waiting to be assigned to the richest bidder. She cannot be bought even by the wealth of a king's treasury. But if there is a woman who can resist the charms of finery, is there one who can stand against the admiration of her personal beauty? A man of Solomon's experience would scarcely believe that such was to be found.

Nevertheless now the sex he estimates too lightly is to be vindicated, while the king himself is to be taught a wholesome lesson. He may call her fair; he may praise her dove-like eyes.[1] His flattery is lost upon her. She only thinks of the beauty of her shepherd lad, and pictures to herself the green bank on which they used to sit, with the cedars and firs for the beams and roof of their trysting-place.[2] Her language carries us away from the gilded splendour and close, perfumed atmosphere of the royal palace to scenes such as Shakespeare presents in the forest of Arden and the haunts of Titania, and Milton in the Mask of *Comus*. Here is a Hebrew lady longing to escape from the clutches of one who for all his glory is not without some of the offensive traits of the monster Comus. She thinks of herself as a wild flower, like the crocus that grows on the plains of Sharon or the lily (literally the anemone) that is sprinkled so freely over the upland valleys.[3] The open country is the natural *habitat* of such a plant, not the stifling court. Solomon catches at her beautiful imagery. Compared with other maidens she is like a lily among thorns.[4]

And now these scenes of nature carry the persecuted girl away in a sort of reverie. If she is like the tender flower, her lover resembles the apple tree at the foot of which it nestles, a tree the shadow of which is delightful and its fruit sweet.[5] She remembers how he brought her to his banqueting house; that rustic bower was a very different place from the grand divan on which she had seen Solomon sitting at his table. No purple hangings like those of the king's palace there

---

[1] i. 15.
[2] i. 16, 17.
[3] ii. 1.
[4] ii. 2.
[5] ii. 3.

screened her from the sun. The only banner her shepherd could spread over her was love, his own love.[1] But what could be a more perfect shelter?

She is fainting. How she longs for her lover to comfort her! She has just compared him to an apple tree; now the refreshment she hungers for is the fruit of this tree; that is to say, his love.[2] Oh that he would put his arms round her and support her, as in the old happy days before she had been snatched away from him![3]

Next follows a verse which is repeated later, and so serves as a sort of refrain.[4] The Shulammite adjures the daughters of Jerusalem not to awaken love. This verse is misrendered in the Authorised Version, which inserts the pronoun "my" before "love" without any warrant in the Hebrew text. The poor girl has spoken of apples. But the court ladies must not misunderstand her. She wants none of their love apples,[5] no philtre, no charm to turn her affections away from her shepherd lover and pervert them to the importunate royal suitor. The opening words of the poem which celebrated the charms of Solomon had been aimed in that direction. The motive of the work seems to be the Shulammite's resistance to various attempts to move her from loyalty to her true love. It is natural, therefore, that an appeal to desist from all such attempts should come out emphatically.

The poem takes a new turn. In imagination the Shulammite hears the voice of her beloved. She pictures him standing at the foot of the lofty rock on which the harem is built, and crying,—

---

[1] ii. 4. [3] ii. 6. [5] See Gen. xxx. 14.
[2] ii. 5. [4] ii. 7.

> "Oh, my dove, that art in the clefts of the rock, in the cover
> of the steep place,
> Let me see thy countenance, let me hear thy voice;
> For sweet is thy voice, and thy countenance is comely."[1]

He is like a troubadour singing to his imprisoned lady-love; and she, in her soliloquys, though not by any means a "high-born maiden," may call to mind the simile in Shelley's *Skylark* :—

> "Like a high-born maiden
> In a palace tower,
> Soothing her love-laden
> Soul in secret hour,
> With music sweet as love, which overflows her bower."

She remembers how her lover had come to her bounding over the hills "like a roe or a young hart,"[2] and peeping in at her lattice; and she repeats the song with which he had called her out—one of the sweetest songs of spring that ever was sung.[3] In our own green island we acknowledge that this is the most beautiful season of all the round year; but in Palestine it stands out in more strongly pronounced contrast to the three other seasons, and it is in itself exceedingly lovely. While summer and autumn are there parched with drought, barren and desolate, and while winter is often dreary with snow-storms and floods of rain, in spring the whole land is one lovely garden, ablaze with richest hues, hill and dale, wilderness and farm-land vying in the luxuriance of their wild flowers, from the red anemone that fires the steep sides of the mountains to the purple and white cyclamen that nestles among the rocks at their feet. Much of the beauty of this poem is found in the fact that it is pervaded by

---

[1] ii. 14. [2] ii. 9. [3] ii. 11-13.

the spirit of an eastern spring. This makes it possible to introduce a wealth of beautiful imagery which would not have been appropriate if any other season had been chosen. Even more lovely in March than England is in May, Palestine comes nearest to the appearance of our country in the former month; so that this poem, that is so completely bathed in the atmosphere of early spring, calls up echoes of the exquisite English garden pictures in Shelley's *Sensitive Plant* and Tennyson's *Maud*. But it is not only beauty of imagery that our poet gains by setting his work in this lovely season. His ideas are all in harmony with the period of the year he describes so charmingly. It is the time of youth and hope, of joy and love—especially of love, for,

"In the spring a young man's fancy
Lightly turns to thoughts of love."

There is even a deeper association between the ideas of the poem and the season in which it is set. None of the freshness of spring is to be found about Solomon and his harem, but it is all present in the Shulammite and her shepherd; and spring scenes and thoughts powerfully aid the motive of the poem in accentuating the contrast between the tawdry magnificence of the court and the pure, simple beauty of the country life to which the heroine of the poem clings so faithfully.

The Shulammite answers her lover in an old ditty about "the little foxes that spoil the vineyards."[1] He would recognise that, and so discover her presence. We are reminded of the legend of Richard's page finding his master by singing a familiar ballad outside the walls of the castle in the Tyrol where the captive crusader

---

[1] ii. 15.

was imprisoned. This is all imaginary. And yet the faithful girl knows in her heart that her beloved is hers and that she is his, although in sober reality he is now feeding his flocks in the far-off flowery fields of her old home.[1] There he must remain till the cool of the evening, till the shadows melt into the darkness of night, when she would fain he returned to her, coming over the rugged mountains "like a roe or a young hart."[2]

Now the Shulammite tells a painful dream.[3] She dreamed that she had lost her lover, and that she rose up at night and went out into the streets seeking him. At first she failed to find him. She asked the watchmen whom she met on their round, if they had seen him whom her soul loved. They could not help her quest. But a little while after leaving them she discovered the missing lover, and brought him safely into her mother's house.

After a repetition of the warning to the daughters of Jerusalem not to awaken love,[4] we are introduced to a new scene.[5] It is by one of the gates of Jerusalem, where the country maiden has been brought in order that she may be impressed by the gorgeous spectacle of Solomon returning from a royal progress. The king comes up from the wilderness in clouds of perfume, guarded by sixty men-at-arms, and borne in a magnificent palanquin of cedar-wood, with silver posts, a floor of gold, and purple cushions, wearing on his head the crown with which his mother had crowned him. Is the mention of the mother of Solomon intended to be specially significant ? Remember—she was Bath-

---

[1] ii. 16.   [3] iii. 1-4.   [5] iii. 6-11.
[2] ii. 17.   [4] iii. 5.

sheba! The allusion to such a woman would not be likely to conciliate the pure young girl who was not in the least degree moved by this attempt to charm her with a scene of exceptional magnificence.

Solomon now appears again, praising his captive in extravagant language of courtly flattery. He praises her dove-like eyes, her voluminous black hair, her rosy lips, her noble brow (not even disguised by her veil), her towering neck, her tender bosom—lovely as twin gazelles that feed among the lilies. Like her lover, who is necessarily away with his flock, Solomon will leave her till the cool of the evening, till the shadows melt into night; but he has no pastoral duties to attend to, and though the delicate balancing and assimilation of phrase and idea is gracefully manipulated, there is a change. The king will go to "mountains of myrrh" and "hills of frankincense,"[1] to make his person more fragrant, and so, as he hopes, more welcome.

If we adopt the "shepherd hypothesis" the next section of the poem must be assigned to the rustic lover.[2] It is difficult to believe that this peasant would be allowed to speak to a lady in the royal harem. We might suppose that here and perhaps also in the earlier scene the shepherd is represented as actually present at the foot of the rock on which the palace stands. Otherwise this also must be taken as an imaginary scene, or as a reminiscence of the dreamy girl. Although a thread of unity runs through the whole poem, Goethe was clearly correct in calling it "a medley." Scenes real and imaginary melting one into another cannot take their places in a regular

---

[1] iv. 6.   [2] iv. 8-15.

drama. But when we grant full liberty to the imaginary element there is less necessity to ask what is subjective and what objective, what only fancied by the Shulammite and what intended to be taken as an actual occurrence. Strictly speaking, nothing is actual ; the whole poem is a highly imaginative series of fancy pictures illustrating the development of its leading ideas.

Next—whether we take it as in imagination or in fact—the shepherd lover calls his bride to follow him from the most remote regions. His language is entirely different from that of the magnificent monarch. He does not waste his breath in formal compliments, high-flown imagery, wearisome lists of the charms of the girl he loves. That was the clumsy method of the king ; clumsy, though reflecting the finished manners of the court, in comparison with the genuine outpourings of the heart of a country lad. The shepherd is eloquent with the inspiration of true love ; his words throb and glow with genuine emotion ; there is a fine, wholesome passion in them. The love of his bride has ravished his heart. How beautiful is her love! He is intoxicated with it more than with wine. How sweet are her words of tender affection, like milk and honey! She is so pure, there is something sisterly in her love with all its warmth. And she is so near to him that she is almost like part of himself, as his own sister. This holy and close relationship is in startling contrast to the only thing known as love in the royal harem. It is as much more lofty and noble as it is more strong and deep than the jaded emotions of the court. The sweet pure maiden is to the shepherd like a garden the gate of which is barred against trespassers, like a spring shut off from 'casual access,' like a sealed fountain—sealed to all but one, and, happy man, he is that one. To him she belongs, to him alone. She is a garden, yes, a most fragrant garden, an orchard of pomegranates full of rich fruit, crowded with sweet-scented plants—henna and spikenard and saffron, calamus and cinnamon and all kinds of frankincense, myrrh and aloes and the best of spices. She is a fountain in the garden, sealed to all others, but not stinted towards the one she loves. To him she is as a well of living waters, like the full-fed streams that flow from Lebanon.

The maiden is supposed to hear the song of love. She replies in fearless words of welcome, bidding the north wind awake, and the south wind too, that the fragrance of which her lover has spoken so enthusiastically may flow out more richly than ever. For his sake she would be more sweet and loving. All she possesses is for him. Let him come and take possession of his own.[1]

What lover could turn aside from such a rapturous invitation? The shepherd takes his bride; he enters his garden, gathers his myrrh and spice, eats his honey and drinks his wine and milk, and calls on his friends to feast and drink with him.[2] This seems to point to the marriage of the couple and their wedding feast; a view of the passage which interpreters who regard Solomon as the lover throughout for the most part take, but one which has this fatal objection, that it leaves the second half of the poem without a motive. On the hypothesis of the shepherd lover it is still more difficult to suppose the wedding to have occurred at the point we have now reached, for the distraction of

---

[1] iv. 16.   [2] v. 1

the royal courtship still proceeds in subsequent passages of the poem. It would seem, then, that we must regard this as quite an ideal scene. It may, however, be taken as a reminiscence of an earlier passage in the lives of the two lovers. It is not impossible that it refers to their wedding, and that they had been married before the action of the whole story began. In that case we should have to suppose that Solomon's officers had carried off a young bride to the royal harem. The intensity of the love and the bitterness of the separation apparent throughout the poem would be the more intelligible if this were the situation. It is to be remembered that Shakespeare ascribes the climax of the love and grief of Romeo and Juliet to a time after their marriage. But the difficulty of accepting this view lies in the improbability that so outrageous a crime would be attributed to Solomon, although it must be admitted that the guilty conduct of his father and mother had gone a long way in setting an example for the violation of the marriage tie. In dealing with vague and dreamy poetry such as that of the Song of Solomon, it is not possible to determine a point like this with precision; nor is it necessary to do so. The beauty and force of the passage now before us centre in the perfect mutual love of the two young hearts that here show themselves to be knit together as one, whether already actually married or not yet thus externally united.

CHAPTER III

LOVE UNQUENCHABLE

CHAPTER v. 1-viii

WE have seen how this strange poem mingles fact and fancy, memory and reverie, in what would be hopeless confusion if we could not detect a common prevailing sentiment and one aim towards which the whole is tending, with all its rapidly shifting scenes and all its perplexingly varying movements. The middle of the poem attains a perfect climax of love and rapture. Then we are suddenly transported to an entirely different scene. The Shulammite recites a second dream, which somewhat resembles her former dream, but is more vivid and intense, and ends very painfully.[1] The circumstances of it will agree most readily with the idea that she is already married to the shepherd. Again it is a dream of the loss of her lover, and of her search for him by night in the streets of Jerusalem. But in the present case he was first close to her, and then he deserted her most unaccountably; and when she went to look for him this time she failed to find him, and met with cruel ill-treatment. In her dream she fancies she hears the bridegroom knocking at her chamber door and calling upon her as his sister, his love, his dove, his undefiled, to open to him. He

---

[1] v. 2-7.

has just returned from tending his flock in the night, and his hair is wet with the dew. The bride coyly excuses herself, on the plea that she has laid aside her mantle and washed her feet; as though it would vex her to put her feet to the ground again. This is but the playful reluctance of love; for no sooner is her beloved really lost than she undertakes the greatest trouble in the search for him. When he puts in his hand to lift the latch, her heart is moved towards him, and she rises to open the door. On touching the lock she finds it covered with liquid myrrh. It has been ingeniously suggested that we have here a reference to the construction of an eastern lock, with a wooden pin dropped into the bolt, which is intended to be lifted by a key, but which may be raised by a man's finger if he is provided with some viscid substance, such as the ointment here mentioned, to adhere to the pin. The little detail shews that the lover or bridegroom had come with the deliberate intention of entering. How strange, then, that when the bride opens the door he is not to be seen! Why has he fled? The shock of this surprise quite overwhelms the poor girl, and she is on the point of fainting. She looks about for her vanished lover, and calls him by name; but there is no answer. She goes out to seek for him in the streets, and there the watchmen cuff and bruise her, and the sentry on the city walls rudely tear off her veil.

Returning from the distressing recollection of her dream to the present condition of affairs, the sorrowful Shulammite adjures the daughters of Jerusalem to tell her if they have found her love.[1] They respond by asking, what is her beloved more than any other

---

[1] v. 8.

beloved?[1] This mocking question of the harem women rouses the Shulammite, and affords an opportunity for descanting on the beauty of her love.[2] He is both fair and ruddy, the chiefest among ten thousand. For this is what he is like: a head splendid as finest gold; massive, curling, raven locks; eyes like doves by water brooks, and looking as though they had been washed in milk—an elaborate image in which the soft iris and the sparkling light on the pupils suggest the picture of the gentle birds brooding on the bank of a flashing stream, and the pure, healthy eyeballs a thought of the whiteness of milk; cheeks fragrant as spices; lips red as lilies (the blood-red anemones); a body like ivory, with blue veins as of sapphire; legs like marble columns on golden bases. The aspect of him is like great Lebanon, splendid as the far-famed cedars; and when he opens his lips his voice is ravishingly sweet. Yes, he is altogether lovely. Such is her beloved, her dearest one.

The mocking ladies ask their victim where then has this paragon gone?[3] She would have them understand that he has not been so cruel as really to desert her. It was only in her dream that he treated her with such unaccountable fickleness. The plain fact is that he is away at his work on his far-off farm, feeding his flock, and perhaps gathering a posy of flowers for his bride.[4] He is far away,—that sad truth cannot be denied; and yet he is not really lost, for love laughs at time and distance; the poor lonely girl can say still that she is her beloved's and that he is hers.[5] The reappearance of this phrase suggests that it is intended

---

[1] v. 9.   [3] vi. 1.   [5] vi. 3.
[2] v. 10-16.   [4] vi. 2.

to serve as a sort of refrain. Thus it comes in with admirable fitness to balance the other refrain to which reference has been made earlier.[1] In the first refrain the daughters of Jerusalem are besought not to attempt to awaken the Shulammite's love for Solomon; this is well balanced by the refrain in which she declares the constancy of the mutual love that exists between herself and the shepherd.

Now Solomon reappears on the scene, and resumes his laudation of the Shulammite's beauty.[2] But there is a marked change in his manner. This most recent capture is quite unlike the sort of girls with whom his harem was stocked from time to time. He had no reverence for any of them; they all considered themselves to be highly honoured by his favour, all adored him with slavish admiration, like that expressed by one of them in the first line of the poem. But he is positively afraid of the Shulammite. She is "terrible as an army with banners." He cannot bear to look at her eyes; he begs her to turn them away from him, for they have overcome him. What is the meaning of this new attitude on the part of the mighty monarch? There is something awful in the simple peasant girl. The purity, the constancy, the cold scorn with which she regards the king, are as humiliating as they are novel in his experience. Yet it is well for him that he is susceptible to their influence. He is greatly injured and corrupted by the manners of a luxurious oriental court. But he is not a seared profligate. The vision of goodness startles him; then there is a better nature in him, and its slumbering powers are partly roused by this unexpected apparition.

---

[1] Page 20.   [2] vi. 4-7.

We have now reached a very important point in the poem. It is almost impossible to reconcile this with the theory that Solomon is the one and only lover referred to throughout. But on the "shepherd hypothesis" the position is most significant. The value of constancy in love is not only seen in the steadfast character of one who is sorely tempted to yield to other influences; it is also apparent in the effects on a spectator of so uncongenial a nature as king Solomon. Thus the poet brings out the great idea of his work most vividly. He could not have done so more forcibly than by choosing the court of Solomon for the scene of the trial, and shewing the startling effect of the noble virtue of constancy on the king himself.

Here we are face to face with one of the rescuing influences of life, which may be met in various forms. A true woman, an innocent child, a pure man, coming across the path of one who has permitted himself to slide down towards murky depths, arrests his attention with a painful shock of surprise. The result is a revelation to him, in the light of which he discovers, to his horror, how far he has fallen. It is a sort of incarnate conscience warning him of the still lower degradation towards which he is sinking. Perhaps it strikes him as a beacon light, shewing the path up to purity and peace; an angel from heaven sent to help him retrace his steps and return to his better self. Few men are so abandoned as never to be visited by some such gleam from higher regions. To many, alas, it comes but as the temporary rift in the clouds through which for one brief moment the blue sky becomes visible even on a wild and stormy day, soon to be lost in deeper darkness. Happy are they who obey its unexpected message.

The concluding words of the passage which opens with Solomon's praises of the Shulammite present another of the many difficulties with which the poem abounds. Mention is made of Solomon's sixty queens, his eighty concubines, his maidens without number; and then the Shulammite is contrasted with this vast seraglio as "My dove, my undefiled," who is "but one"—"the only one of her mother."[1] Who is speaking here? If this is a continuation of Solomon's speech, as the flow of the verses would suggest, it must mean that the king would set his newest acquisition quite apart from all the ladies of the harem, as his choice and treasured bride. Those who regard Solomon as the lover, think they see here what they call his conversion, that is to say, his turning away from polygamy to monogamy. History knows of no such conversion; and it is hardly likely that a poet of the northern kingdom would go out of his way to whitewash the matrimonial reputation of a sovereign from whom the house of Judah was descended. Besides, the occurrence here represented bears a very dubious character when we consider that all the existing denizens of the harem were to be put aside in favour of a new beauty. It would have been more like a genuine conversion if Solomon had gone back to the love of his youth, and confined his affections to his neglected first wife.

On the shepherd hypothesis it is most natural to attribute the passage to the shepherd himself. But since it is difficult to imagine him present at this scene between Solomon and the Shulammite, it seems that we must fall back on the idealising character of the poem.

---

[1] vi. 8, 9.

In this figurative way the true lover expresses his contempt for the monstrous harem at the palace. He is content with his one ewe lamb; nay, she is more to him than all Solomon's bevy of beauties; even these ladies of the court are now constrained to praise the noble qualities of his bride.

Solomon's expression of awe for the terrible purity and constancy of the Shulammite is repeated,[1] and then she tells the story of her capture.[2] She had gone down to the nut garden to look at the fresh green on the plants, and to see whether the vines were budding and the pomegranates putting forth their lovely scarlet blossoms, when suddenly, and all unawares, she was pounced upon by the king's people and whisked away in one of his chariots. It is a vivid scene, and, like other scenes in this poem, the background of it is the lovely aspect of nature in early spring.

The Shulammite now seems to be attempting a retreat, and the ladies of the court bid her return; they would see the performance of a favourite dance, known as "The Dance of Mahanaim."[3] Thereupon we have a description of the performer, as she was seen during the convolutions of the dance, dressed in a transparent garment of red gauze,—perhaps such as is represented in Pompeian frescoes,—so that her person could be compared to pale wheat surrounded by crimson anemones.[4] It is quite against the tenor of her conduct to suppose that the modest country girl would degrade herself by ministering to the amusement of a corrupt court in this shameless manner. It is more reasonable to conclude

---

[1] vi. 10.
[2] Vers. 11, 12.
[3] vi. 13. This is obscured in the Authorised Version.
[4] vii. 1-9.

that the entertainment was given by a professional dancer from among the women of the harem. We have a hint that this is the case in the title applied to the performer, in addressing whom Solomon exclaims, "O prince's daughter,"[1] an expression never used for the poor Shulammite, and one from which we should gather that she was a captive princess who had been trained as a court dancer. The glimpse of the manners of the palace helps to strengthen the contrast of the innocent, simple country life in which the Shulammite delights.

It has been suggested, with some degree of probability, that the Shulammite is supposed to make her escape while the attention of the king and his court is diverted by this entrancing spectacle. It is to be observed, at all events, that from this point onwards to the end of the poem, neither Solomon nor the daughters of Jerusalem take any part in the dialogue, while the scene appears to be shifted to the Shulammite's home in the country, where she and the shepherd are now seen together in happy companionship. The bridegroom has come to fetch his bride. Again she owns that she is his, and delights in the glad thought that his heart goes out to her.[2] She bids him come with her into the field, and lodge in the villages. They will get them early into the vineyards and see whether the vines are blooming, and whether the pomegranates are in blossom.[3] It is still early spring. It was early spring when she was snatched away. Unless she had been a whole year at the palace,—an impossible situation with the king continuing his ineffectual courtship for so long a time,—we have no movement of time. But

---

[1] vii. 1.   [2] vii. 10.   [3] vii. 11-13.

the series of events from the day when the Shulammite was seized in her nut garden, till she found herself back again in her home in the north country, after the trying episode of her temporary residence in the royal palace, must have occupied some weeks. And yet the conclusion of the story is set in precisely the same stage of spring, the time when people look for the first buds and blossoms, as the opening scenes. It has been proposed to confine the whole action to the northern district, where Solomon might have had a country house adjoining his vineyard.[1] The presence of the "daughters of Jerusalem," and allusions to the streets of the city, its watchmen, and the guard upon the walls, are against this notion. It is better to conclude that we have here another instance of the idealism of the poem. Since early spring is the season that harmonises most perfectly with the spirit of the whole work, the author does not trouble himself with adapting its scenes in a realistic manner to the rapidly changing aspects of nature.

The shepherd has addressed the Shulammite as his sister;[2] she now reciprocates the title by expressing her longing that he had been as her brother.[3] This singular mode of courtship between two lovers who are so passionately devoted to one another that we might call them the Hebrew Romeo and Juliet, is not without significance. Its recurrence, now on the lips of the bride, helps to sharpen still more the contrast between what passes for love in the royal harem, and the true emotion experienced by a pair of innocent young people, unsullied by the corruptions of the court —illustrating, as it does at once, its sweet intimacy and its perfect purity.

---

[1] viii. 11.   [2] viii. 1.   [3] viii. 1.

The proud bride would now lead her swain to her mother's house.[1] There is no mention of her father; apparently he is not living. But the fond way in which this simple girl speaks of her mother reveals another lovely trait in her character. She has witnessed the wearisome magnificence of Solomon's palace. It was impossible to associate the idea of *home* with such a place. We never hear the daughters of Jerusalem, those poor degraded women of the harem, speaking of their mothers. But to the Shulammite no spot on earth is so dear as her mother's cottage. There her lover shall have spiced wine and pomegranate juice— simple home-made country beverages.[2] Repeating one of the early refrains of the poem, the happy bride is not afraid to say that there too her husband shall support her in his strong embrace.[3] She then repeats another refrain, and for the last time—surely one would say now, quite superfluously—she adjures the daughters of Jerusalem not to awaken any love for Solomon in her, but to leave love to its spontaneous course.[4]

Now the bridegroom is seen coming up from the wilderness with his bride leaning upon him, and telling how he first made love to her when he found her asleep under an apple tree in the garden of the cottage where she was born.[5] As they converse together we reach the richest gem of the poem, the Shulammite's impassioned eulogy of love.[6] She bids her husband set her as a seal upon his heart in the inner sanctuary of his being, and as a seal upon his arm—always owning her, always true to her in the outer world. She is to be his closely, his openly, his for ever. She has proved her

---

[1] viii. 2.　　[3] viii. 3.　　[5] viii. 5.
[2] viii. 2.　　[4] viii. 4.　　[6] viii. 6, 7.

constancy to him; now she claims his constancy to her. The foundation of this claim rests on the very nature of love. The one essential characteristic here dwelt upon is strength—"Love is strong as death." Who can resist grim death? who escape its iron clutches? Who can resist mighty love, or evade its power? The illustration is startling in the apparent incompatibility of the two things drawn together for comparison. But it is a stern and terrible aspect of love to which our attention is now directed. This is apparent as the Shulammite proceeds to speak of jealousy which is "hard as the grave." If love is treated falsely, it can flash out in a flame of wrath ten times more furious than the raging of hatred—"a most vehement flame of the Lord." This is the only place in which the name of God appears throughout the whole poem. It may be said that even here it only comes in according to a familiar Hebrew idiom, as metaphor for what is very great. But the Shulammite has good reason for claiming God to be on her side in the protection of her love from cruel wrong and outrage. Love as she knows it is both unquenchable and unpurchasable. She has tested and proved these two attributes in her own experience. At the court of Solomon every effort was made to destroy her love for the shepherd, and all possible means were employed for buying her love for the king. Both utterly failed. All the floods of scorn which the harem ladies poured over her love for the country lad could not quench it; all the wealth of a kingdom could not buy it for Solomon. Where true love exists, no opposition can destroy it; where it is not, no money can purchase it. As for the second idea—the purchasing of love—the Shulammite flings it away with the utmost contempt. Yet this was the too common means employed by a king such as Solomon for replenishing the stock of his harem. Then the monarch was only pursuing a shadow; he was but playing at love-making; he was absolutely ignorant of the reality.

The vigour, one might say the rigour, of this passage distinguishes it from nearly all other poetry devoted to the praises of love. That poetry is usually soft and tender; sometimes it is feeble and sugary. And yet it must be remembered that even the classical Aphrodite could be terribly angry. There is nothing morbid or sentimental in the Shulammite's ideas. She has discovered and proved by experience that love is a mighty force, capable of heroic endurance, and able, when wronged, to avenge itself with serious effect.

Towards the conclusion of the poem fresh speakers appear in the persons of the Shulammite's brothers, who defend themselves from the charge of negligence in having permitted their little sister to be snatched away from their keeping, explaining how they have done their best to guard her. Or perhaps they mean that they will be more careful in protecting a younger sister. They will build battlements about her. The Shulammite takes up the metaphor. She is safe now, as a wall well embattled; at last she has found peace in the love of her husband. Solomon may have a vineyard in her neighbourhood, and draw great wealth from it with which to buy the wares in which he delights.[1] It is nothing to her. She has her own vineyard. This reference to the Shulammite's vineyard recalls the mention of it at the beginning of the poem, and suggests the idea that in both cases the image

---

[1] viii. 11.

represents the shepherd lover. In the first instance she had not kept her vineyard,[1] for she had lost her lover. Now she has him, and she is satisfied.[2] He calls to her in the garden, longing to hear her voice there,[3] and she replies, bidding him hasten and come to her as she has described him coming before,—

> "Like to a roe or a young hart
> Upon the mountains of spices."[4]

And so the poem sinks to rest in the happy picture of the union of the two young lovers.

---

[1] i. 6. [2] viii. 12. [3] viii. 13. [4] viii. 14.

CHAPTER IV

MYSTICAL INTERPRETATIONS

THUS far we have been considering the bare, literal sense of the text. It cannot be denied that, if only to lead up to the metaphorical significance of the words employed, those words must be approached through their primary physical meanings. This is essential even to the understanding of pure allegory such as that of *The Faerie Queen* and *The Pilgrim's Progress*; we must understand the adventures of the Red Cross Knight and the course of Christian's journey before we can learn the moral of Spenser's and Bunyan's elaborate allegories. Similarly it is absolutely necessary for us to have some idea of the movement of the Song of Solomon as a piece of literature, in its external form, even if we are persuaded that beneath this sensuous exterior it contains the most profound ideas, before we can discover any such ideas. In other words, if it is to be considered as a mass of symbolism the symbols must be understood in themselves before their significance can be drawn out of them.

But now we are confronted with the question whether the book has any other meaning than that which meets the eye. The answers to this question are given on three distinct lines :—First, we have the *allegorical* schemes of interpretation, according to which the poem is not to be taken literally at all, but is to be regarded as a purely metaphorical representation of national or Church history, philosophical ideas, or spiritual experiences. In the second place, we meet with various forms of double interpretation, described as *typical* or *mystical*, in which a primary meaning is allowed to the book as a sort of drama or idyl, or as a collection of Jewish love-songs, while a secondary signification of an ideal or spiritual character is added. Distinct as these lines of interpretation are in themselves, they tend to blend in practice, because even when two meanings are admitted the symbolical signification is considered to be of so much greater importance than the literal that it virtually occupies the whole field. In the third place there is the *purely literal* interpretation, that which denies the existence of any symbolical or mystical intention in the poem.

Allegorical interpretations of the Song of Solomon are found among the Jews early in the Christian era. The Aramaic Targum, probably originating about the sixth century A.D., takes the first half of the poem as a symbolical picture of the history of Israel previous to the captivity, and the second as a prophetic picture of the subsequent fortunes of the nation. The recurrence of the expression "the congregation of Israel" in this paraphrase wherever the Shulammite appears, and other similar adaptations, entirely destroy the fine poetic flavour of the work, and convert it into a dreary, dry-as-dust composition.

Symbolical interpretations were very popular among Christian Fathers—though not with universal approval, as the protest of Theodore of Mopsuestia testifies. The great Alexandrian Origen is the founder and patron of this method of interpreting the Song of Solomon in the Church. Jerome was of opinion that

Origen "surpassed himself" in his commentary on the poem—a commentary to which he devoted ten volumes. According to his view, it was originally an epithalamium celebrating the marriage of Solomon with Pharaoh's daughter; but it has secondary mystical meanings descriptive of the relation of the Redeemer to the Church or the individual soul. Thus "the little foxes that spoil the grapes" are evil thoughts in the individual, or heretics in the Church. Gregory the Great contributes a commentary of no lasting interest. Very different is the work of the great mediæval monk St. Bernard of Clairvaux, who threw himself into it with all the passion and rapture of his enthusiastic soul, and in the course of eighty-six homilies only reached the beginning of the third chapter in this to him inexhaustible mine of spiritual wealth, when he died, handing on the task to his faithful disciple Gilbert Porretanus, who continued it on the same portentous scale, and also died before he had finished the fifth chapter. Even while reading the old monkish Latin in this late age we cannot fail to feel the glowing devotion that inspires it. Bernard is addressing his monks, to whom he says he need not give the milk for babes, and whom he exhorts to prepare their throats not for this milk but for bread. As a schoolman he cannot escape from metaphysical subtleties—he takes the kiss of the bridegroom as a symbol of the incarnation. But throughout there burns the perfect rapture of love to Jesus Christ which inspires his well-known hymns. Here we are at the secret of the extraordinary popularity of mystical interpretations of the Song of Solomon. It has seemed to many in all ages of the Christian Church to afford the best expression for the deepest spiritual relations of Christ and His people. Nevertheless, the mystical method has been widely disputed since the time of the Reformation. Luther complains of the "many wild and monstrous interpretations" that are attached to the Song of Solomon, though even he understands it as symbolical of Solomon and his state. Still, not a few of the most popular hymns of our own day are saturated with ideas and phrases gathered from this book, and fresh expositions of what are considered to be its spiritual lessons may still be met with.

It is not easy to discover any justification for the rabbinical explanation of the Song of Solomon as a representation of successive events in the history of Israel, an explanation which Jewish scholars have abandoned in favour of simple literalism. But the mystical view, according to which the poem sets forth spiritual ideas, has pleas urged in its favour that demand some consideration. We are reminded of the analogy of Oriental literature, which delights in parable to an extent unknown in the West. Works of a kindred nature are produced in which an allegorical signification is plainly intended. Thus the Hindoo *Gitagovinda* celebrates the loves of Chrishna and Radha in verses that bear a remarkable resemblance to the Song of Solomon. Arabian poets sing of the love of Joseph for Zuleikha, which mystics take as the love of God towards the soul that longs for union with Him. There is a Turkish mystical commentary on the Song of Hafiz.

The Bible itself furnishes us with suggestive analogies. Throughout the Old Testament the idea of a marriage union between God and His people occurs repeatedly, and the most frequent metaphor for religious apostasy is drawn from the crime of adultery.[1] This symbolism

---

[1] *E.g.* Exod. xxxiv. 15, 16; Numb. xv. 39; Psalm lxxiii. 27; Ezek. xvi. 23, etc.

is especially prominent in the writings of Jeremiah[1] and Hosea.[2] The forty-fifth psalm is an epithalamium commonly read with a Messianic signification. John the Baptist describes the coming Messiah as the Bridegroom,[3] and Jesus Christ accepts the title for Himself.[4] Our Lord illustrates the blessedness of the Kingdom of Heaven in a parable of a wedding feast.[5] With St. Paul the union of husband and wife is an earthly copy of the union of Christ and His Church. The marriage of the Lamb is a prominent feature in the Book of the Revelation.[7]

Further, it may be maintained that the experience of Christians has demonstrated the aptness of the expression of the deepest spiritual truths in the imagery of the Song of Solomon. Sad hearts disappointed in their earthly hopes have found in the religious reading of this poem as a picture of their relation to their Saviour the satisfaction for which they have hungered, and which the world could never give them. Devout Christians have read in it the very echo of their own emotions. Samuel Rutherford's *Letters*, for example, are in perfect harmony with the religious interpretation of the Song of Solomon; and these letters stand in the first rank of devotional works. There is certainly some force in the argument that a key which seems to fit the lock so well must have been designed to do so.

On the other hand, the objections to a mystical, religious interpretation are very strong. In the first place, we can quite account for its appearance apart from any justification of it in the original intention of

---

[1] *E.g.* Jer. iii. 1-11.
[2] Hosea ii. 2; iii. 3.
[3] John iii. 29.
[4] Mark. ii. 19.
[5] Matt. xxii. 1-14.
[6] Eph. v. 22-33.
[7] Rev. xxi. 9.

the author. Allegory was in the air at the time when, as far as we know, secondary meanings were first attached to the ideas of the Song of Solomon. They sprang from Alexandria, the home of allegory. Origen, who was the first Christian writer to work out a mystical explanation of this book, treated other books of the Old Testament in exactly the same way; but we never dream of following him in his fantastical interpretations of those works. There is no indication that the poem was understood allegorically or mystically as early as the first century of the Christian era. Philo is the prince of allegorists; but while he explains the narratives of the Pentateuch according to his favourite method, he never applies that method to this very tempting book, and never even mentions the work or makes any reference to its contents. The Song of Solomon is not once mentioned or even alluded to in the slightest way by any writer of the New Testament. Since it is never noticed by Christ or the Apostles, of course we cannot appeal to their authority for reading it mystically; and yet it was undoubtedly known to them as one of the books in the canon of the sacred Scriptures to which they were in the habit of appealing repeatedly. Consider the grave significance of this fact. All secondary interpretations of which we know anything, and, as far as we can tell, all that ever existed, had their origin in post-apostolic times. If we would justify this method by authority it is to the Fathers that we must go, not to Christ and His apostles, not to the sacred Scriptures. It is a noteworthy fact, too, that the word *Eros*, the Greek name for the love of man and woman, as distinguished from *Agape*, which stands for love in the widest sense of the word, is first applied to our Lord by Ignatius. Here we have the faint beginning of the stream of erotic religious fancies which sometimes manifests itself most objectionably in subsequent Church history. There is not a trace of it in the New Testament.

If the choice spiritual ideas which some people think they see in the Song of Solomon are not imported by the reader, but form part of the genuine contents of the book, how comes it that this fact was not recognised by one of the inspired writers of the New Testament? or, if privately recognised, that it was never utilised? In the hands of the mystical interpreter this work is about the most valuable part of the Old Testament. He finds it to be an inexhaustible mine of the most precious treasures. Why, then, was such a remunerative lode never worked by the first authorities in Christian teaching? It may be replied that we cannot prove much from a bare negative. The apostles may have had their own perfectly sufficient reasons for leaving to the Church of later ages the discovery of this valuable spiritual store. Possibly the converts of their day were not ripe for the comprehension of the mysteries here expounded. Be that as it may, clearly the *onus probandi* rests with those people of a later age who introduce a method of interpretation for which no sanction can be found in Scripture.

Now the analogies that have been referred to are not sufficient to establish any proof. In the case of the other poems mentioned above there are distinct indications of symbolical intentions. Thus in the *Gitagovinda* the hero is a divinity whose incarnations are acknowledged in Hindoo mythology; and the concluding verse of that poem points the moral by a direct assertion of the religious meaning of the whole composition. This is not the case with the Song of

Solomon. We must not be misled by the chapter-headings in our English Bibles, which of course are not to be found in the original Hebrew text. From the first line to the last there is not the slightest hint in the poem itself that it was intended to be read in any mystical sense. This is contrary to the analogy of all allegories. The parable may be difficult to interpret, but at all events it must suggest that it is a parable; otherwise it defeats its own object. If the writer never drops any hint that he has wrapped up spiritual ideas in the sensuous imagery of his poetry, what right has he to expect that anybody will find them there, so long as his poem admits of a perfectly adequate explanation in a literal sense? We need not be so dense as to require the allegorist to say to us in so many words: "This is a parable." But we may justly expect him to furnish us with some hint that his utterance is of such a character. Æsop's fables carry their lessons on the surface of them, so that we can often anticipate the concluding morals that are attached to them. When Tennyson announced that the *Idyls of the King* constituted an allegory most people were taken by surprise; and yet the analogy of *The Faerie Queen*, and the lofty ethical ideas with which the poems are inspired, might have prepared us for the revelation. But we have no similar indications in the case of the Song of Solomon. If somebody were to propound a new theory of *The Vicar of Wakefield*, which should turn that exquisite tale into a parable of the Fall, it would not be enough for him to exercise his ingenuity in pointing out resemblances between the eighteenth-century romance and the ancient narrative of the serpent's doings in the Garden of Eden. Since he could not shew that Goldsmith had the slightest intention of teaching anything of the kind, his exploit could be regarded as nothing but a piece of literary trifling.

The Biblical analogies already cited, in which the marriage relation between God or Christ and the Church or the soul are referred to, will not bear the strain that is put upon them when they are brought forward in order to justify a mystical interpretation of the Song of Solomon. At best they simply account for the emergence of this view of the book at a later time, or indicate that such a notion might be maintained if there were good reasons for adopting it. They cannot prove that in the present case it should be adopted. Moreover, they differ from it on two important points. *First*, in harmony with all genuine allegories and metaphors, they carry their own evidence of a symbolical meaning, which as we have seen the Song of Solomon fails to do. *Second*, they are not elaborate compositions of a dramatic or idyllic character in which the passion of love is vividly illustrated. Regarded in its entirety, the Song of Solomon is quite without parallel in Scripture. It may be replied that we cannot disprove the allegorical intention of the book. But this is not the question. That intention requires to be proved; and until it is proved, or at least until some very good reasons are urged for adopting it, no statement of bare possibilities counts for anything.

But we may push the case further. There is a positive improbability of the highest order that the spiritual ideas read into the Song of Solomon by some of its Christian admirers should have been originally there. This would involve the most tremendous anachronism in all literature. The Song of Solomon is dated among the earlier works of the Old Testament.

But the religious ideas now associated with it represent what is regarded as the fruit of the most advanced saintliness ever attained in the Christian Church. Here we have a flat contradiction to the growth of revelation manifested throughout the whole course of Scripture history. We might as well ascribe the Sistine Madonna to the fresco-painters of the catacombs; or, what is more to the point, our Lord's discourse with His disciples at the paschal meal to Solomon or some other Jew of his age.

No doubt the devoted follower of the mystical method will not be troubled by considerations such as these. To him the supposed fitness of the poem to convey his religious ideas is the one sufficient proof of an original design that it should serve that end. So long as the question is approached in this way, the absence of clear evidence only delights the prejudiced commentator with the opportunity it affords for the exercise of his ingenuity. To a certain school of readers the very obscurity of a book is its fascination. The less obvious a meaning is, the more eagerly do they set themselves to expound and defend it. We could leave them to what might be considered a very harmless diversion if it were not for other considerations. But we cannot forget that it is just this ingenious way of interpreting the Bible in accordance with preconceived opinions that has encouraged the quotation of the Sacred Volume in favour of absolutely contradictory propositions, an abuse which in its turn has provoked an inevitable reaction leading to contempt for the Bible as an obscure book which speaks with no certain voice.

Still, it may be contended, the analogy between the words of this poem and the spiritual experience of

Christians is in itself an indication of intentional connection. Swedenborg has shewn that there are correspondences between the natural and the spiritual, and this truth is illustrated by the metaphorical references to marriage in the Bible which have been adduced for comparison with the Song of Solomon. But their very existence shows that analogies between religious experience and the love story of the Shulammite may be traced out by the reader without any design on the part of the author to present them. If they are natural they are universal, and any love song will serve our purpose. On this principle, if the Song of Solomon admits of mystical adaptation, so do Mrs. Browning's *Sonnets from the Portuguese.*

We have no alternative, then, but to conclude that the mystical interpretation of this work is based on a delusion. Moreover, it must be added that the delusion is a mischievous one. No doubt to many it has been as meat and drink. They have found in their reading of the Song of Solomon real spiritual refreshment, or they believe they have found it. But there is another side. The poem has been used to minister to a morbid, sentimental type of religion. More than any other influence, the mystical interpretation of this book has imported an effeminate element into the notion of the love of Christ, not one trace of which can be detected in the New Testament. The Catholic legend of the marriage of St. Catherine is somewhat redeemed by the high ascetic tone that pervades it ; and yet it indicates a decline from the standpoint of the apostles. Not a few unquestionable revelations of immorality in convents have shed a ghastly light on the abuse of erotic religious fervour. Among Protestants it cannot be said that the most wholesome hymns are those which are composed on the model of the Song of Solomon. In some cases the religious use of this book is perfectly nauseous, indicating nothing less than a disease of religion. When—as sometimes happens—frightful excesses of sensuality follow close on seasons of what has been regarded as the revival of religion, the common explanation of these horrors is that in some mysterious way spiritual emotion lies very near to sensual appetite, so that an excitement of the one tends to rouse the other. A more revolting hypothesis, or one more insulting to religion, cannot be imagined. The truth is, the two regions are separate as the poles. The explanation of the phenomena of their apparent conjunction is to be found in quite another direction. It is that their victims have substituted for religion a sensuous excitement which is as little religious as the elation that follows indulgence in alcoholism. There is no more deadly temptation of the devil than that which hoodwinks deluded fanatics into making this terrible mistake. But it can scarcely be denied that the mystical reading of the Song of Solomon by unspiritual persons, or even by any persons who are not completely fortified against the danger, may tend in this fatal direction.

CHAPTER V

CANONICITY

IT is scarcely to be expected that the view of the Song of Solomon expounded in the foregoing pages will meet with acceptance from every reader. A person who has been accustomed to resort to this book in search of the deepest spiritual ideas cannot but regard the denial of their presence with aversion. While, however, it is distressing to be compelled to give pain to a devout soul, it may be necessary. If there is weight in the considerations that have been engaging our attention, we cannot shut our eyes to them simply because they may be disappointing. The mystical interpreter will be shocked at what he takes for irreverence. But, on the other hand, he should be on his guard against falling into this very fault from the opposite side. Reverence for truth is a primary Christian duty. The iconoclast is certain to be charged with irreverence by the devotee of the popular idol which he feels it his duty to destroy; and yet, if his action is inspired by loyalty to truth, reverence for what he deems highest and best may be its mainspring.

If the Song of Solomon were not one of the books of the Bible, questions such as these would never arise. It is its place in the sacred canon that induces people to resent the consequences of the application of criticism to it. It is simply owing to its being a part of the

Bible that it has come to be treated mystically at all. Undoubtedly this is why it was allegorised by the Jews. But, then, the secondary signification thus acquired reacted upon it, and served as a sort of buoy to float it over the rocks of awkward questions. The result was that in the end the book attained to an exceptionally high position in the estimation of the rabbis. Thus the great Rabbi Akiba says : "The course of the ages cannot vie with the day on which the Song of Songs was given to Israel. All the *Kethubim* (*i.e.*, the *Hagiographa*) are holy, but the Song of Songs is a holy of holies."

Such being the case, it is manifest that the rejection of the mystical signification of its contents must revive the question of the canonicity of the book. We have not, however, to deal with the problem of its original insertion in the canon. We find it there. Some doubts as to its right to the place it holds seem to have been raised among the Jews during the first century of the Christian era; but these doubts were effectually borne down. As far as we know, the Song of Solomon has always been a portion of the Hebrew Scriptures from the obscure time when the collection of those Scriptures was completed. It stands as the first of the five *Megilloth*, or sacred rolls—the others being Ruth, Lamentations, Esther, and Ecclesiastes. We are not now engaged in the difficult task of constructing a new canon. The only possibility is that of the expulsion of a book already in the old canon. But the attempt to disturb in any way such a volume as the Old Testament, with all its incomparable associations, is not one to be undertaken lightly or without adequate reason.

In order to justify this radical measure it would not be enough to shew that the specific religious meanings that some have attached to the Song of Solomon do not really belong to it. If it is said that the secular tone it acquires under the hands of criticism shews it to be unworthy of a place in the sacred Scriptures, this assertion goes upon an unwarrantable assumption. We have no reason to maintain that all the books of the Old Testament must be of equal value. The Book of Esther does not reach a very high level of moral or religious worth; the pessimism of Ecclesiastes is not inspiring; even the Book of Proverbs contains maxims that cannot be elevated to a first place in ethics. If we could discover no distinctively enlightening or uplifting influence in the Song of Solomon, this would not be a sufficient reason for raising a cry against it; because if it were simply neutral in character, like nitrogen in the atmosphere, it would do no harm, and we could safely let it be. The one justification for a radical treatment of the question would be the discovery that the book was false in doctrine or deleterious in character. As to doctrine, it does not trench on that region at all. It would be as incongruous to associate it with the grave charge of heresy as to bring a similar accusation against the *Essays of Elia* or Keats's poetry. And if the view expressed in these pages is at all correct, it certainly cannot be said that the moral tendency of the book is injurious; the very reverse must be affirmed.

Since there is no reason to believe that the Song of Solomon had received any allegorical interpretation before the commencement of the Christian era, we must conclude that it was not on the ground of some such interpretation that it was originally admitted into the Hebrew collection of Scripture. It was placed in the canon before it was allegorised. It was only allegorised because it had been placed in the canon. Then why was it set there? The natural conclusion to arrive at under these circumstances is that the scribes who ventured to put it first among the sacred *Megilloth* saw that there was a distinctive value in it. Perhaps, however, it is too much to say this of them. The word "Solomon" being attached to the book would seem to justify its inclusion with other literature which had received the hall-mark of that great name. Still we can learn to appreciate it on its own merits, and in so doing perceive that there is something in it to justify its right to a niche in the glorious temple of scripture.

Assuredly it was much to make clear in the days of royal polygamy among the Jews that this gross imitation of the court life of heathen monarchies was a despicable and degrading thing, and to set over against it an attractive picture of true love and simple manners. The prophets of Israel were continually protesting against a growing dissoluteness of morals: the Song of Solomon is a vivid illustration of the spirit of their protest. If the two nations had been content with the rustic delights so beautifully portrayed in this book, they might not have fallen into ruin as they did under the influence of the corruptions of an effete civilisation. If their people had cherished the graces of purity and constancy that shine so conspicuously in the character of the Shulammite they might not have needed to pass through the purging fires of the captivity.

But while this can be said of the book as it first appeared among the Jews, a similar estimate of its function in later ages may also be made. An ideal representation of fidelity in love under the greatest provocation to surrender at discretion has a message for every age. We need not shrink from reading it in the pages of the Bible. Our Lord teaches us that next to the duty of love to God comes that of love to one's neighbour. But a man's nearest neighbour is his wife. Therefore after his God his wife has the first claim upon him. But the whole conception of matrimonial duty rests on the idea of constancy in the love of man and woman.

If this book had been read in its literal signification and its wholesome lesson absorbed by Christendom in the Middle Ages, the gloomy cloud of asceticism that then hung over the Church would have been somewhat lightened, not to give place to the outburst of licentiousness that accompanied the *Renaissance*, but rather to allow of the better establishment of the Christian home. The absurd legends that follow the names of St. Anthony and St. Dunstan would have lost their motive. Hildebrand would have had no occasion to hurl his thunderbolt. The Church was making the huge mistake of teaching that the remedy for dissoluteness was unnatural celibacy. This book taught the lesson—truer to nature, truer to experience, truer to the God who made us—that it was to be found in the redemption of love.

Can it be denied that the same lesson is needed in our own day? The realism that has made itself a master of a large part of popular literature reveals a state of society that perpetuates the manners of the court of Solomon, though under a thin veil of decorum. The remedy for the awful dissoluteness of large portions of society can only be found in the cultivation of such lofty ideas on the relation of the sexes that this abomination shall be scouted with horror. It is neither necessary, nor right, nor possible to contradict nature. What has to be shewn is that man's true nature is not bestial, that satyrs and fauns are not men, but degraded caricatures of men. We cannot crush the strongest passion of human nature. The moral of the Song of Solomon is that there is no occasion to attempt to crush it, because the right thing is to elevate it by lofty ideals of love and constancy.

This subject also deserves attention on its positive side. The literature of all ages is a testimony to the fact that nothing in the world is so interesting as love. What is so old as love-making? and what so fresh? At least ninety-nine novels out of a hundred have a love-story for plot; and the hundredth is always regarded as an eccentric experiment. The pedant may plant his heel on the perennial flower; but it will spring up again as vigorous as ever. This is the poetry of the most commonplace existence. When it visits a dingy soul the desert blossoms as the rose. Life may be hard, and its drudgery a grinding yoke; but with love "all tasks are sweet." "And Jacob served seven years for Rachel; and they seemed unto him but a few days, for the love he had to her."[1] That experience of the patriarch is typical of the magic power of true love in every age, in every clime. To the lover it is always "the time of the singing of birds." Who shall tell the value of the boon that God has given so freely to mankind, to sweeten the lot of the toiler and shed music into his heart? But this boon requires to be jealously guarded and sheltered from abuse, or its honey will be turned into gall. It is for the toiler—the shepherd whose locks are wet with the dew that has fallen upon him while guarding his flock by night, the maiden who has been working in the vineyard; it is beyond the

---

[1] Gen. xxix. 20.

reach of the pleasure-seeking monarch and the indolent ladies of his court. This boon is for the pure in heart; it is utterly denied to the sensual and dissolute. Finally, it is reserved for the loyal and true as the peculiar reward of constancy.

But while a poem that contains these principles must be allowed to have an important mission in the world, it does not follow that it is suitable for public or indiscriminate reading. The fact that the key to it is not easily discovered is a warning that it is liable to be misunderstood. When it is read superficially, without any comprehension of its drift and motive, it may be perverted to mischievous ends. The antique Oriental pictures with which it abounds, though natural to the circumstances of its origin, are not in harmony with the more reserved manners of our own conditions of society. As all the books of the Bible are not of the same character, so also they are not all to be used in the same way.

THE LAMENTATIONS OF JEREMIAH

CHAPTER I

HEBREW ELEGIES

THE book which is known by the title "The Lamentations of Jeremiah" is a collection of five separate poems, very similar in style, and all treating of the same subject—the desolation of Jerusalem and the sufferings of the Jews after the overthrow of their city by Nebuchadnezzar. In our English Bible it is placed among the prophetical works of the Old Testament, standing next to the acknowledged writings of the man whose name it bears. This arrangement follows the order in the Septuagint, from which it was accepted by Josephus and the Christian Fathers. And yet the natural place for such a book would seem to be in association with the Psalms and other poetical compositions of a kindred character. So thought the Rabbis who compiled the Jewish canon. In the Hebrew Bible the Book of Lamentations is assigned to the third collection, that designated *Hagiographa*, not to the part known as the *Prophets*.

In form as well as in substance this book is a remarkable specimen of a specific order of poetry. The difficulty of recovering the original pronunciation of the language has left our conception of Hebrew metres in a state of obscurity. It has been generally supposed that the rhythm was more of sight than of sound, but that it consisted essentially in neither, depending mainly on the balance of ideas. The metre, it has been stated, might strike the eye in the external aspect of the sentences; it was designed much more to charm the mind by the harmony and music of the thoughts. But while these general principles are still acknowledged, some further progress has been made in the examination of the structure of the verses, with the result that both more regularity of law and more variety of metre have been discovered. The elegy in particular is found to be shaped on special lines of its own. It has been pointed out that a peculiar metre is reserved for poems of mournful reflection.

The first feature of this metre to be noted is the unusual length of the line. In Hebrew poetry, according to the generally accepted pronunciation, the lines vary from about six syllables to about twelve. In the elegy the line most frequently runs to the extreme limit, and so acquires a slow, solemn movement.

A second feature of elegiac poetry is the breaking of the lengthy line into two unequal parts—the first part being about as long as a whole line in an average Hebrew lyric, and the second much shorter, reading like another line abbreviated, and seeming to suggest that the weary thought is waking up and hurrying to its conclusion. Sometimes this short section is a thin echo of the fuller conception that precedes, sometimes the completion of that conception. In the English version, of course, the effect is frequently lost; still occasionally it is very marked, even after passing through this foreign medium. Take, for example, the lines,

"Her princes are become like harts—that find no pasture,
And they are gone without strength—before the pursuer;"[1]

---

[1] i. 6.

or again the very long line,

"It is of the Lord's mercies that we are not consumed—because His compassions fail not."[1]

Now although this is only a structural feature it points to inferences of deeper significance. It shews that the Hebrew poets paid special attention to the elegy as a species of verse to be treated apart, and therefore that they attached a peculiar significance to the ideas and feelings it expresses. The ease with which the transition to the elegiac form of verse is made whenever an occasion for using it occurs is a hint that this must have been familiar to the Jews. Possibly it was in common use at funerals in the dirge. We meet with an early specimen of this verse in Amos, when, just after announcing that he is about to utter a *lamentation* over the house of Israel, the herdsman of Tekoa breaks into elegiacs with the words,

"The virgin daughter of Israel is fallen—she shall no more rise:
She is cast down upon her land—there is none to raise her up."[2]

Similarly constructed elegiac pieces are scattered over the Old Testament scriptures from the eighth century B.C. onwards. Several illustrations of this peculiar kind of metre are to be found in the Psalms. It is employed ironically with terrible effect in the Book of Isaiah, where the mock lament over the death of the king of Babylon is constructed in the form of a true elegy. When the prophet made a sudden transition from his normal style to sombre funereal measures his purpose would be at once recognised, for his words would sound like the tolling bell and the muffled drums that announce

---

[1] iii. 22.   [2] Amos v. 2.

the march of death; and yet it would be known that this solemn pomp was not really a demonstration of mourning or a symbol of respect, but only the pageantry of scorn and hatred and vengeance. The sarcasm would strike home with the more force since it fell on men's ears in the heavy, lingering lines of the elegy, as the exultant patriot exclaimed,

> "How hath the oppressor ceased—the golden city ceased!
> The Lord hath broken the staff of the wicked—the sceptre of the rulers," etc.[1]

A special characteristic of the five elegies that make up the Book of Lamentations is their alphabetical arrangement. Each elegy consists of twenty-two verses, the same number as that of the letters in the Hebrew alphabet. All but the last are acrostics, the initial letter of each verse following the order of the alphabet. In the third elegy every line in the verse begins with the same letter. According to another way of reckoning, this poem consists of sixty-six verses arranged in triplets, each of which not only follows the order of the alphabet with its first letter, but also has this initial letter repeated at the beginning of each of its three verses. Alphabetical acrostics are not unknown elsewhere in the Old Testament; there are several instances of them in the Psalms.[2] The method is generally thought to have been adopted as an expedient to assist the memory. Clearly it is a somewhat artificial arrangement, cramping the imagination of the poet; and it is regarded by some as a sign of literary decadence. Whatever view we may take of it from the standpoint of purely artistic criticism, we can

---

[1] Isa. xiv. 4 *ff.*
[2] *E.g.*, Psalms ix., x., xxv., xxxiv., xxxvii., cxix., cxlv.

derive one important conclusion concerning the mental attitude of the writer from a consideration of the elaborate structure of the verse. Although this poetry is evidently inspired by deep emotion—emotion so profound that it cannot even be restrained by the stiffest vesture—still the author is quite self-possessed : he is not at all over-mastered by his feelings; what he says is the outcome of deliberation and reflection.

Passing from the form to the substance of the elegy, our attention is arrested on the threshold of the more serious enquiry by another link of connection between the two. In accordance with a custom of which we have other instances in the Hebrew Bible, the first word in the text is taken as the title of the book. The haphazard name is more appropriate in this case than it sometimes proves to be, for the first word of the first chapter—the original Hebrew for which is the Jewish title of the book—is "How." Now this is a characteristic word for the commencement of an elegy. Three out of the five elegies in Lamentations begin with it; so does the mock elegy in Isaiah. Moreover, it is not only suggestive of the form of a certain kind of poetry; it is a hint of the spirit in which that poetry is conceived; it strikes the key-note for all that follows. Therefore it may not be superfluous for us to consider the significance of this little word in the present connection.

In the first place, it is a sort of note of exclamation prefixed to the sentence it introduces. Thus it infuses an emotional element into the statements which follow it. The word is a relic of the most primitive form of language. Judging from the sounds produced by animals and the cries of little children, we should conclude that the first approach to speech would be a simple expression of excitement—a scream of pain, a shout of delight, a yell of rage, a shriek of surprise. Next to the mere venting of feeling comes the utterance of desire—a request, either for the possession of some coveted boon, or for deliverance from something objectionable. Thus the dog barks for his bone, or barks again to be freed from his chain; and the child cries for a toy, or for protection from a terror. If this is correct it will be only at the third stage of speech that we shall reach statements of fact pure and simple. Conversely, it may be argued that as the progress of cultivation develops the perceptive and reasoning faculties and corresponding forms of speech, the primitive emotional and volitional types of language must recede. Our phlegmatic English temperament predisposes us to take this view. It is not easy for us to sympathise with the expressiveness of an excitable Oriental people. What to them is perfectly natural and not at all inconsistent with true manliness strikes us as a childish weakness. Is not this a trifle insular? The emotions constitute as essential a part of human nature as the observing and reasoning faculties, and it cannot be proved that to stifle them beneath a calm exterior is more right and proper than to give them a certain adequate expression. That this expression may be found even among ourselves is apparent from the singular fact that the English, who are the most prosaic people in their conduct, have given the world more good poetry than any other nation of modern times; a fact which, perhaps, may be explained on the principle that the highest poetry is not the rank outgrowth of irregulated passions, but the cultivated fruit of deep-rooted ideas. Still these ideas must be warmed with feeling before they will germinate.

Much more, when we are not merely interested in poetic literature, when we are in earnest about practical actions, an artificial restraint of the emotions must be mischievous. No doubt the unimpassioned style has its mission—in allaying a panic, for example. But it will not inspire men to attempt a forlorn hope. Society will never be saved by hysterics; but neither will it ever be saved by statistics. It may be that the exclamation *how* is a feeble survival of the savage *howl*. Nevertheless the emotional expression, when regulated as the taming of the sound suggests, will always play a very real part in the life of mankind, even at the most highly developed stage of civilisation.

In the second place, it is to be observed that this word introduces a tone of vagueness into the sentences which it opens. A description beginning as these elegies begin would not serve the purpose of an inventory of the ruins of Jerusalem such as an insurance society would demand in the present day. The facts are viewed through an atmosphere of feeling, so that their chronological order is confused and their details melt one into another. That is not to say that they are robbed of all value. Pure impressionism may reveal truths which no hard, exact picture can render clear to us. These elegies make us see the desolation of Jerusalem more vividly than the most accurate photographs of the scenes referred to could have done, because they help us to enter into the passion of the event.

With this idea of vagueness, however, there is joined a sense of vastness. The note of exclamation is also a note of admiration. The language is indefinite in part for the very reason that the scene beggars description. The cynical spirit which would reduce all life to the level of a Dutch landscape is here excluded by the overwhelming mass of the troubles bewailed. The cataract of sorrow awes us with the greatness of its volume and the thunder of its fall.

From suggestions thus rising out of a consideration of the opening word of the elegy we may be led on to a perception of similar traits in the body of this poetry. It is emotional in character; it is vague in description; and it sets before us visions of vast woe.

But now it is quite clear that poetry such as this must be something else than the wild expression of grief. It is a product of reflection. The acute stage of suffering is over. The writer is musing upon a sad past; or if at times he is reflecting on a present state of distress, still he is regarding this as the result of more violent scenes, in the midst of which the last thing a man would think of doing would be to sit down and compose a poem. This reflective poetry will give us emotion, still warm, but shot with thought.

The reflectiveness of the elegy does not take the direction of philosophy. It does not speculate on the mystery of suffering. It does not ask such obstinate questions, or engage in such vexatious dialectics, as circle about the problem of evil in the Book of Job. Leaving those difficult matters to the theologians who care to wrestle with them, the elegist is satisfied to dwell on his theme in a quiet, meditative mood, and to permit his ideas to flow on spontaneously as in a reverie. Thus it happens that, artificial as is the form of his verse, the underlying thought seems to be natural and unforced. In this way he represents to us the afterglow of sunset which follows the day of storm and terror.

The afterglow is beautiful—that is what the elegy

makes evident. It paints the beauty of sorrow. It is able to do so only because it contemplates the scene indirectly, as portrayed in the mirror of thought. An immediate vision of pain is itself wholly painful. If the agony is intense, and if no relief can be offered, we instinctively turn aside from the sickening sight. Only a brutalised people could find amusement in the ghastly spectacle of the Roman amphitheatre. It is cited as a proof of Domitian's diabolical cruelty that the emperor would have dying slaves brought before him in order that he might watch the facial expression of their last agonies. Such scenes are not fit subjects for art. The famous group of the *Laocoon* is considered by many to have passed the boundaries of legitimate representation in the terror and torment of its subject; and *Ecce Homos* and pictures of the crucifixion can only be defended from a similar condemnation when the profound spiritual significance of the subjects is made to dominate the bare torture. Faced squarely, in the glare of day, pain and death are grim ogres, the ugliness of which no amount of sentiment can disguise. You can no more find poetry in a present Inferno than flowers in the red vomit of a live volcano. Men who have seen war tell us they have discovered nothing attractive in its dreadful scenes of blood and anguish and fury. What could be more revolting to contemplate than the sack of a city,—fire and sword in every street, public buildings razed to the ground, honoured monuments defaced, homes ravaged, children torn from the arms of their parents, young girls dragged away to a horrible fate, lust, robbery, slaughter rampant without shame or restraint, the wild beast in the conquerors let loose, and a whole army, suddenly freed from all rules of discipline, behaving like a swarm of demons just escaped from hell. To think of cultivating art or poetry in the presence of such scenes would be as absurd as to attempt a musical entertainment among the shrieks of lost souls.

The case assumes another aspect when we pass from the region of personal observation to that of reflection. There is no beauty in the sight of a captured castle immediately after the siege which ended in its fall, its battlements shattered, its walls seamed with cracks, here and there a breach, rough and ragged, and strewn with stones and dust. And yet, by slow degrees and in imperceptible ways, time and nature will transform the scene until moss-grown walls and ivy-covered towers acquire a new beauty only seen among ruins. Nature heals and time softens, and between them they throw a mantle of grace over the scars of what were once ugly, gaping wounds. Pain as it recedes into memory is transmuted into pathos; and pathos always fascinates us with some approach to beauty. If it is true that

"Poets learn in sorrow what they teach in song,"

must it not be also the fact that sorrow while inspiring song is itself glorified thereby? To use suffering merely as the food of æstheticism would be to degrade it immeasurably. We should rather put the case the other way. Poetry saves sorrow from becoming sordid by revealing its beauty, and in epic heroism even its sublimity. It helps us to perceive how much more depth there is in life than was apparent under the glare and glamour of prosperity. Some of us may recollect how shallow and shadowy our own lives were felt to be in the simple days before we had tasted the bitter cup. There was a hunger then for some deeper experience which seemed to lie beyond our reach. While we naturally shrank from entering the *via dolorosa*, we were dimly conscious that the pilgrims who trod its rough stones had discovered a secret that remained hidden from us, and we coveted their attainment, although we did not envy the bitter experience by which it had been acquired. This feeling may have been due in part to the foolish sentimentality that is sometimes indulged in by extreme youth; but that is not the whole explanation of it, for when our path conducts us from the flat, monotonous plain of ease and comfort into a region of chasms and torrents, we do indeed discover an unsuspected depth in life. Now it is the mission of the poetry of sorrow to interpret this discovery to us. At least it should enable us to read the lessons of experience in the purest light. It is not the task of the poet to supply a categorical answer to the riddle of the universe; stupendous as that task would be, it must be regarded as quite a prosaic one. Poetry will not fit exact answers to set questions, for poetry is not science; but poetry will open deaf ears and anoint blind eyes to receive the voices and visions that haunt the depths of experience. Thus it leads on to—

> "that blessed mood,
> In which the burden of the mystery,
> In which the heavy and the weary weight
> Of all this unintelligible world
> Is lightened."

It may not be obvious to the reader of an elegy that this function is discharged by such a poem, for elegiac poetry seems to aim at nothing more than the thoughtful expression of grief. Certainly it is neither didactic nor metaphysical. Nevertheless in weaving a wreath of imagination round the sufferings it bewails it cannot but clothe them with a rich significance. It would seem to be the mission of the five inspired elegies contained in the Book of Lamentations thus to interpret the sorrows of the Jews, and through them the sorrows of mankind.

CHAPTER II

THE ORIGIN OF THE POEMS

AS we pass out of Jerusalem by the Damascus Gate, and follow the main north road, our attention is immediately arrested by a low hill of grey rock sprinkled with wild flowers, which is now attracting peculiar notice because it has been recently identified with the "Golgotha" on which our Lord was crucified. In the face of this hill a dark recess—faintly suggestive of the eye-socket, if we may suppose the title "Place of a skull" to have arisen from a fancied resemblance to a goat's skull—is popularly known as "Jeremiah's grotto," and held by current tradition to be the retreat where the prophet composed the five elegies that constitute our Book of Lamentations. Clambering with difficulty over the loose stones that mark the passage of winter torrents, and reaching the floor of the cave, we are at once struck by the suspicious aptness of the "sacred site." In a solitude singularly retired, considering the proximity of a great centre of population, the spectator commands a full view of the whole city, its embattled walls immediately confronting him, with clustered roofs and domes in the rear. What place could have been more suitable for a poetic lament over the ruins of fallen Jerusalem? Moreover, when we take into account the dread associations derived from the later history of the Crucifixion, what could be more fitting than that the mourning patriot's tears for the woes of his city should have been shed so near to the very spot where her rejected Saviour was to suffer? But unfortunately history cannot be constructed on the lines of harmonious sentiments. When we endeavour to trace the legend that attributes the Lamentations to Jeremiah back to its source we lose the stream some centuries before we arrive at the time of the great prophet. No doubt for ages the tradition was undisputed; it is found both in Jewish and in Christian literature—in the Talmud and in the Fathers. Jerome popularised it in the Church by transferring it to the Vulgate, and before this Josephus set it down as an accepted fact. It is pretty evident that each of these parallel currents of opinion may have been derived from the Septuagint, which introduces the book with the sentence, "And it came to pass, after Israel had been carried away captive, and Jerusalem had become desolate, that Jeremiah sat weeping, and lamented with this lamentation over Jerusalem, and said," etc. Here our upward progress in tracking the tradition is stayed; no more ancient authority is to be found. Yet we are still three hundred years from the time of Jeremiah! Of course it is only reasonable to suppose that the translators of the Greek version did not make their addition to the Hebrew text at random, or without what they deemed sufficient grounds. Possibly they were following some documentary authority, or, at least, some venerable tradition. Of this we know nothing. Meanwhile, it must be observed that no such statement exists in the Hebrew Bible; and it would never have been omitted if it had been there originally.

One other witness has been adduced, but only to furnish testimony of an obscure and ambiguous character.

In 2 Chron. xxxv. 25 we read, "And Jeremiah lamented for Josiah; and all the singing men and singing women spake of Josiah in their lamentations, unto this day; and they made them an ordinance in Israel; and, behold, they are written in the lamentations." Josephus, and Jerome after him, appear to assume that the chronicler is here referring to our Book of Lamentations. That is very questionable; for the words describe an elegy on Josiah, and our book contains no such elegy. Can we suppose that the chronicler assumed that inasmuch as Jeremiah was believed to have written a lament for the mourners to chant in commemoration of Josiah, this would be one of the poems preserved in the collection of Jerusalem elegies familiar to readers of his day? Be that as it may, the chronicler wrote in the Grecian period, and therefore his statements come some long time after the date of the prophet.

In this dearth of external testimony we turn to the book itself for indications of origin and authorship. The poems make no claim to have been the utterances of Jeremiah; they do not supply us with their author's name. Therefore there can be no question of genuineness, no room for an ugly charge of "forgery," or a delicate ascription of "pseudonymity." The case is not comparable to that of 2 Peter, or even to that of Ecclesiastes—the one of which directly claims apostolic authority, and the other a "literary" association with the name of Solomon. It is rather to be paralleled with the case of the Epistle to the Hebrews, a purely anonymous work. Still there is much which seems to point to Jeremiah as the author of these intensely pathetic elegies. They are not like MacPherson's *Ossian*; nobody can question their antiquity. If they were not quite contemporaneous with the scenes they describe so graphically they cannot have originated much later; for they are like the low wailings with which the storm sinks to rest, reminding us how recently the thunder was rolling and the besom of destruction sweeping over the land. Among the prophets of Israel Jeremiah was the voice crying in the wilderness of national ruin; it is natural to suppose that he too was the poet who poured out sad thoughts of memory in song at a later time when sorrow had leisure for reflection. His prophecies would lead us to conclude that no Jew of those dark days could have experienced keener pangs of grief at the incomparable woes of his nation. He was the very incarnation of patriotic mourning. Who then would be more likely to have produced the national lament? Here we seem to meet again none other than the man who exclaimed, "Oh that I could comfort myself against sorrow! my heart is faint within me,"[1] and again, "Oh that my head were waters, and mine eyes a fountain of tears, that I might weep day and night for the slain of the daughter of my people."[2] Many points of resemblance between the known writings of Jeremiah and these poems may be detected. Thus Jeremiah's "Virgin daughter" of God's people reappears as the "Virgin daughter of Judah." In both the writer is oppressed with fear as well as grief; in both he especially denounces clerical vices, the sins of the two rival lines of religious leaders, the priests and the prophets; in both he appeals to God for retribution. There is a remarkable likeness in tone and temper throughout between the two series of writings. It would be possible to adduce many purely verbal marks of similarity; the commentator on

---

[1] Jer. viii. 18.   [2] Jer. ix. 1.

Lamentations most frequently illustrates the meaning of a word by referring to a parallel usage in Jeremiah.

On the other hand, several facts raise difficulties in the way of our accepting of the hypothesis of a common authorship. The verbal argument is precarious at best; it can only be fully appreciated by the specialist, and if accepted by the general reader, it must be taken on faith. Of course this last point is no valid objection to the real worth of the argument in itself; it cannot be maintained that nothing is true which may not be reduced to the level of the "meanest intelligence," or the "differential calculus" would be a baseless fable. But when the specialists disagree, even the uninitiated have some excuse for holding the case to be not proved for either side; and it is thus with the resemblances and the differences between Jeremiah and Lamentations, long lists of phrases used in common being balanced with equally long lists of peculiarities found in one only of the two books in question. The strongest objection to the theory that Jeremiah was the author of the Lamentations, however, is one that can be more readily grasped. These poems are most elaborately artistic in form, not to say artificial. Now the objection which is roused by that fact is not simply due to the loose and less shapely construction of the prophecies; for it may justly be urged that the literary designs entertained by the prophet in the leisure of his later years may have led him to cultivate a style which would have been quite unsuitable for his practical preaching or for the political pamphlets he used to fling off in the heat of conflict. It originates in deeper psychological contradictions. Is it possible that the man who had shed bitterest tears, as from his very heart, in the dismal reality of misery, could play with his troubles in fanciful acrostics? Can we imagine a leading actor in the tragedy turning the events through which he had passed into materials for æsthetic treatment? Can we credit this of so intense a soul as Jeremiah? The composition of *In Memoriam* may be cited as an instance of the production of highly artistic poetry under the influence of keen personal sorrow. But the case is not parallel; for Tennyson was a passive mourner over the loss of a friend under circumstances with which he had no connection, while Jeremiah had contended strenuously for years on the field of action. Could a man with such a history have set himself to work up its most doleful experiences into the embroidery of a peculiarly artificial form of versification? That is the gravest difficulty. Other objections of minor weight follow. In the third elegy Jeremiah would seem to be giving more prominence to his own personality than we should have expected of the brave, unselfish prophet. In the fourth the writer appears to associate himself with those Jews who were disappointed in expecting deliverance from an Egyptian alliance, when he complains—

"Our eyes do yet fail in looking for our vain help:
In watching we have watched for a nation that could not save."[1]

Would Jeremiah, who bade the Jews bow to the scourge of Jehovah's chastisement and look for no earthly deliverer, thus confess participation in the worldly policy which he, in common with all the true prophets, had denounced as faithless and disobedient? Then, while sharing Jeremiah's condemnation of the priests and prophets, the writer appears to have only commiseration

---

[1] iv. 17.

for the fate of the poor weak king Zedekiah.[1] This is very different from Jeremiah's treatment of him.[2]

It is not a serious objection that our poet says of Zion,

"Yea, her prophets find no vision from the Lord,"[3]

while we know that Jeremiah had visions after the destruction of Jerusalem,[4] because the general condition may still have been one characterised by the silencing of the many prophets with whose oracles the Jews had been accustomed to solace themselves in view of threatened calamities; nor that he exclaims,

"Shall the priest and the prophet be slain in the sanctuary of the Lord?"[5]

although Jeremiah makes no mention of this twofold assassination, because we have no justification for the assumption that he recorded every horror of the great tragedy; nor, again, that the author is evidently familiar with the Book of Deuteronomy, and refers frequently to the "Song of Moses" in particular, for this is just what we might have expected of Jeremiah; and yet these and other similar but even less conclusive points have been brought forward as difficulties. Perhaps it is a more perplexing fact, in view of the traditional hypothesis, that the poet appears to have made use of the writings of Ezekiel. Thus the allusion to the prophets who have "seen visions . . . of vanity and foolishness,"[6] points to the fuller description of these men in the writings of the prophet of the exile, where the completeness of the picture shews that the priority is

---

[1] iv. 20.
[2] Jer. lii. 2, 3.
[3] ii. 9.
[4] *E.g.* Jer. xlii. 7.
[5] ii. 20.
[6] ii. 14.

with Ezekiel.[1] Similarly the "perfection of beauty" ascribed to the daughter of Jerusalem in the second elegy[2] reminds us of the similar phrase that occurs more than once in Ezekiel.[3] Still, that prophet wrote before the time to which the Lamentations introduce us, and it cannot be affirmed that Jeremiah could not have seen his writings, or would not have condescended to echo a phrase from them. A difficulty of a broader character must be felt in the fact that the poems themselves give us no hint of Jeremiah. The appearance of the five elegies in the *Hagiographa* without any introductory notice is a grave objection to the theory of a Jeremiah authorship. If so famous a prophet had composed them, would not this have been recorded? Even in the Septuagint, where they are associated with Jeremiah, they are not translated by the same hand as the version of the prophet's acknowledged works. It may be that none of the objections which have been adduced against the later tradition can be called final; nor when regarded in their total force do they absolutely forbid the possibility that Jeremiah was the author of the Lamentations. But then the question is not so much one of possibility as one of probability. We must remember that we are dealing with anonymous poems that make no claim upon any particular author, and that we have no pleas whatever, special or more general, on which to defend the guesses of a much later and quite uncritical age, when people cultivated a habit of attaching every shred of literature that had come down from their ancestors to some famous name.

---

[1] *E.g.* Ezek. xii. 24, xiii. 6, 7, xxii. 28.   [2] Lam. ii. 15.
[3] Ezek. xxvii. 3, xxviii. 12.

Failing Jeremiah, it is not possible to hit upon any other known person with the least assurance. Some have followed Bunsen in his conjecture that Baruch the scribe may have been the author of the poems. Others have suggested a member of the family of Shaphan, in which Jeremiah found his most loyal friends.[1]

It is much questioned whether the five elegies are the work of one man. The second, the third, and the fourth follow a slightly different alphabetical arrangement from that which is employed in the first—in reversing the order of two letters,[2] while the internal structure of the verses in the third shews another variation—the threefold repetition of the acrostic. Then the personality of the poet emerges more distinctly in the third elegy as the centre of interest—a marked contrast to the method of the other poems. Lastly, the fifth differs from its predecessors in several respects. Its lines are shorter; it is not an acrostic; it is chiefly devoted to the insults heaped upon the Jews by their enemies; and it seems to belong to a later time, for while the four previous poems treat of the siege of Jerusalem and its accompanying troubles, this one is concerned with the subsequent state of servitude, and reflects on the ruin of the nation across some interval of time. Thus the poet cries—

"Wherefore doest thou forget us for ever,
And forsake us *so long time*?"[3]

A recent attempt to assign the last two elegies to the age of the Maccabees has entirely broken down. The

---

[1] See Jer. xxvi. 24, xxix. 3 *ff*, xl. 5.   [2] ע and פ.
[3] v. 20.

points of agreement with that age which have been adduced will fit the Babylonian period equally well, and the most significant marks of the later time are entirely absent. Is it conceivable that a description of the persecution by Antiochus Epiphanes would contain no hint of the martyr fidelity of the devout Jews to their law which was so gloriously maintained under the Maccabees? The fourth and fifth elegies are as completely silent on this subject as the earlier elegies.

The evidence that points to any diversity of authorship is very feeble. The fifth elegy may have been written years later than the rest of the book, and yet it may have come from the same source, for the example of Tennyson shews that the gift of poetry is not always confined to but a brief interval in the poet life. The other distinctions are not nearly so marked as some that may be observed in the recognised poems of a single author—for example, the amazing differences between the smooth style of *The Idylls of the King* and the quaint dialect of *The Northern Farmer*. Though some differences of vocabulary have been discovered, the resemblances between all the five poems are much more striking. In motive and spirit and feeling they are perfectly agreed. While therefore in our ignorance of the origin of the Lamentations, and in recognition of the variations that have been indicated, we cannot deny that they may have been collected from the utterances of two or even three inspired souls, neither are we by any means forced to assent to this opinion; and under these circumstances it will be justifiable as well as convenient to refer to the authorship of Lamentations in terms expressive of a single individual. One thing is fairly certain. The author was a contemporary, an eye-witness of the frightful calamities he bewailed.

With all their artificiality of structure these elegies are the outpourings of a heart moved by a near vision of the scenes of the Babylonian invasion. The swift, vivid pictures of the siege and its accompanying miseries force upon our minds the conclusion that the poet must have moved in the thick of the events he narrates so graphically, although, unlike Jeremiah, he does not seem to have been a leading actor in them. Children cry to their mothers for bread, and faint with hunger at every street corner; the ghastly rumour goes forth that a mother has boiled her baby; elders sit on the ground in silence; young maidens hang their heads despairing; princes tremble in their helplessness; the enemy break through the walls, carry havoc into the city, insolently trample the sacred courts of the temple; even the priest and the prophet do not escape in the indiscriminate carnage; wounded people are seen, with blood upon their garments, wandering aimlessly like blind men; the temple is destroyed, its rich gold bedimmed with smoke, and the city herself left waste and desolate, while the exultant victors pour ridicule over the misery of their prey. A later generation would have blurred the outline of these scenes, regarding them through the shifting mists of rumour, with more or less indistinctness. Besides, the motive for the composition of such elegies would vanish with the lapse of time. Still some few years must be allowed for the patriot's brooding over the scenes he had witnessed, until the memory of them had mellowed sufficiently for them to become the subjects of song. The fifth elegy, at all events, implies a considerable interval. Jerusalem was destroyed in the year B.C. 587; therefore we may safely date the poems from about B.C. 550 onwards—*i.e.*, at some time during the second half of the sixth century. What is of more moment for us to know is that we have here no falsetto notes, such as we may sometimes detect in Virgil's exquisite descriptions of the siege of Troy, for the poet has witnessed the fiery ordeal the recollection of which now inspires his song. Thus out of the unequalled woes of Jerusalem destroyed he has provided for all ages the typical, divinely inspired expression of sorrow—primarily the expression of sorrow—and then associated with this some pregnant hints both of its dark relationship to sin and of its higher connection with the purposes of God.

CHAPTER III

THE THEME

NO more pathetic subject ever inspired a poet than that which became the theme of the Lamentations. Wave after wave of invasion had swept over Jerusalem, until at length the miserable city had been reduced to a heap of ruins. After the decisive defeat of the Egyptians at the great battle of Carchemish during the reign of Jehoiakim, Nebuchadnezzar broke into Jerusalem and carried off some of the sacred vessels from the temple, leaving a disorganised country at the mercy of the wild tribes of Bedouin from beyond the Jordan. Three months after the accession of Jehoiakin, the son of Jehoiakim, the Chaldæans again visited the city, pillaged the temple and the royal palace, and sent the first band of captives, consisting of the very *élite* of the citizens, with Ezekiel among them, into captivity at Babylon. This was only the beginning of troubles. Zedekiah, who was set up as a mere vassal king, intrigued with Pharaoh Hophra, a piece of folly which called down upon himself and his people the savage vengeance of Nebuchadnezzar. Jerusalem now suffered all the horrors of a siege, which lasted for a year and a half. Famine and pestilence preyed upon the inhabitants; and yet the Jews were holding out with a stubborn resistance, when the invaders effected an entrance by night, and were encamped in the temple court before the astonished king was aware of their presence. Zedekiah then imitated the secrecy of his enemies. With a band of followers he crept out of one of the eastern gates, and fled down the defile towards the Jordan; but he was overtaken near Jericho, and conveyed a prisoner to Riblah; his sons were killed in his very presence, his eyes were burnt out, and the wretched man sent in chains to Babylon. The outrages perpetrated against the citizens at Jerusalem as well as the sufferings of the fugitives were such as are only possible in barbarous warfare. Finally the city was razed to the ground and her famous temple burnt.

The Lamentations bewail the fall of a city. In this respect they are unlike the normal type of elegiac poetry. As a rule, the elegy is personal in character and individualistic, mourning the untimely death of some one beloved friend of the writer. It is the revelation of a private grief, although with a poet's privilege its author calls upon his readers to share his sorrow. In the classic model of this order of verse Milton justifies the intrusion of his distress upon the peace of nature by exclaiming—

> "For Lycidas is dead, dead ere his prime,
> Young Lycidas, and hath not left his peer.
> Who would not sing for Lycidas?"

And Shelley, while treating his theme in an ethereal, fantastic way, still represents Alastor, the Spirit of Solitude, in the person of one who has just died, when he cries—

> "But thou art fled,
> Like some frail exhalation which the dawn
> Robes in its golden beams,—ah! thou hast fled!
> The brave, the gentle, and the beautiful,
>   he child of grace and genius."

Gray's well-known elegy, it is true, is not confined to the fate of a single individual; the churchyard suggests the pathetic reflections of the poet on the imaginary lives and characters of many past inhabitants of the village. Nevertheless these cross the stage one by one; the village itself has not been destroyed, like Goldsmith's "Sweet Auburn." Jeremiah's lamentation on the death of Josiah must have been a personal elegy; so was the scornful lament over the king of Babylon in Isaiah. But now we have a different kind of subject in the Book of Lamentations. Here it is the fate of Jerusalem, the fate of the city itself as well as that of its citizens, that is deplored. To rouse the imagination and awaken the sympathy of the reader Zion is personified, and thus the poetry is assimilated in form to the normal elegy. Still it is important for us to take note of this distinguishing trait of the Lamentations; they bewail the ruin of a city.

Poetry inspired with this intention must acquire a certain breadth not found in more personal effusions. Too much indulgence in private grief cannot but produce a narrowing effect upon the mind. Intense pain is as selfish as intense pleasure. We may mourn our dead until we have no room left in our sympathies for the great ocean of troubles among the living that surges round the little island of our personal interests.

This misfortune is escaped in the Lamentations. Close as is the poet's relations with the home of his childhood, there is still some approach to altruism in his lament over the desolation of Jerusalem viewed as a whole, rather than over the death of his immediate friends alone. There is a largeness, too, in it. We find it difficult to recover the ancient feeling for the city. Our more important towns are so huge and shapeless that the inhabitants fail to grasp the unity, the wholeness of the wilderness of streets and houses; and yet they so effectually overshadow the smaller towns that these places do not venture to assume much civic pride. Besides, the general tendency of modern life is individualistic. Even the more recent attempts to rouse interest in comprehensive social questions are conceived in a spirit of sympathy for the individual rights and needs of the people, and do not spring from any great concern for the prosperity of the corporation as such. No doubt this is an indication of a movement in a right direction. The old civic idea was too abstract; it sacrificed the citizens to the city, beautifying the public buildings in the most costly manner, while the people were crowded in miserable dens to rot and die unseen and unpitied. We substitute sanitation for splendour. This is more sensible, more practical, more humane, if it is more prosaic; for life is something else than poetry. Still it may be worth while asking whether in aiming at a useful, homely object it is so essential to abandon the old ideal altogether, because it cannot be denied that the price we pay is seen in a certain dinginess and commonness of living. Is it necessary that philanthropy should always remain Philistine?

The largeness of view which breaks upon us when we begin to think of the city as a whole rather than only of a number of isolated individuals is more than a perception of mass and magnitude. The city is an organism; and not like an animal of the lower orders, such as the *anelids* or *centipedes*, in which every segment is simply a *replica* of its neighbour, it is an organism maintained in efficiency by means of a great variety of mutual ministeries. Thus it is a unit in itself more elaborately differentiated, and therefore in a sense higher in the scale of being than its constituent elements, the individual inhabitants. The destruction of a city constituted in this way is a serious loss to the world. Even if no one inhabitant is killed, and quite apart from the waste of property and the ruin of commerce, the dissolution of the organism leaves a tremendous gap. The scattered people may acquire a new prosperity in the land of their exile, but still the city will have vanished. The Jews survived the destruction of Jerusalem; yet who shall estimate the loss that this destruction of their national capital involved?

Then the city being a definite organic unit has its own history, a history which is immensely more than the sum of the biographies of its inhabitants—stretching down from remote ages, and joining the distant past with present days. Here, then, time adds to the largeness of the city idea. The brevity of life seems to assign a petty part to the individual. But that brevity vanishes in the long, continuous story of an ancient city. A man may well be proud of his connection with such a record, unless it be one of wickedness and shame; and even in that case his relations to a great city deepen and widen his life, though the result may be, as it was with the devout Jew, to induce grief and humiliation. But Jerusalem had her records of glory as well as her tales of shame. The city of David and Solomon held garnered stores of legend and history, in the rich memories of which each of her children had a heritage. The overthrow of Jerusalem was the dissipation of a great inheritance.

And this is not all. The city has its own peculiar character—a character which is not only more than a summary of the morals and manners of the men and women who live in it, but also unique when compared with other cities. Every city that can boast of real civic life has its distinctive individuality; and often this is as striking as the individuality of any private person. Birmingham is very unlike Manchester; nobody could mistake Glasgow for Edinburgh. London, Paris, Berlin, Rome, Melbourne, New York—each of these cities is unique. The particular city may be said to be the only specimen of its kind. If one is blotted out the type is lost; there is no duplicate. Athens and Sparta, Rome and Carthage, Florence and Venice, were rivals which could never take the place of one another. Most assuredly Jerusalem stood alone, stamped with a character which no other place in the world approached, and charged with a perfectly unique mission. For such a city to vanish off the face of the earth was the impoverishment of the world in the loss of what no nation in all the four continents could ever supply.

In saying this we must be careful to avoid the anachronism of reading into the present situation the after history of the sacred city and the character therein evolved. In the days before the exile Jerusalem was not the holy place that Ezra and Nehemiah subsequently laboured to make of it. Still looking back across the centuries we can see what perhaps the contemporaries could not discover, that the peculiar destiny of Jerusalem was already shaping itself in history. At the time, to the patriotic devotion of the mourning Jews, she was their old home, the happy dwelling-place of their childhood, the shrine of their fathers' sepulchres—Nehemiah's thought about the city even at a later date;[1] in a word, the ancient centre

---
[1] Neh. ii. 3.

of national life and union, strength and glory. But another and a higher meaning was beginning to gather about the word Jerusalem, a meaning which has come in course of time to give this city a place quite solitary and unrivalled in all history. Jerusalem is now revered as the religious centre of the world's life. Even in this early age she was beginning to earn her lofty character. Josiah's reformation had so far succeeded that the temple of Solomon had been pronounced the centre of the worship of Jehovah. Then these elegies bear witness to the importance of the national festivals, which were all held at the capital, and which were all of a religious nature. It is impossible to conjecture what would have been the course of the religious history of the world if Jerusalem had been blotted out for ever at this period of the life of the city. More than five centuries later Jesus Christ declared that the *time* had come when neither at the Samaritan mountain nor at Jerusalem should men worship the Father, because God is spirit and can only be worshipped in spirit and in truth. Thus the possibility of this spiritual worship which was independent of the sanctity of any place was a question of time. The time for it had only just arrived when our Lord made His great declaration. Of course the calendar could not rule this matter; it was not essentially an affair of dates. But the world required all those intervening ages to ripen into fitness for the lofty act of purely spiritual worship; and even then the great advance was not made by a process of simple development. It was necessary for Christ to come, both to reveal the higher nature of worship by revealing the higher nature of Him who was the object of worship, and also to bestow the spiritual grace through which men and women could practise the true worship. Therefore these very words of our Lord which proclaim the absolute spirituality of worship for those who have attained to His teaching most plainly imply that such worship must have been beyond the reach of average people, at all events, in earlier ages. Jerusalem, then, was needed to serve as the cradle of the religion revealed through her prophets. When her wings had grown religion could dispense with the nest; but in her unfledged condition the destruction of the local shelter threatened the death of the broodling.

There is a hopeful side to these reflections. A city with such a character may be said to bear the seeds of her own revival. Her individuality has that within it which fights against extinction. To put it another way, the idea of the city is too marked and too attractive for its privileged custodians to let it fade out of their minds, or to rest satisfied without attempting once more to have it realised in visible form. Carthage might perish; for Carthage had few graces wherewith to stir the enthusiasm of her citizens. Rome, on the other hand, had developed a character and a corresponding destiny of her own; and therefore she could not be blotted out by savage Huns or Vandal hosts. The genius for government, unapproached by any other city, could not be suppressed by the worst ravages of the invader. Even when political supremacy had passed away in consequence of the vices and weakness of the degenerate citizens, the power that had ruled the world simply took another shape and ruled the Church, the supremacy of Rome in the papacy succeeding to the supremacy of Rome in the empire. So was it with Jerusalem. There was immortality in this wonderful city.

We may look at the subject from two points of view. First, faith in God encourages the hope that such a destiny as is here foreshadowed should not be allowed to fail. So felt the prophets who were permitted to read the counsels of God by inspired insight into the eternal principles of His nature. These men were sure that Jerusalem must rise again from her ashes because they knew for a certainty that her Lord would not let His purposes concerning her be frustrated.

Then even with the limited vision which is all that can be attained from the lower platform of historical criticism, we may see that Jerusalem had acquired such an immortal place in the estimation of the Jews, that the people must have clung to the idea of a restoration till it was realised. To say this is to shew that the realisation could not but be accomplished. Such passionate regrets as those of the Lamentations are seeds of hope.

May we go one step further? Is not every true and deep regret a prophecy of restoration? There is an irrecoverable past, it must be owned. That is to say, the days that are gone cannot return, nor can deeds once done ever be undone; the future will never be an exact repetition of the past. But all this does not forbid the assurance that there may be genuine restoration. Jerusalem restored was very unlike the city whose fate the elegist bewailed; nevertheless she was restored, and that with her essential characteristics more pronounced than ever. Henceforth she was to be most completely what her earlier history had only faintly adumbrated—the typical seat of religion. Thus, though the Lamentations are not at all cheering or prophetic in tone, or even in intention, but the very reverse, wholly mournful and despondent, we may still detect, in the very intensity and persistence of the sorrow they portray, gleams of hope for better days. There is no hope in stolid indifference; it is in the penitent's tears that we discover the prospect of his amendment. Repentance weeps for the past, but at the same time it looks forward with a changed mind that is the promise of better things to come. Why should not we apply these ideas that spring from a consideration of the five Hebrew elegies to other elegies—to the dirges that mourn the loved and dead ? If we could willingly let the departed drop out of thought we might have little ground for believing we should ever see them again. But sorrow for the dead immortalises them in memory. In a materialistic view of the universe that might mean nothing but the perpetuity of a sentiment. But then it may by itself help us to perceive the superficiality, the utter falseness of such a view. Thus Tennyson sees the answer to the crushing doubts of materialism and the assurance of immortality for the departed in the strength of the love with which they are cherished :

"What is it all if we all of us end but in being our own corpse coffins at last,
Swallowed in Vastness, lost in Silence, drowned in the deeps of a meaningless Past !
What but a murmur of gnats in the gloom, or a moment's anger of bees in their hive ?

. . . . . .

Peace, let it be ! for I loved him, and love him for ever. The dead are not dead, but alive."

CHAPTER IV

DESOLATION

i. 1-7.

THE first elegy is devoted to moving pictures of the desolation of Jerusalem and the sufferings of her people. It dwells upon these disasters themselves, with fewer references to the causes of them or the hope of any remedy than are to be found in the subsequent poems, simply to express the misery of the whole story. Thus it is in the truest sense of the word a "Lamentation." It naturally divides itself into two parts—one with the poet speaking in his own person,[1] the other representing the deserted city herself appealing to passing strangers and neighbouring nations, and lastly to God, to take note of her woes.[2]

The poem opens with a very beautiful passage in which we have a comparison of Jerusalem to a widow bereft of her children, sitting solitary in the night, weeping sorely. It would not be just to read into the image of widowhood ideas collected from utterances of the prophets about the wedded union of Israel and her Lord; we have no hint of anything of the sort here. Apparently the image is selected in order to express the more vividly the utter lonesomeness of the city. It is clear that the attribute "soli-

---

[1] i. 1-11.   [2] i. 12-22.

tary" has no bearing on the external relations of Jerusalem—her isolation among the Syrian hills, or the desertion of her allies, mentioned a little later;[1] it points to a more ghostly solitude, streets without traffic, tenantless houses. The widow is solitary because she has been robbed of her children. And in this, her desolation, *she sits*. The attitude, so simple and natural and easy under ordinary circumstances, here suggests a settled continuance of wretchedness; it is helpless and hopeless. The first wild agony of the severance of the closest natural ties has passed, and with it the stimulus of conflict; now there has supervened the dull monotony of despair. This is the lowest depth of misery, because it allows leisure when leisure is least welcome, because it gives the reins to the imagination to roam over regions of heart-rending memory or sombre apprehension, above all because there is nothing to be done, so that the whole range of consciousness is abandoned to pain. Many a sufferer has been saved by the healing ministry of active duties, sometimes resented as an intrusion. It is a fearful thing simply to sit in sorrow.

The mourner sits *in the night*, while the world around lies in the peace of sleep. The darkness has fallen, yet she does not stir, for day and night are alike to her—both dark. She is statuesque in sorrow, petrified by pain, and yet unhappily not dead; benumbed, but alive in every sensitive fibre of her being and terribly awake. In this dread night of misery her one occupation is weeping. The mourner knows how the hidden fountains of tears which have been sealed to the world for the day will break out in the silent

---

[1] i. 2.

solitude of night; then the bravest will "wet his couch with his tears." The forlorn woman "weepeth *sore*"; to use the expressive Hebraism, "weeping she weepeth." "Her tears are on her cheeks"; they are continually flowing; she has no thought of drying them; there is no one else to wipe them away. This is not the frantic torrent of youthful tears, soon to be forgotten in sudden sunshine, like a spring shower; it is the dreary winter rain, falling more silently, but from leaden clouds that never break. The Hebrew poet's picture is illustrated with singular aptness by a Roman coin, struck off in commemoration of the destruction of Jerusalem by the army of Titus, which represents a woman seated under a palm tree with the legend *Judæa capta*. Is it too much to imagine that some Greek artist attached to the court of Vespasian may have borrowed the idea for the coin from the Septuagint version of this very passage?

The woe of Jerusalem is intensified by reason of its contrast with the previous splendour of the proud city. She had not always appeared as a lonely widow. Formerly she had held a high place among the neighbouring nations—for did she not cherish memories of the great days of her shepherd king and Solomon the magnificent? Then she ruled provinces; now she is herself tributary. She had lovers in the old times— a fact which points to faults of character not further pursued at present. How opposite is the utterly deserted state into which she is now sunk! This thought of a tremendous fall gives the greatest force to the portrait. It is Rembrandtesque; the black shadows on the foreground are the deeper because they stand sharply out against the brilliant radiance that streams in from the sunset of the past. The pitiableness of the comfortless present lies in this, that there had been lovers whose consolations would now have been a solace; the bitterness of the enmity now experienced is its having been distilled from the dregs of poisoned friendship. Against the protests of her faithful prophets Jerusalem had courted alliance with her heathen neighbours, only to be cruelly deserted in her hour of need. It is the old story of friendship with the world, keenly accentuated in the life of Israel, because this favoured people had already seen glimpses of a rich, rare privilege, the friendship of Heaven. This is the irony of the situation; it is the tragic irony of all Hebrew history. Why were these people so blindly infatuated that they would be perpetually forsaking the living waters, and hewing out to themselves broken cisterns that could hold no water? The question is only surpassed by that of the similar folly on the part of those of us who follow their example in spite of the warning their fate affords, failing to see that true friendship is too exacting for ties spun from mere convenience or superficial pleasantness to bear the strain of its more serious claims.

Passing on from the poetic image to a more direct view of the drear facts of the case, the author describes the hardships of the fugitives—people who had fled to Egypt, the retreat of Jeremiah and his companions. This must be the bearing of the passage which our translators render—

"Judah is gone into captivity because of affliction, and because of great servitude."

For if the topic were the captivity at Babylon it would be difficult to see how "affliction" and "great servitude" could be treated as the *causes* of that disaster; were they not rather its effects? Two solutions of this difficulty have been proposed. It has been suggested that the captivity is here presented as a consequence of the misconduct of the Jews in oppressing peoples subject to them. But the abstract words will not readily bear any such meaning; we should have expected some more explicit charge. Then it has been proposed to read the words "out of affliction," etc., in place of the phrase "because of affliction," etc., as though in escaping from trouble at home the Jews had only passed into a new misfortune abroad. This is not so simple an explanation of the poet's language as that at which we arrive by the perfectly legitimate substitution of the word "exile" for "captivity." It may seem strange that the statement should be affirmed of "Judah," as though the whole nation had escaped to Egypt; but it would be equally inexact to say that "Judah" was carried captive to Babylon, seeing that only a selection from the upper classes was deported, while the majority of the people was probably left in the land. But so many of the Jews, especially those best known to the poet, were in voluntary exile, that it was quite natural for him to regard them as virtually the nation. Now upon these refugees three troubles fall. First, the asylum is a heathen country, abominable to pious Israelites. Second, even here the fugitives have no rest; they are not allowed to settle down; they are perpetually molested. Third, on the way thither they are harassed by the enemy. They are overtaken by pursuers "within the straits," a statement which may be read literally; bands of Chaldæans would hover about the mountains, ready to pounce upon the disorganised groups of fugitives as they made their way through the narrow defiles that led out of the hill country to the southern plains. But the phrase is a familiar Hebraism for difficulties generally. No doubt it was true of the Jews in this larger sense that their opponents took advantage of their straitened circumstances to vex them in every possible way. This is just in accordance with the common experience of mankind all the world over. But while the fact of the experience is obvious, the inference to which it points like an arrow is obstinately eluded. Thus a commercial man in financial straits loses his credit at the very moment when he most needs it. We cannot say that this is a proof of spite, or even a sign of cynical indifference; because the needy person is really most untrustworthy, though his moral integrity may be unshaken, seeing that his circumstances make it probable that he will be unable to fulfil his obligations. But now it is the deeper significance of this fact that is so persistently ignored. There is perceptible at times in nature a law of compensation by the operation of which misfortune is mitigated; but that merciful law is frequently thwarted by the overbearing influence of the terrible law of the "survival of the fittest," the gospel of the fortunate, but the death-knell for all failures. If this is so in nature, much more does it obtain in human society so long as selfish greed is unchecked by higher principles. Then the world, the Godless world, can be no asylum for the miserable and unfortunate, because it will be hard upon them in exact proportion to the extremity of their necessities. Moreover, the perception that this bitter truth is not a fruit of temporary passions which may be restrained by education, but the outcome of certain persistent principles which cannot be set aside while society retains its present constitution, gives to it the adamantine strength of destiny.

Coming nearer to the city in his mental vision, the poet next bewails deserted roads; " those ways of Zion " up which the holiday folks used to troop, clad in gay garments, with songs of rejoicing, are left so lonely that it seems as though they themselves must be mourning. It is in keeping with the imagery of these poems which personify the city, to endow the very roads with fancied consciousness. This is a natural result of intense emotion, and therefore a witness to its very intensity. It seems as though the very earth must share in the feelings of the man whose heart is stirred to its depths; as though all things must be filled with the passion the waves of which flow out to the horizon of his consciousness, till the very stones cry out.

As he approaches the city, the poet is struck with a strange, sad sight. There are no people about the gates; yet here, if anywhere, we should expect to meet not only travellers passing through, but also groups of men, merchants at their traffic, arbitrators settling disputes, friends exchanging confidences, idlers lounging about and chewing the cud of the latest gossip, beggars whining for alms; for by the gates are markets, *al fresco* tribunals, open spaces for public meetings. Formerly the life of the city was here concentrated; now no trace of life is to be seen even at these social ganglia. The desertion and silence of the gateways gives a shock of distress to the visitor on entering the ruined city. More disappointments await him within the walls. Still keeping in mind the idea of the national festivals, and accompanying the course of them in imagination, the poet goes up to the temple. No services are proceeding; any priests who may be found still haunting the precincts of the charred ruins can only sigh over their enforced idleness; the girl-choristers whose voices would ring through the porticoes in the old times, are silent and desolate, for their mother, Jerusalem, is herself "in bitterness."

In this part of the elegy our attention is directed to the cessation of the happy national assemblies with their accompaniment of public worship in songs of praise for harvest and vintage and in the awful symbolism of the altar. The name "Zion" was associated with two things, festivity and worship. It was a happy privilege for Israel to have had the inspired insight as well as the courage of faith to realise the conjunction. Even with the fuller light and larger liberty of Christianity it is rarely acknowledged among us. Our services have too much of the funeral dirge about them. The devout Israelite reserved his dirge for the death of his worship. It does not seem to have occurred to the poet that anybody could come to regard worship as an irksome duty from which he would gladly be liberated. Are we, then, to suppose that the Israelites who practised the crude cult that was prevalent before the Exile, even among the true servants of Jehovah, were indeed more devout than Christians who enjoy the privileges of their richer revelation? Scarcely so; for it must be remembered that we are called to a more spiritual and therefore a more difficult worship. Inward sincerity is here of supreme importance; if this is missing there is no worship, and without it the miserable unreality becomes inexpressibly wearisome. No doubt it is the failure to reach the rare altitude of its lofty ideal that makes Christian worship to appear in the eyes of many to be a melancholy performance. But this explanation should not be permitted to obscure the fact that true, living, spiritual worship must be a very delightful exercise of the soul. Perhaps one reason why this truth is not sufficiently appreciated may be found in the very facility with which the outward means of worship are presented to us. People who are seldom out of the sound of church bells are inclined to grow deaf to their significance. The Roman Christian hunted in the catacombs, the Waldensian hiding in his mountain cave, the Covenanter meeting his fellow members of the kirk in a remote highland glen, the backwoodsman walking fifty miles to attend Divine service once in six months, are led by difficulty and deprivation to perceive the value of public worship in a degree which is surprising to people among whom it is merely an incident of every-day life. When Zion was in ashes the memory of her festivals was encircled with a halo of regret.

In accordance with the principle of construction which he follows throughout—the heightening of the effect of the picture by presenting a succession of contrasts—the poet next sets the prosperity of the enemies of Jerusalem in close juxtaposition to the misery of those of her people in whom it is most pitiable and startling, the children and the princes. Men with any heart in them would wish above all things that the innocent young members of their families should be spared; yet the captives carried off to Babylon consisted principally of boys and girls torn from their homes, conveyed hundreds of miles across the desert, many of them dragged down to hideous degradation by the vices that luxuriated in the corrupt empire of the Euphrates. The other class of victims specially commented on is that of the princes. Not only is the present humiliation of the nobility in sharp contrast to their former elevation of rank, and therefore their sufferings the more acute, but it is also to be observed that their old position of leadership has been completely reversed. The reference must be to Zedekiah and his courtiers.[1] These proud princes who formerly exercised command over the multitude have become a shameful flock of fugitives. In the expressive image of the poet, they are compared to "harts that find no pasture"; they are like fleet wild deer, so cowed by hunger that they meekly permit themselves to be driven by their enemies just as if they were a herd of tame cattle.

In the middle of this comparison between the success of the conquerors and the fate of their victims the poet inserts a pregnant sentence which suddenly carries us off to regions of far more profound reflection, touching upon the two sources of the ruin of Jerusalem that lie behind the visible hand of Nebuchadnezzar and his hosts, her own sin and the consequent wrath of her God. It flashes out as a momentary thought, and then retires with equal suddenness, permitting the previous current of reflections to be resumed as though unaffected by the startling interruption. This thought will reappear, however, with increasing fulness, shewing that it is always present to the mind of the poet and ready to come to the surface at any moment, even when it would seem to be inappropriate, although it can never be really inappropriate, because it is the key to the mystery of the whole tragedy.

Lastly, while the sense of a strong contrast is excited objectively by a comparison of the placid security of the invaders with the degradation of the fugitives, subjectively it is most vividly realised by the sufferers themselves when they call to mind their former happiness. Jerusalem is supposed to fall into a reverie in which she follows the recollection of the whole series

---

[1] Jer. xxxix. 4, 5.

of her pleasant experiences from far-off bygone times through all the succeeding ages down to the present era of calamities. This is to indulge in the pains of memory—pains which are decidedly more acute than the corresponding pleasures celebrated by Samuel Rogers. These pains are doubly intense owing to the inevitable fact that the contrast is unnaturally strained. Viewed in the softened lights of memory, the past is strangely simplified, its mixed character is forgotten, and many of its unpleasant features are smoothed out, so that an idyllic charm hovers over the dream, and lends it an unearthly beauty. This is why so many people foolishly damp the hopes of children, who, if they are healthily constituted, ought to be anticipating the future with eagerness, by solemnly exhorting them to make hay while the sun shines, with the gloomy warning that the sunny season must soon pass. Their application of the motto *carpe diem* is not only pagan in spirit; it is founded on an illusion. Happily there is some unreality about most of our yearning regrets for the days that have gone. That sweet, fair past was not so radiant as its effigy in the dreamland of memory now appears to be; nor is the hard present so free from mitigating circumstances as we suppose. And yet, when all is said, we cannot find the consolation we hunger after in hours of darkness among bare conclusions of common-sense. The grave is not an illusion, at least when only viewed in the light of the past—though even this chill, earthy reality begins to melt into a shadow immediately the light of the eternal future falls upon it. The melancholy that laments the lost past can only be perfectly mastered by that Christian grace, the hope which presses forward to a better future.

CHAPTER V

SIN AND SUFFERING

i. 8-11

THE doctrinaire rigour of Judaism in its uncompromising association of moral and physical evils has led to an unreasonable disregard for the solid truth which lies behind this mistake. It can scarcely be said that men are now perplexed by the problem that inspired the Book of Job. The fall of the tower of Siloam or the blindness of a man from his birth would not start among us the vexatious questions which were raised in the days of our Lord. We have not accepted the Jewish theory that the punishment of sin always overtakes the sinner in this life, much less have we assented to the by no means necessary corollary that all calamities are the direct penalties of the misconduct of the sufferers, and therefore sure signs of guilt. The modern tendency is in the opposite direction; it goes to ignore the existence of any connection whatever between the course of the universe and human conduct. No interference with the uniformity of the laws of nature for retributive or disciplinary purposes can be admitted. The machinery runs on in its grooves never deflected by any regard for our good or bad deserts. If we dash ourselves against its wheels they will tear us to pieces, grind us to powder; and we may reasonably consider this treatment to be the natural punishment of our folly. But here we are not beyond physical causation, and the drift of thought is towards holding the belief in anything more to be a simple survival from primitive anthropomorphic ideas of nature, a pure superstition. Is it a pure superstition? It is time we turned to another side of the question.

Every strong conviction that has obtained wide recognition, however erroneous and mischievous it may be, can be traced back to the abuse of some solid truth. It is not the case that the universe is constructed without any regard for moral laws. Even the natural punishment of the violation of natural laws contains a certain ethical element. Other considerations apart, clearly it is wrong to injure one's health or endanger one's life by rushing headlong against the constituted order of the universe; therefore the consequences of such conduct may be taken as signs of its condemnation. In the case of the sufferings of the Jews lamented by our poet the calamities were not primarily of a physical origin; they grew out of human acts—the accompaniments of the Chaldæan invasion. When we come to the evolution of history we are introduced to a whole world of moral forces that are not at work in the material universe. Nebuchadnezzar did not know that he was the instrument of a Higher Power for the chastisement of Israel; but the corruptions of the Jews, so ruthlessly exposed by their prophets, had undermined the national vigour which is the chief safeguard of a state, as surely as at a later time the corruptions of Rome opened her gates to devastating hosts of Goths and Huns. May we not go further, and, passing beyond the region of common observation, discover richer indications of the ethical meanings of events in the application to them of a real faith in God? It was his profound theism that lay at the base of the Jew's conception of temporal retribution, crude, hard, and narrow as this was. If we believe that God is supreme over nature and history as well as over individual lives, we must conclude that He will use every province of His vast dominion so as to further His righteous purposes. If the same Spirit reigns throughout there must be a certain harmony between all parts of His government. The mistake of the Jew was his claim to interpret the details of this Divine administration with a sole regard for the minute fraction of the universe that came under his own eyes, with blank indifference to the vast realm of facts and principles of which he could know nothing. His idea of Providence was too shortsighted, too parochial, in every respect too small; yet it was true in so far as it registered the conviction that there must be an ethical character in the government of the world by a righteous God, that the divinely ordered course of events cannot be out of all relation to conduct.

It does not fall in with the plan of the Lamentations for this subject to be treated so fully in these poems as it is in the stirring exhortations of the great prophets. Yet it comes to the surface repeatedly. In the fifth verse of the first elegy the poet attributes the affliction of Zion to "the multitude of her transgressions"; and he introduces the eighth verse with the clear declaration—

"Jerusalem hath grievously sinned; therefore she has become an unclean thing."

The powerful |Hebrew idiom according to which the cognate substance follows the verb is here employed. Rendered literally, the opening phrase is, "sinned sin." The experience of the chastisement leads to a keen perception of the guilt that precedes it. This is more than a consequence of the application of the accepted doctrine of the connection of sin with suffering to a particular case. No intellectual theory is strong enough by itself to awaken a slumbering conscience. The logic may be faultless; and yet even though the point of the syllogism is not evaded it will be coolly ignored. Trouble arouses a torpid conscience in a much more direct and effectual way. In the first place, it shatters the pride which is the chief hindrance to the confession of sin. Then it compels reflection; it calls a halt, and makes us look back over the path we may have been following too heedlessly. Sometimes it seems to exercise a distinctly illuminating influence. It is as though scales had fallen from the sufferer's eyes; he sees all things in a new light, and some ugly facts which had been lying at his side for years disregarded suddenly glare upon him as horrible discoveries. Thus the "Prodigal Son" perceives that he has sinned both against Heaven and against his father when he is in the lowest depths of misery, not so much because he recognises a penal character in his troubles, but more on account of the fact that he has *come to himself*. This subjective, psychological connection between suffering and sin is independent of any dogma of retribution; for the ends of practical discipline it is the most important connection. We may waive all discussion of the ancient Jewish problem, and still be thankful to recognise the Elijah-like ministry of adversity.

The immediate effect of this vision of sin is that a new colour is given to the picture of the desolation of Jerusalem. The image of a miserable woman is preserved, but the dignity of the earlier scene is missing here. Pathos and poetry gather round the picture of the forlorn widow weeping for the loss of her children. Neglected and humbled as she is in worldly estate, the tragic vastness of her sorrow has exalted her to an altitude of moral sublimity. Such suffering breaks through those barriers of conventional experience which make many lives look mean and trivial. It is so awful that we cannot but regard it with reverence. But all this is altered in the aspect of Jerusalem which follows the confession of her great sin. In the freedom of ancient language the poet ventures on an illustration that would be regarded as too gross for modern literature. The limits of our art exclude subjects which excite a sensation of disgust; but this is just the sensation the author of the elegy deliberately aims at producing. He paints a picture which is simply intended to sicken his readers. The utter humiliation of Jerusalem is exhibited in the unavoidable exposure of a condition which natural modesty would conceal at any cost. Another contrast between the reserve of our modern style and the rude bluntness of antiquity is here apparent. It is not only that we have grown more refined in language—a very superficial change which might be no better than the whitewashing of sepulchres; over and above this civilising of mere manners, the effect of Teutonic habits, strengthened by Christian sentiments, has been to develop a respect for woman undreamed of in the old Eastern world. It may be added that the scientific temper of recent times has taught us that there is nothing really dishonouring in purely natural processes. The ancient world could not distinguish between delicacy and shame. We should regard a poor suffering woman whose modesty had been grievously wounded with simple commiseration; the ancient Jews treated such a person with disgust as an unclean creature, quite unable to see that their conduct was simply brutal.

The new aspect of the misery of Jerusalem is thus set forth as one of degradation and ignominy. The vision of sin is immediately followed by a scene of shame. Commentators have been divided over the question whether this picture of the humiliated woman is intended to apply to the sin of the city or only to her misfortunes. In favour of the former view, it may be remarked that uncleanness is distinctly associated with moral corruption: the connection is the more appropriate here inasmuch as a confession of sin immediately precedes. On the other hand, the attendant circumstances point to the second interpretation. It is the humiliation of the condition of the sufferer, rather than that condition itself, which is dwelt upon. Jerusalem is despised, "she sigheth," "is come down wonderfully," "hath no comforter," and is generally afflicted and oppressed by her enemies. But while we are led to regard the pitiable picture as a representation of the woful plight into which the proud city has fallen, we cannot conclude it to be an accident that this particular phase of her misery succeeds the mention of her great guilt. After all, it is only the underlying guilt that can justify a verdict which carries disgrace as well as suffering for its penalty. Even when the judgments of men are too confused to recognise this truth with regard to other people, it should be apparent to the conscience of the humiliated person himself. The humiliation which follows nothing worse than a fall into external misfortunes is but a superficial trouble, and the consciousness of innocence can enable one to submit to it without any sense of inward shame. The sting of contempt lies in the miserable consciousness that it is deserved.

8

Thus we see the punishment of sin consisting in exposure. The exposure which simply hurts natural modesty is acutely painful to a refined, sensitive spirit; and yet the very dignity which it outrages is a shield against the point of the insult. But where the exposure follows sin this shield is absent. In that case the degradation of it is without any mitigation. Nothing more may be necessary to constitute a very severe punishment. When the secrets of all hearts are revealed the very revelation will be a penal process. To lay bare the quivering nerves of memory to the searching sunlight must be to torture the guilty soul with inconceivable horrors. Nevertheless it is a matter for profound thankfulness that there is no question of a surprising revelation of the sinner's guilt being made to God at some future time, some shocking discovery which might turn His lovingkindness into wrath or contempt. We cannot have a firmer ground of joy and hope than the fact that God knows everything about us, and yet loves us at our worst, patiently waiting for repentance with His offer of unlimited forgiveness. Exposure before God is like a surgical examination; the hope of a cure, if it does not dispel the sense of humiliation—and that is impossible in the case of guilt, the disgrace of which to a healthy conscience is more intense before the holiness of God than before the eyes of fellow-sinners—still encourages confidence.

The recognition of a moral lapse at the root of the shame of Jerusalem, though not perhaps in the shame itself, is confirmed by a phrase which reflects on the culpable heedlessness of the Jews. The elegy deplores how the city has "come down wonderfully" on account of the fact that "she remembered not her latter end." It is quite confusing and incorrect to render this expression in the present tense as it stands in the Authorised English Version. The poet cannot mean that the Jews in exile and captivity have already forgotten the recent horrors of the siege of Jerusalem. This would be flatly contrary to the motive of the elegy, which is to give tongue to the sufferings of the Jews flowing out of that disaster. It would be impossible to say that the calamity that inspired the elegy was no longer even remembered by its victims. What an anti-climax this would be ! Clearly the poet is bewailing the culpable folly of the people in not giving a thought to the certain consequences of such a course as they were following ; a course that had been denounced by the faithful prophets of Jehovah, who, alas! had been but voices crying in the wilderness, unnoted, or even scouted and suppressed, like the stormy petrels hated by sailors as birds of ill-omen. In her ease and prosperity, her self-indulgence and sin, the doomed city had failed to recollect what must be the end of such things. The idea of remembrance is peculiarly apt and forcible in this connection, although it has a relation to the future, because the Jews had been through experiences which should have served as warnings if they had duly reflected on them. This was not a matter for wild guesses or vague apprehensions. Not only were there the distinct utterances of Jeremiah and his predecessors to rouse the thoughtless ; events had been speaking louder than words. Jerusalem was already a city with a history, and that history had even by this time accumulated some tragic lessons. These were subjects for memory. Thus memory can become prophecy, because the laws which are revealed in the past will govern the future. We are none of us so wholly inexperienced but that in the knowledge of what we have already been through we may gain wisdom to anticipate the consequences of our present actions. The heedless person is one who forgets, or at all events one who will not attend to his own memories. Such recklessness is its own condemnation; it cannot plead the excuse of ignorance.

But now it may be objected that this reference to the mere thought of consequences suggests considerations that are too low to furnish the reasons for the ruin of Jerusalem. Would the city have been spared if only her inhabitants had been a little more foreseeing? It should be observed that though mere prudence is never a very lofty virtue, imprudence is sometimes a very serious fault. It cannot be right to be simply reckless, to ignore all lessons of the past and fling oneself blindly into the future. The hero who is sure that he is inspired by a lofty motive may walk straight into the very jaws of death, and be all the stronger for his noble indifference to his fate; but he who is no hero, he who is not influenced by any great or unselfish ideas, has no excuse for neglecting the warnings of common prudence. All wise actions must be more or less guided with a view to their issues in the future, although in the case of the best of them the aims will be pure and unselfish. It is our prerogative to "look before and after"; and just in proportion as we take long views do our deeds acquire gravity and depth. Our Lord characterised the two ways by their ends. While the example of the careless Jews is followed on all sides—and who of us can deny that he has ever fallen into the negligence?—is it not a little superfluous to discuss abstract, unpractical problems about a remote altruism?

Intermingled with his painful picture of the humiliation and shame of the fallen city, the poet supplies indications of the effect of all this on the suffering citizens. Despised by all who had formerly honoured her, Jerusalem sighs and longs to retire into obscurity, away from the rude gaze of her oppressors.

In particular, two further signs of her distress are here given.

The first is *spoliation*. Her enemies have laid hands on "all her pleasant things." It may strike us that, after the miseries just narrated, this is but a minor trouble. Job's calamities began with the loss of his property, and rose from this by degrees to the climax of agony. If his first trouble had been the sudden death of all his children, stunned by that awful blow, he would have cared little about the fate of his flocks and herds. It is not according to the method of the Lamentations, however, to move on to any climax. The thoughts are set forth as they well up in the mind of the poet, now passionate and intense, then again of a milder cast, yet altogether combining to colour one picture of intolerable woe. But there is an aspect of this idea of the robbery of the "pleasant things" which heightens the sense of misery. It is another instance of the force of contrast so often manifested in these elegies. Jerusalem had been a home of wealth and luxury in the merry old days. But hoarded money, precious jewellery, family heirlooms, products of art and skill, accumulated during generations of prosperity and treated as necessaries of life—all had been swept away in the sack of the city, and scattered among strangers who could not prize them as they had been prized by their owners; and now these victims of spoliation, stripped of everything, were in want of daily bread. Even what little could be saved from the wreck they had to give up in exchange for common food, bought dearly in the market of necessity.

The second sign of the great distress here noted is *desecration.* Gentiles invade the sacred precincts of the temple. Considering that the sanctuary had been already much more effectually desecrated by the blood-stained hands and lustful hearts of impious worshippers, such as those "rulers of Sodom" denounced by Isaiah for "trampling" the courts of Jehovah with their "vain oblations,"[1] we do not find it easy to sympathise with this horror of a supposed defilement from the mere presence of heathen persons. Yet it would be unjust to accuse the shocked Israelites of hypocrisy. They ought to have been more conscious of the one real corruption of sin; but we cannot add that therefore their notions of external uncleanness were altogether foolish and wrong. To judge the Jews of the age of the Captivity by a standard of spirituality which few Christians have yet attained to would be a cruel anachronism. The Syrian invasion of the temple in the time of the Maccabees was called by a very late prophet an "abomination of desolation,"[2] and a similar insult to be offered to the sacred place by the Romans is described by our Lord in the same terms.[3] All of us must be conscious at times of the sacredness of associations. To botanise on his mother's grave may be a proof of a man's freedom from superstition, but it cannot be taken as an indication of the fineness of his feelings. The Israelite exclusiveness which shunned the intrusion of foreigners simply because they were foreigners was combined both with a patriotic anxiety to preserve the integrity of the nation, and in

---

[1] Isa. i. 10-17.   [2] Dan. xi. 31.   [3] Mark xiii. 14.

some cases with a religious dread of idolatry. It is true the nominal contamination of the mere presence of Gentiles was generally more dreaded than the real contagion of their corrupt examples. Still the very idea of desecration, even when it is superficial, together with a sense of pain at its presence, is higher than the materialism which despises it not because this materialism has the grace to sanctify everything, but for the opposite reason, because it counts nothing holy, because to it all things are common and unclean.

Before we pass from this portion of the elegy there is one curious characteristic of it which calls for notice. The poet suddenly drops the construction in the third person and writes in the first person. This he does twice—at the end of the ninth verse, and again at the end of the eleventh. He might be speaking in his own person, but the language points to the personified city. Yet in each case the outburst is quite abrupt, sprung upon us without any introductory formula. Possibly the explanation of this anomaly must be sought in the liturgical use for which the poem was designed. If it was to be sung antiphonally we may conjecture that at these places a second chorus would break in. The result would be a startling dramatic effect—as though the city had sat listening to the lament over her woes until the piteous tale had compelled her to break her silence and cry aloud. In each case the cry is directed to heaven. It is an appeal to God; and it simply prays for His attention—" Behold, O Lord," "See, O Lord, and behold." In the first case the Divine attention is called to the insolence of the enemy, in the second to the degradation of Jerusalem. Still it is only an appeal for notice. Will God but look upon all this misery? That is sufficient.

CHAPTER VI

ZION'S APPEAL

i. 12-22

IN the latter part of the second elegy Jerusalem appears as the speaker, appealing for sympathy, first to stray, passing travellers, then to the larger circle of the surrounding nations, and lastly to her God. Already the suffering city has spoken once or twice in brief interruptions of the poet's descriptions of her miseries, and now she seems to be too impatient to permit herself to be represented any longer even by this friendly advocate; she must come forward in person and present her case in her own words.

There is much difference of opinion among commentators about the rendering of the phrase with which the appeal begins. The Revisers have followed the Authorised Version in taking it as a question—"Is it nothing to you, all ye that pass by?"[1] But it may be treated as a direct negative—"It is nothing," etc., or, by a slightly different reading of the Hebrew text, as a simple call for attention—"O all ye that pass by," etc., as in the Vulgate "*O vos,*" etc. The usual rendering is the finest in literary feeling, and it is in accordance with a common usage. Although the sign of an interrogation, which would set this meaning beyond

---

[1] i. 12.

dispute, is absent, there does not seem to be sufficient reason for rejecting it in favour of one of the proposed alternatives. But in any case the whole passage evidently expresses a deep yearning for sympathy. Mere strangers, roving Bedouin, any people who may chance to be passing by Jerusalem, are implored to behold her incomparable woes. The wounded animal creeps into a corner to suffer and die in secret, perhaps on account of the habit of herds, in tormenting a suffering mate. But among mankind the instinct of a sufferer is to crave sympathy, from a friend, if possible; but if such be not available, then even from a stranger. Now although where it is possible to give effectual aid, merely to cast a pitying look and pass by on the other side, like the priest and the Levite in the parable, is a mockery and a cruelty, although unpretentious indifference is better than that hypocrisy, it would be a great mistake to suppose that in those cases for which no direct relief can be given sympathy is of no value. This sympathy, if it is real, would help if it could; and under all circumstances it is the reality of the sympathy that is most prized, not its issues.

It should be remembered, further, that the first condition of active aid is a genuine sense of compassion, which can only be awakened by means of knowledge and the impressions which a contemplation of suffering produce. Evil is wrought not only from want of thought, but also from lack of knowledge; and good-doing is withheld for the same reason. Therefore the first requisite is to arrest attention. A royal commission is the reasonable precursor of a state remedy for some public wrong. Misery is permitted to flourish in the dark because people are too indolent to search it out. No doubt the knowledge of sufferings which we might remedy implies a grave responsibility; but we cannot escape our obligations by simply closing our eyes to what we do not wish to see. We are responsible for our ignorance and its consequences wherever the opportunity of knowledge is within our reach.

The appeal to all who pass by is most familiar to us in its later association with our Lord's sufferings on the cross. But this is not in any sense a Messianic passage; it is confined in its purpose to the miseries of Jerusalem. Of course there can be no objection to illustrating the grief and pain of the Man of Sorrows by using the classic language of an ancient lament if we note that this is only an illustration. There is a kinship in all suffering, and it is right to consider that He who was tried in all points as we are tried passed through sorrows which absorbed all the bitterness even of such a cup of woe as that which was drunk by Jerusalem in the extremity of her misfortunes. If never before there had been sorrow like unto her sorrow, at length that was matched, nay, surpassed at Gethsemane and Golgotha. Still it would be a mistake to confine these words to their secondary application—not only an exegetical mistake, but one of deeper significance. Jesus Christ restrained the wailing of the women who offered Him their compassion on His way to the cross, bidding them weep not for Him, but for themselves and their children.[1] Much more when His passion is long past and He is reigning in glory must it be displeasing to Him for His friends to be wasting idle tears over the sufferings of His earthly life. The morbid sentimentality which broods over the ancient wounds of Christ, the nail prints and the spear thrust,

---

[1] Luke xxiii. 28.

but ignores the present wounds of society—the wounds of the world for which He bled and died, or the wounds of the Church which is His body now, must be wrong in His sight. He would rather we gave a cup of cold water to one of His brethren than an ocean of tears to the memory of Calvary. If then we would make use of the ruined city's appeal for sympathy by applying it to some later object it would be more in agreement with the mind of Christ to think of the miseries of mankind in our own day, and to consider how a sympathetic regard for them may point to some ministry of alleviation.

In order to impress the magnitude of her miseries on the minds of the strangers whose attention she would arrest, the city, now personified as a suppliant, describes her dreadful condition in a series of brief, pointed metaphors. Thus the imagination is excited; and the imagination is one of the roads to the heart. It is not enough that people know the bald facts of a calamity as these may be scheduled in an inspector's report. Although this preliminary information is most important, if we go no further the report will be replaced in its pigeon-hole, and lie there till it is forgotten. If it is to do something better than gather the dust of years it must be used as a foundation for the imagination to work upon. This does not imply any departure from truth, any false colouring or exaggeration; on the contrary, the process only brings out the truth which is not really seen until it is imagined. Let us look at the various images under which the distress of Jerusalem is here presented.

It is like a fire in the bones.[1] It burns, consumes,

---

[1] i. 13.

pains with intolerable torment; it is no skin-deep trouble, it penetrates to the very marrow. This fire is overmastering; it is not to be quenched, neither does it die out; it "prevaileth" against the bones. There is no getting such a fire under.

It is like a net.[1] The image is changed. We see a wild creature caught in the bush, or perhaps a fugitive arrested in his flight and flung down by hidden snares at his feet. Here is the shock of surprise, the humiliation of deceit, the vexation of being thwarted. The result is a baffled, bewildered, helpless condition.

It is like faintness.[2] The desolate sufferer is ill. It is bad enough to have to bear calamities in the strength of health. Jerusalem is made sick and kept faint "all the day"—with a faintness that is not a momentary collapse, but a continuous condition of failure.

It is like a yoke[3] which is wreathed upon the neck—fixed on, as with twisted withes. The poet is here more definite. The yoke is made out of the transgressions of Jerusalem. The sense of guilt does not lighten its weight; the band that holds it most closely is the feeling that it is deserved. It is natural that the sinful sufferer should exclaim that God, who has bound this terrible yoke upon her, has made her strength to fail. As there is nothing so invigorating as the assurance that one is suffering for a righteous cause, so there is nothing so wretchedly depressing as the consciousness of guilt.

Lastly, it is like a winepress.[4] This image is elaborated with more detail, although at the expense of unity of design. God is said to have called a "solemn assembly" to oppress the Jews, by an ironical reversal

---

[1] i. 13. [2] Ibid. [3] i. 14. [4] i. 15.

of the common notion of such an assembly. The language recalls the idea of one of the great national festivals of Israel. But now instead of the favoured people their enemies are summoned, and the object is not the glad praise of God for His bounties in harvest or vintage, but the crushing of the Jews. They are to be victims, not guests as of old. They are themselves the harvest of judgment, the vintage of wrath. The wine is to be made, but the grapes crushed to produce it are the people who were accustomed to feast and drink of the fruits of God's bounty in the happy days of their prosperity. So the mighty men are set at nought, their prowess counting as nothing against the brutal rush of the enemy; and the young men are crushed, their spirit and vigour failing them in the great destruction.

The most terrible trait in these pictures, one that is common to all of them, is the Divine origin of the troubles. It was God who sent fire into the bones, spread the net, made the sufferer desolate and faint. The yoke was bound by His hands. It was He who set at nought the mighty men, and summoned the assembly of foes to crush His people. The poet even goes so far as to make the daring statement that it was the Lord Himself who trod the virgin daughter of Judah as in a winepress. It is a ghastly picture— a dainty maiden trampled to death by Jehovah as grapes are trampled to squeeze out their juice! This horrible thing is ascribed to God! Yet there is no complaint of barbarity, no idea that the Judge of all the earth is not doing right. The miserable city does not bring any railing accusation against her Lord; she takes all the blame upon herself. We must be careful to bear in mind the distinction between poetic imagery and prosaic narrative. Still it remains true that Jerusalem here attributes her troubles to the will and action of God. This is vital to the Hebrew faith. To explain it away is to impoverish the religion of Israel, and with it the Old Testament revelation. That revelation shews us the absolute sovereignty of God, and at the same time it brings out the guilt of man, so that no room is allowed for complaints against the Divine justice. The grief is all the greater because there is no thought of rebellion. The daring doubts that struggle into expression in Job never obtrude themselves here to check the even flow of tears. The melancholy is profound, but comparatively calm, since it does not once give place to anger. It is natural that the succession of images of misery conceived in this spirit should be followed by a burst of tears. Zion weeps because the comforter who should refresh her soul is far away, and she is left utterly desolate.[1]

Here the supposed utterance of Jerusalem is broken for the poet to insert a description of the suppliant making her piteous appeal.[2] He shews us Zion spreading out her hands, that is to say, in the well-known attitude of prayer. She is comfortless, oppressed by her neighbours in accordance with the will of her God, and treated as an unclean thing; she who had despised the idolatrous Gentiles in her pride of superior sanctity has now become foul and despicable in their eyes!

The semi-dramatic form of the elegy is seen in the reappearance of Jerusalem as speaker without any formula of introduction. After the poet's brief interjection describing the suppliant, the personified city continues her plaintive appeal, but with a considerable

---

[1] i. 16.   [2] i. 17.

enlargement of its scope. She makes the most distinct acknowledgment of the two vital elements of the case— God's righteousness and her own rebellion.[1] These carry us beneath the visible scenes of trouble so graphically illustrated earlier, and fix our attention on deep-seated principles. It cannot be supposed that the faith and penitence unreservedly confessed in the elegy were truly experienced by all the fugitive citizens of Jerusalem, though they were found in the devout " remnant" among whom the author of the poem must be reckoned. But the reasonable interpretation of these utterances is that which accepts them as the inspired expressions of the thoughts and feelings which Jerusalem ought to possess, as ideal expressions, suitable to those who rightly appreciate the whole situation. This fact gives them a wide applicability. The ideal approaches the universal. Although it cannot be said that all trouble is the direct punishment of sin, and although it is manifestly insincere to make confession of guilt one does not inwardly admit, to be firmly settled in the conviction that God is right in what He does even when it all looks most wrong, that if there is a fault it must be on man's side, is to have reached the centre of truth. This is very different from the admission that God has the right of an absolute sovereign to do whatever He chooses, like mad Caligula when intoxicated with his own divinity; it even implies a denial of that supposed right, for it asserts that He acts in accordance with something other than His will, viz., righteousness.

Enlarging the area of her appeal, no longer content to snatch at the casual pity of individual travellers on

---

[1] i, 18.

the road, Jerusalem now calls upon all the "peoples"—
i.e., all neighbouring tribes—to hear the tale of her woes.[1]
This is too huge a tragedy to be confined to private
spectators; it is of national proportions, and it claims
the attention of whole nations. It is curious to observe
that foreigners, whom the strict Jews sternly exclude
from their privileges, are nevertheless besought to
compassionate their distresses. These uncircumcised
heathen are not now thrust contemptuously aside; they
are even appealed to as sympathisers. Perhaps this
is meant to indicate the vastness of the misery of
Jerusalem by the suggestion that even aliens should be
affected by it; when the waves spread far in all directions
there must have been a most terrible storm at the centre
of disturbance. Still it is possible to find in this widening
outlook of the poet a sign of the softening and enlarging
effects of trouble. The very need of much sympathy
breaks down the barriers of proud exclusiveness, and
prepares one to look for gracious qualities among people
who have been previously treated with churlish indifference or positive animosity. Floods and earthquakes
tame savage beasts. On the battlefield wounded men
gratefully accept relief from their mortal enemies.
Conduct of this sort may be self-regarding, perhaps
weak and cowardly; still it is an outcome of the natural
brotherhood of all mankind, any confession of which,
however reluctant, is a welcome thing.

The appeal to the nations contains three particulars.
It deplores the captivity of the virgins and young men;
the treachery of allies—"lovers" who have been called
upon for assistance, but in vain; and the awful fact that
men of such consequence as the elders and priests, the

---

[1] i. 18.

very aristocracy of Jerusalem, had died of starvation after an ineffectual search for food—a lurid picture of the horrors of the siege.[1] The details repeat themselves with but very slight variations. It is natural for a great sufferer to revolve his bitter morsel continuously. The action is a sign of its bitterness. The monotony of the dirge is a sure indication of the depth of the trouble that occasions it. The theme is only too interesting to the mourner, however wearisome it may become to the listener.

In drawing to a close the appeal goes further, and, rising altogether above man, seeks the attention of God.[2] It is not enough that every passing traveller is arrested, nor even that the notice of all the neighbouring nations is sought; this trouble is too great for human shoulders to bear. It will absorb the largest mass of sympathy, and yet thirst for more. Twice before in the first part of the elegy the language of the poet speaking in his own person was interrupted by an outcry of Jerusalem to God.[3] Now the elegy closes with a fuller appeal to Heaven. This is an utterance of faith where faith is tried to the uttermost. It is distinctly recognised that the calamities bewailed have been sent by God; and yet the stricken city turns to God for consolation. And the appeal is not at all in the form of a cry to a tormentor for mercy; it seeks friendly sympathy and avenging actions. Nothing could more clearly prove the consciousness that God is not doing any wrong to His people. Not only is there no complaint against the justice of His acts; in spite of them all He is still regarded as the greatest Friend and Helper of the victims of His wrath.

---

[1] i. 18, 19.   [2] i. 20-2.   [3] i. 9, 11.

9

This apparently paradoxical position issues in what might otherwise be a contradiction of thought. The ruin of Jerusalem is attributed to the righteous judgment of God, against which no shadow of complaint is raised; and yet God is asked to pour vengeance on the heads of the human agents of His wrath! These people have been acting from their own evil, or at all events their own inimical motives. Therefore it is not held that they deserve punishment for their conduct any the less on account of the fact that they have been the unconscious instruments of Providence. The vengeance here sought for cannot be brought into line with Christian principles; but the poet had never heard the Sermon on the Mount. It would not have occurred to him that the spirit of revenge was not right, any more than it occurred to the writers of maledictory Psalms.

There is one more point in this final appeal to God which should be noticed, because it is very characteristic of the elegy throughout. Zion bewails her friendless condition, declaring, "there is none to comfort me."[1] This is the fifth reference to the absence of a comforter.[2] The idea may be merely introduced in order to accentuate the description of utter desolation. And yet when we compare the several allusions to it the conclusion seems to be forced upon us that the poet has a more specific intention. In some cases, at least, he seems to have one particular comforter in mind, as, for example, when he says, "The comforter that should refresh my soul is far from me."[3] Our thoughts instinctively turn to the Paraclete of St. John's Gospel. It would not be reasonable to suppose that the elegist had attained to any definite conception of the Holy Spirit

---

[1] i. 21.　　　[2] See i. 2, 9, 16, 17, 21.　　　[3] i. 16.

such as that of the ripe Christian revelation. But we have his own words to witness that God is to him the supreme Comforter, is the Lord and Giver of life who refreshes his soul. It would seem, then, that the poet's thought is like that of the author of the twenty-second Psalm, which was echoed in our Lord's cry of despair on the cross.[1] When God our Comforter hides the light of His countenance the night is most dark. Yet the darkness is not always perceived, or its cause recognised. Then to miss the consolations of God consciously, with pain, is the first step towards recovering them.

---

[1] Mark xv. 34.

CHAPTER VII

GOD AS AN ENEMY

ii. 1-9

THE elegist, as we have seen, attributes the troubles of the Jews to the will and action of God. In the second poem he even ventures further, and with daring logic presses this idea to its ultimate issues. If God is tormenting His people in fierce anger it must be because He is their enemy—so the sad-hearted patriot reasons. The course of Providence does not shape itself to him as a merciful chastisement, as a veiled blessing; its motive seems to be distinctly unfriendly. He drives his dreadful conclusion home with great amplitude of details. In order to appreciate the force of it let us look at the illustrative passage in two ways—first, in view of the calamities inflicted on Jerusalem, all of which are here ascribed to God, and then with regard to those thoughts and purposes of their Divine Author which appear to be revealed in them.

First, then, we have the earthly side of the process. The daughter of Zion is covered with a cloud.[1] The metaphor would be more striking in the brilliant East than it is to us in our habitually sombre climate. There it would suggest unwonted gloom—the loss of the customary light of heaven, rare distress, and ex-

---

[1] ii. 1.

cessive melancholy. It is a general, comprehensive image intended to overshadow all that follows. Terrible disasters cover the aspect of all things from zenith to horizon. The physical darkness that accompanied the horrors of Golgotha is here anticipated, not indeed by any actual prophecy, but in idea.

But there is more than gloom. A mere cloud may lift, and discover everything unaltered by the passing shadow. The distress that has fallen on Jerusalem is not thus superficial and transient. She herself has suffered a fatal fall. The beauty of Israel has been cast down from heaven to earth. The language is now varied; instead of " the daughter of Zion " we have " the beauty of Israel."[1] The use of the larger title, "Israel," is not a little significant. It shews that the elegist is alive to the idea of the fundamental unity of his race, a unity which could not be destroyed by centuries of inter-tribal warfare. Although in the ungracious region of politics Israel stood aloft from Judah, the two peoples were frequently treated as one by poets and prophets when religious ideas were in mind. Here apparently the vastness of the calamities of Jerusalem has obliterated the memory of jealous distinctions. Similarly we may see the great English race—British and American—forgetting national divisions in pursuit of its higher religious aims, as in Christian missions ; and we may be sure that this blood-unity would be felt most keenly under the shadow of a great trouble on either side of the Atlantic. By the time of the destruction of Jerusalem the northern tribes had been scattered, but the use of the distinctive name of these people is a sign that the ancient oneness of all who traced back their

---

[1] ii. 1.

pedigree to the patriarch Jacob was still recognised. It is some compensation for the endurance of trouble to find it thus breaking down the middle wall of partition between estranged brethren.

It has been suggested with probability that by the expression "the beauty of Israel" the elegist intended to indicate the temple. This magnificent pile of buildings, crowning one of the hills of Jerusalem, and shining with gold in "barbaric splendour," was the central object of beauty among all the people who revered the worship it enshrined. Its situation would naturally suggest the language here employed. Jerusalem rises among the hills of Judah, some two thousand feet above the sea-level; and when viewed from the wilderness in the south she looks indeed like a city built in the heavens. But the physical exaltation of Jerusalem and her temple was surpassed by exaltation in privilege, and prosperity, and pride. Capernaum, the vain city of the lake that would raise herself to heaven, is warned by Jesus that she shall be cast down to Hades.[1] Now not only Jerusalem, but the glory of the race of Israel, symbolised by the central shrine of the national religion, is thus humiliated.

Still keeping in mind the temple, the poet tells us that God has forgotten His footstool. He seems to be thinking of the Mercy-Seat over the ark, the spot at which God was thought to shew Himself propitious to Israel on the great Day of Atonement, and which was looked upon as the very centre of the Divine presence. In the destruction of the temple the holiest places were outraged, and the ark itself carried off or broken up, and never more heard of. How different

---

[1] Matt. xi. 23.

was this from the story of the loss of the ark in the days of Eli, when the Philistines were constrained to send it home of their own accord! Now no miracle intervenes to punish the heathen for their sacrilege. Yes, surely God must have forgotten His footstool! So it seems to the sorrowful Jew, perplexed at the impunity with which this crime has been committed.

But the mischief is not confined to the central shrine. It has extended to remote country regions and simple rustic folk. The shepherd's hut has shared the fate of the temple of the Lord. All the habitations of Jacob—a phrase which in the original points to country cottages—have been swallowed up.[1] The holiest is not spared on account of its sanctity, neither is the lowliest on account of its obscurity. The calamity extends to all districts, to all things, to all classes.

If the shepherd's cot is contrasted with the temple and the ark because of its simplicity, the fortress may be contrasted with this defenceless hut because of its strength. Yet even the strongholds have been thrown down. More than this, the action of the Jews' army has been paralysed by the God who had been its strength and support in the glorious olden time. It is as though the right hand of the warrior had been seized from behind and drawn back at the moment when it was raised to strike a blow for deliverance. The consequence is that the flower of the army, "all that were pleasant to the eye,"[2] are slain. Israel herself is swallowed up, while her palaces and fortresses are demolished.

The climax of this mystery of Divine destruction is reached when God destroys His own temple. The

---

[1] ii. 2.   [2] ii. 4.

elegist returns to the dreadful subject as though fascinated by the terror of it. God has violently taken away His tabernacle.[1] The old historic name of the sanctuary of Israel recurs at this crisis of ruin; and it is particularly appropriate to the image which follows, an image which possibly it suggested. If we are to understand the metaphor of the sixth verse as it is rendered in the English Authorised and Revised Versions, we have to suppose a reference to some such booth of boughs as people were accustomed to put up for their shelter during the vintage, and which would be removed as soon as it had served its temporary purpose. The solid temple buildings had been swept away as easily as though they were just such flimsy structures, as though they had been "of a garden." But we can read the text more literally, and still find good sense in it. According to the strict translation of the original, God is said to have violently taken away His tabernacle "as a garden." At the siege of a city the fruit gardens that encircle it are the first victims of the destroyer's axe. Lying out beyond the walls they are entirely unprotected, while the impediments they offer to the movements of troops and instruments of war induce the commander to order their early demolition. Thus Titus had the trees cleared from the Mount of Olives, so that one of the first incidents in the Roman siege of Jerusalem must have been the destruction of the Garden of Gethsemane. Now the poet compares the ease with which the great, massive temple—itself a powerful fortress, and enclosed within the city walls—was demolished, with the simple process of scouring the outlying gardens. So the place of assembly disappears,

---

[1] ii. 6.

and with it the assembly itself, so that even the sacred Sabbath is passed over and forgotten. Then the two heads of the nation—the king, its civil ruler, and the priest, its ecclesiastical chief—are both despised in the indignation of God's anger.

The central object of the sacred shrine is the altar, where earth seems to meet heaven in the high mystery of sacrifice. Here men seek to propitiate God; here too God would be expected to shew Himself gracious to men. Yet God has even cast off His altar, abhorring His very sanctuary.[1] Where mercy is most confidently anticipated, there of all places nothing but wrath and rejection are to be found. What prospect could be more hopeless?

The deeper thought that God rejects His sanctuary because His people have first rejected Him is not brought forward just now. Yet this solution of the mystery is prepared by a contemplation of the utter failure of the old ritual of atonement. Evidently that is not always effective, for here it has broken down entirely; then can it ever be inherently efficacious? It cannot be enough to trust to a sanctuary and ceremonies which God Himself destroys. But further, out of this scene which was so perplexing to the pious Jew, there flashes to us the clear truth that nothing is so abominable in the sight of God as an attempt to worship Him on the part of people who are living at enmity with Him. We can also perceive that if God shatters our sanctuary, perhaps He does so in order to prevent us from making a fetich of it. Then the loss of shrine and altar and ceremony may be the saving of the superstitious worshipper who is thereby taught to turn to some more stable source of confidence.

---

[1] ii. 7.

This, however, is not the line of reflections followed by the elegist in the present instance. His mind is possessed with one dark, awful, crushing thought. All this is God's work. And why has God done it? The answer to that question is the idea that here dominates the mind of the poet. It is because *God has become an enemy*! There is no attempt to mitigate the force of this daring idea. It is stated in the strongest possible terms, and repeated again and again at every turn— Israel's cloud is the effect of God's anger; it has come in the day of His anger; God is acting with fierce anger, with a flaming fire of wrath. This must mean that God is decidedly inimical. He is behaving as an adversary; He bends His bow; He manifests violence. It is not merely that God permits the adversaries of Israel to commit their ravages with impunity; God commits those ravages; He is Himself the enemy. He shews indignation, He despises, He abhors. And this is all deliberate. The destruction is carried out with the same care and exactitude that characterise the erection of a building. It is as though it were done with a measuring line. God surveys to destroy.

The first thing to be noticed in this unhesitating ascription to God of positive enmity is the striking evidence it contains of faith in the Divine power, presence, and activity. These were no more visible to the mere observer of events in the destruction of Jerusalem than in the shattering of the French empire at Sedan. In the one case as in the other all that the world could see was a crushing military defeat and its fatal consequences. The victorious army of the Babylonians filled the field as completely in the old time as that of the Germans in the modern event. Yet the poet simply ignores its existence. He passes it with sublime indifference, his mind filled with the thought of the unseen Power behind. He has not a word for Nebuchadnezzar, because he is assured that this mighty monarch is nothing but a tool in the hands of the real Enemy of the Jews. A man of smaller faith would not have penetrated sufficiently beneath the surface to have conceived the idea of Divine enmity in connection with a series of occurrences so very mundane as the ravages of war. A heathenish faith would have acknowledged in this defeat of Israel a triumph of the might of Bel or Nebo over the power of Jehovah. But so convinced is the elegist of the absolute supremacy of his God that no such idea is suggested to him even as a temptation of unbelief. He knows that the action of the true God is supreme in everything that happens, whether the event be favourable or unfavourable to His people. Perhaps it is only owing to the dreary materialism of current thought that we should be less likely to discover an indication of the enmity of God in some huge national calamity.

Still, although this idea of the elegist is a fruit of his unshaken faith in the universal sway of God, it startles and shocks us, and we shrink from it almost as though it contained some blasphemous suggestion. Is it ever right to think of God as the enemy of any man? It would not be fair to pass judgment on the author of the Lamentations on the ground of a cold consideration of this abstract question. We must remember the terrible situation in which he stood—his beloved city destroyed, the revered temple of his fathers a mass of charred ruins, his people scattered in exile and captivity, tortured, slaughtered; these were not circumstances to encourage a course of calm and measured reflection. We must not expect the sufferer to carry out an exact chemical analysis of his cup of woe before uttering an exclamation on its quality; and if it should be that the burning taste induces him to speak too strongly of its ingredients, we who only see him swallow it without being required to taste a drop ourselves should be slow to examine his language too nicely. He who has never entered Gethsemane is not in a position to understand how dark may be the views of all things seen beneath its sombre shade. If the Divine sufferer on the cross could speak as though His God had actually deserted Him, are we to condemn an Old Testament saint when he ascribes unspeakably great troubles to the enmity of God?

Is this, then, but the rhetoric of misery? If it be no more, while we seek to sympathise with the feelings of a very dramatic situation, we shall not be called upon to go further and discover in the language of the poet any positive teaching about God and His ways with man. But are we at liberty to stop short here? Is the elegist only expressing his own feelings? Have we a right to affirm that there can be no objective truth in the awful idea of the enmity of God?

In considering this question we must be careful to dismiss from our minds the unworthy associations that only too commonly attach themselves to notions of enmity among men. Hatred cannot be ascribed to One whose deepest name is Love. No spite, malignity, or evil passion of any kind can be found in the heart of the Holy God. When due weight is given to these negations very much that we usually see in the practice of enmity disappears. But this is not to say that the idea itself is denied, or the fact shown to be impossible.

In the first place, we have no warrant for asserting that God will never act in direct and intentional opposition to any of His creatures. There is one obvious occasion when He certainly does this. The man who resists the laws of nature finds those laws working against Him. He is not merely running his head against a stone wall; the laws are not inert obstructions in the path of the transgressor; they represent forces in action. That is to say, they resist their opponent with vigorous antagonism. In themselves they are blind, and they bear him no ill-will. But the Being who wields the forces is not blind or indifferent. The laws of nature are, as Kingsley said, but the ways of God. If they are opposing a man God is opposing that man. But God does not confine His action to the realm of physical processes. His providence works through the whole course of events in the world's history. What we see evidently operating in nature we may infer to be equally active in less visible regions. Then if we believe in a God who rules and works in the world, we cannot suppose that His activity is confined to aiding what is good. It is unreasonable to imagine that He stands aside in passive negligence of evil. And if He concerns Himself to thwart evil, what is this but manifesting Himself as the enemy of the evildoer?

It may be contended, on the other side, that there is a world of difference between antagonistic actions and unfriendly feelings, and that the former by no means imply the latter. May not God oppose a man who is doing wrong, not at all because He is his Enemy, but just because He is his truest Friend? Is it not an act of real kindness to save a man from himself when his own will is leading him astray? This of course must be granted, and being granted, it will certainly affect our views of the ultimate issues of what we may be compelled to regard in its present operation as nothing short of Divine antagonism. It may remind us that the motives lying behind the most inimical action on God's part may be merciful and kind in their aims. Still, for the time being, the opposition is a reality, and a reality which to all intents and purposes is one of enmity, since it resists, frustrates, hurts.

Nor is this all. We have no reason to deny that God can have real anger. Is it not right and just that He should be "angry with the wicked every day"?[1] Would He not be imperfect in holiness, would He not be less than God if He could behold vile deeds springing from vile hearts with placid indifference? We must believe that Jesus Christ was as truly revealing the Father when He was moved with indignation as when He was moved with compassion. His life shows quite clearly that He was the enemy of oppressors and hypocrites, and He plainly declared that He came to bring a sword.[2] His mission was a war against all evil, and therefore, though not waged with carnal weapons, a war against evil men. The Jewish authorities were perfectly right in perceiving this fact. They persecuted Him as their enemy; and He was their enemy. This statement is no contradiction to the gracious truth that He desired to save all men, and therefore even these men. If God's enmity to any soul were eternal it would conflict with His love. It cannot be that He wishes the ultimate ruin of one of His own children. But if He is at the present time actively opposing a man, and if He is doing this in anger, in the wrath of righteousness against sin, it is only quibbling with words to deny that

---

[1] Psalm vii. 11.   [2] Matt. x. 34.

for the time being He is a very real enemy to that man.

The current of thought in the present day is not in any sympathy with this idea of God as an Enemy, partly in its revulsion from harsh and un-Christlike conceptions of God, partly also on account of the modern humanitarianism which almost loses sight of sin in its absorbing love of mercy. But the tremendous fact of the Divine enmity towards the sinful man so long as he persists in his sin is not to be lightly brushed aside. It is not wise wholly to forget that "our God is a consuming fire."[1] It is in consideration of this dread truth that the atonement wrought by His Son according to His own will of love is discovered to be an action of vital efficacy, and not a mere scenic display.

---

[1] Heb. xii. 29.

CHAPTER VIII

THE CRY OF THE CHILDREN

ii. 10-17

PASSION and poetry, when they fire the imagination, do more than personify individual material things. By fusing the separate objects in the crucible of a common emotion which in some way appertains to them all, they personify this grand unity, and so lift their theme into the region of the sublime. Thus while in his second elegy the author of the Lamentations first dwells on the desolation of inanimate objects, —the temple, fortresses, country cottages,—these are all of interest to him only because they belong to Jerusalem, the city of his heart's devotion, and it is the city herself that moves his deepest feelings; and when in the second part of the poem he proceeds to describe the miserable condition of living persons—men, women, and children—profoundly pathetic as the picture he now paints appears to us in its piteous details, it is still regarded by its author as a whole, and the people's sufferings are so very terrible in his eyes because they are the woes of Jerusalem.

Some attempt to sympathise with the large and lofty view of the elegist may be a wholesome corrective to the intense individualism of modern habits of thought. The difficulty for us is to see that this view is not merely ideal, that it represents a great, solid truth, the truth that the perfect human unit is not an individual, but a more or less extensive group of persons, mutually harmonised and organised in a common life, a society of some sort—the family, the city, the state, mankind. By bearing this in mind we shall be able to perceive that sufferings which in themselves might seem sordid and degrading can attain to something of epic dignity.

It is in this spirit that the poet deplores the exile of the king and the princes. He is not now concerned with the private troubles of these exalted persons. Judah was a limited monarchy, though not after the pattern of government familiar to us, but rather in the style of the Plantagenet rule, according to which the sovereign shared his authority with a number of powerful barons, each of whom was lord over his own territory. The men described as "the princes of Israel" were not, for the most part, members of the royal family; they were the heads of tribes and families. Therefore the banishment of these persons, together with the king, meant for the Jews who were left behind the loss of their ruling authorities. Then it seems most reasonable to connect the clause which follows the reference to the exile with the sufferings of Jerusalem rather than with the hardships of the captives, because the whole context is concerned with the former subject. This phrase read literally is, "The law is not."[1] Our Revisers have followed the Authorised Version in connecting it with the previous expression, "among the nations," which describes the place of exile, so as to lead us to read it as a statement that the king and the princes were enduring the hardship of residence in a land where their sacred *Torah* was

---

[1] ii. 9.

not observed. If, however, we take the words in harmony with the surrounding thoughts, we are reminded by them that the removal of the national rulers involved to the Jews the cessation of the administration of their law. The residents still left in the land were reduced to a condition of anarchy; or, if the conquerors had begun to administer some sort of martial law, this was totally alien to the revered *Torah* of Israel. Josiah had based his reformation on the discovery of the sacred law-book. But the mere possession of this was little consolation if it was not administered, for the Jews had not fallen to the condition of the Samaritans of later times who came to worship the roll of the Pentateuch as an idol. They were not even like the scribes and Talmudists among their own descendants, to whom the law itself was a religion, though only read in the cloister of the student. The loss of good government was to them a very solid evil. In a civilised country, in times of peace and order, we breathe law as we breathe air, unconsciously, too familiar with it to appreciate the immeasurable benefits it confers upon us.

With the banishment of the custodians of law the poet associates the accompanying silence of the voice of prophecy. This, however, is so important and significant a fact, that it must be reserved for separate and fuller treatment.[1]

Next to the princes come the elders, to whom was intrusted the administration of justice in the minor courts. These were not sent into captivity; for at first only the aristocracy was considered sufficiently important to be carried off to Babylon. But though the elders were left in the land, the country was too

---

[1] See next chapter.

disorganised for them to be able to hold their local tribunals. Perhaps these were forbidden by the invaders; perhaps the elders had no heart to decide cases when they saw no means of getting their decisions executed. Accordingly instead of appearing in dignity as the representatives of law and order among their neighbours the most respected citizens sit in silence on the ground, girded in sackcloth, and casting dust over their heads, living pictures of national mourning.[1]

The virgins of Jerusalem are named immediately after the elders. Their position in the city is very different from that of the "grave and reverend signiors"; but we are to see that while the dignity of age and rank affords no immunity from trouble, the gladsomeness of youth and its comparative irresponsibility are equally ineffectual as safeguards. The elders and the virgins have one characteristic in common. They are both silent. These young girls are the choristers whose clear, sweet voices used to ring out in strains of joy at every festival. Now both the grave utterances of magistrates and the blithe singing of maidens are hushed into one gloomy silence. Formerly the girls would dance to the sound of song and cymbal. How changed must things be that the once gay dancers sit with their heads bowed to the ground, as still as the mourning elders!

But now, like Dante when introduced by his guide to some exceptionally agonising spectacle in the infernal regions, the poet bursts into tears, and seems to feel his very being melting away at the contemplation of the most heart-rending scene in the many mournful tableaux of the woes of Jerusalem. Breaking off from his recital

---

[1] ii. 10.

of the facts to express his personal distress in view of the next item, he prepares us for some rare and dreadful exhibition of misery; and the tale that he has to tell is quite enough to account for the start of horror with which it is ushered in. The poet makes us listen to the cry of the children. There are babies at the breast fainting from hunger, and older children, able to speak, but not yet able to comprehend the helpless circumstances in which their miserable parents are placed, calling to their mothers for food and drink—a piercing appeal, enough to drive to the madness of grief and despair. Crying in vain for the first necessaries of life, these poor children, like the younger infants, faint in the streets, and cast themselves on their mothers' bosoms to die.[1] This, then, is the picture in contemplation of which the poet completely breaks down—children swooning in sight of all the people, and dying of hunger in their mothers' arms! He must be recalling scenes of the late siege. Then the fainting little ones, as they sank down pale and ill, resembled the wounded men who crept back from the fight by the walls to fall and die in the streets of the beleaguered city.

This is just the sharpest sting in the sufferings of the children. They share the fearful fate of their seniors, and yet they have had no part in the causes that led to it. We are naturally perplexed as well as distressed at this piteous spectacle of childhood. The beauty, the simplicity, the weakness, the tenderness, the sensitiveness, the helplessness of infancy appeal to our sympathies with peculiar force. But over and above these touching considerations there is a

---

[1] ii. 11, 12.

mystery attaching to the whole subject of the presence of pain and sorrow in young lives that baffles all reasoning. It is not only hard to understand why the bud should be blighted before it has had time to open to the sunshine : this haste in the march of misery to meet her victims on the threshold of life is to our minds a very amazing sight. And yet it is not the most perplexing part of the problem raised by the mystery of the suffering of children.

When we turn to the moral elements of the case we encounter its most serious difficulties. Children may not be accounted innocent in the absolute sense of the word. Even unconscious infants come into the world with hereditary tendencies to the evil habits of their ancestors ; but then every principle of justice resists the attachment of guilt or responsibility to an unsought and undeserved inheritance. And although children soon commit offences on their own account, it is not the consequences of these youthful follies that here trouble us. The cruel wrongs of childhood that overshadow the world's history with its darkest mystery have travelled on to their victims from quite other regions—regions of which the poor little sufferers are ignorant with the ignorance of perfect innocence. Why do children thus share in evils they had no hand in bringing upon the community ?

It is perhaps well that we should acknowledge quite frankly that there are mysteries in life which no ingenuity of thought can fathom. The suffering of childhood is one of the greatest of these apparently insoluble riddles of the universe. We have to learn that in view of such a problem as is here raised we too are but infants crying in the night.

Still there is no occasion for us to aggravate the riddle

by adding to it manufactured difficulties; we may even admit such mitigation of its severity as the facts of the case suggest. When little children suffer and die in their innocence they are free at least from those agonies of remorse for the irrecoverable past, and of apprehension concerning the doom of the future, that haunt the minds of guilty men, and frequently far exceed the physical pains endured. Beneath their hardest woes they have a peace of God that is the counterpart of the martyr's serenity.

Nevertheless, when we have said all that can be said in this direction, there remains the sickening fact that children do suffer and pine and die. Still though this cannot be explained away, there are two truths that we should set beside it before we attempt to form any judgment on the whole subject. The first is that taught so emphatically by our Lord when He declared that the victims of an accident or the sufferers in an indiscriminate slaughter were not to be accounted exceptional sinners.[1] But if suffering is by no means a sign of sin in the victim we may go further, and deny that it is in all respects an evil. It may be impossible for us to accept the Stoic paradox in the case of little children whom even the greatest pedant would scarcely attempt to console with philosophic maxims. In the endurance of them, the pain and sorrow and death of the young cannot but seem to us most real evils, and it is our plain duty to do all in our power to check and stay everything of the kind. We must beware of the indolence that lays upon Providence the burden of troubles that are really due to our own inconsiderateness. In pursuing the policy that led to the disastrous siege of their city the Jews

---

[1] Luke xiii 1-5.

should have known how many innocent victims would be dragged into the vortex of misery if the course they had chosen were to fail. The blind obstinacy of the men who refused to listen to the warnings so emphatically pronounced by the great prophets of Jehovah, the desperate self-will of these men, pitted against the declared counsel of God, must bear the blame. It is monstrous to charge the providence of God with the consequences of actions that God has forbidden.

A second truth must be added, for there still remains the difficulty that children are placed, by no choice of their own, in circumstances that render them thus liable to the effects of other people's sins and follies. We can never understand human life if we persist in considering each person by himself. That we are members one of another, so that if one member suffers all the members suffer, is the law of human experience as well as the principle of Christian churchmanship. Therefore we must regard the wrongs of children that so disturb us as part of the travail and woe of mankind. Bad as it is in itself that these innocents should be thus involved in the consequences of the misconduct of their elders, it would not be any improvement for them to be cut off from all connection with their predecessors in the great family of mankind. Taken on the whole, the solidarity of man certainly makes more for the welfare of childhood than for its disadvantage. And we must not think of childhood alone, deeply as we are moved at the sight of its unmerited sufferings. If children are part of the race, whatever children endure must be taken as but one element in the vast experience that goes to make up the life-history of mankind.

All this is very vague, and if we offer it as a consolation to a mother whose heart is torn with anguish at the sight of her child's pain, it is likely she will think our balm no better than the wormwood of mockery. It would be vain for us to imagine that we have solved the riddle, and vainer to suppose that any views of life could be set against the unquestionable fact that innocent children suffer, as though they in the slightest degree lessened the amount of this pain or made it appreciably easier to endure. But then, on the other hand, the mere existence of all this terrible agony does not justify us in bursting out into tremendous denunciations of the universe. The thoughts that rise from a consideration of the wider relations of the facts should teach us lessons of humility in forming our judgment on so vast a subject. We cannot deny the existence of evils that cry aloud for notice; we cannot explain them away. But at least we can follow the example of the elders and virgins of Israel, and be silent.

The portrait of misery that the poet has drawn in describing the condition of Jerusalem during the siege is painful enough when viewed by itself; and yet he proceeds further, and seeks to deepen the impression he has already made by setting the picture in a suitable frame. So he directs attention to the behaviour of surrounding peoples. Jerusalem is not permitted to hide her grief and shame. She is flung into an arena while a crowd of cruel spectators gloat over her agonies. These are to be divided into two classes, the unconcerned and the known enemies. There is not any great difference between them in their treatment of the miserable city. The unconcerned "hiss and wag their heads";[1] the enemies "hiss and gnash their teeth."[2]

---

[1] ii. 15.   [2] ii. 16.

That is to say, both add to the misery of the Jews—
the one class in mockery, the other in hatred. But
what are these men at their worst? Behind them is
the real Power that is the source of all the misery.
If the enemy rejoices it is only because God has given
him the occasion. The Lord has been carrying out
His own deliberate intentions; nay, these events are
but the execution of commands He issued in the days
of old.[1] This reads like an anticipation of the Calvinistic decrees. But perhaps the poet is referring to the
solemn threatening of Divine Judgment pronounced
by a succession of prophets. Their message had been
unheeded by their contemporaries. Now it has been
verified by history. Remembering what that message
was—how it predicted woes as the punishment of
sins, how it pointed out a way of escape, how it threw
all the responsibility upon those people who were
so infatuated as to reject the warning—we cannot
read into the poet's lines any notion of absolute pre-
destination.

In the midst of this description of the miseries of
Jerusalem the elegist confesses his own inability to
comfort her. He searches for an image large enough
for a just comparison with such huge calamities as he
has in view. His language resembles that of our Lord
when He exclaims, "Whereunto shall I liken the
kingdom of God?"[2] a similarity which may remind us
that if the troubles of man are great beyond earthly
analogy, so also are the mercies of God. Compare
these two, and there can be no question as to which
way the scale will turn. Where sin and misery abound
grace much more abounds. But now the poet is con-

---

[1] ii. 17.   [2] Luke xiii. 20.

cerned with the woes of Jerusalem, and he can only find one image with which these woes are at all comparable. Her breach, he says, "is great like the sea,"[1] meaning that her calamities are vast and terrible as the sea; or perhaps that the ruin of Jerusalem is like that produced by the breaking in of the sea—a striking image in its application to an inland mountain city; for no place was really safer from any such cataclysm than Jerusalem. The analogy is intentionally far-fetched. What might naturally happen to Tyre, but could not possibly reach Jerusalem, is nevertheless the only conceivable type of the events that have actually befallen this ill-fated city. The Jews were not a maritime people. To them the sea was no delight such as it is to us. They spoke of it with terror, and shuddered to hear from afar of its ravages. Now the deluge of their own troubles is compared to the great and terrible sea.

The poet can offer no comfort for such misery as this. His confession of helplessness agrees with what we must have perceived already, namely, that the Book of Lamentations is not a book of consolations. It is not always easy to see that the sympathy which mourns with the sufferer may be quite unable to relieve him. The too common mistake of the friend who comes to show sympathy is Bildad's and his companions' notion that he is called upon to offer advice. Why should one who is not in the school of affliction assume the function of pedagogue to a pupil of that school, who by reason of the mere fact of his presence there should rather be deemed fit to instruct the outsider?

If he cannot comfort Jerusalem, however, the elegist

---

[1] ii. 13.

will pray with her. His latest reference to the Divine source of the troubles of the Jews leads him on to a cry to God for mercy on the miserable people. Though he may not yet see the gospel of grace which is the only thing greater than the sin and misery of man, he can point towards the direction in which that glorious gospel is to dawn on the eyes of weary sufferers. Here, if anywhere, is the solution of the mystery of misery.

CHAPTER IX

PROPHETS WITHOUT A VISION

ii. 9, 14

IN deploring the losses suffered by the daughter of Zion the elegist bewails the failure of her prophets to obtain a vision from Jehovah. His language implies that these men were still lingering among the ruins of the city. Apparently they had not been considered by the invaders of sufficient importance to require transportation with Zedekiah and the princes. Thus they were within reach of inquirers, and doubtless they were more than ever in request at a time when many perplexed persons were anxious for pilotage through a sea of troubles. It would seem, too, that they were trying to execute their professional functions. They sought light; they looked in the right direction—to God. Yet their quest was vain; no vision was given to them; the oracles were dumb.

To understand the situation we must recollect the normal place of prophecy in the social life of Israel. The great prophets whose names and works have come down to us in Scripture were always rare and exceptional men—voices crying in the wilderness. Possibly they were not more scarce at this time than at other periods. Jeremiah had not been disappointed in his search for a Divine message.[1] The greatest seer of

---

[1] See Jer. xlii. 4, 7.

visions ever known to the world, Ezekiel, had already appeared among the captives by the waters of Babylon. Before long the sublime prophet of the restoration was to sound his trumpet blast to awaken courage and hope in the exiles. Though pitched in a minor key, these very elegies bear witness to the fact that their gentle author was not wholly deficient in prophetic fire. This was not an age like the time of Samuel's youth, barren of Divine voices.[1] It is true that the inspired voices were now scattered over distant regions far from Jerusalem, the ancient seat of prophecy. Yet the idea of the elegist is that the prophets who might be still seen at the site of the city were deprived of visions. These must have been quite different men. Evidently they were the professional prophets, officials who had been trained in music and dancing to appear as choristers on festive occasions, the equivalent of the modern dervishes; but who were also sought after like the seer of Ramah, to whom young Saul resorted for information about his father's lost asses, as simple soothsayers. Such assistance as these men were expected to give was no longer forthcoming at the request of troubled souls.

The low and sordid uses to which every-day prophecy was degraded may incline us to conclude that the cessation of it was no very great calamity, and perhaps to suspect that from first to last the whole business was a mass of superstition affording large opportunities for charlatanry. But it would be rash to adopt this extreme view without a fuller consideration of the subject. The great messengers of Jehovah frequently speak of the professional prophets with the contempt of Socrates

---

[1] See 1 Sam. iii. 1.

for the professional sophists; and yet the rebukes which they administer to these men for their unfaithfulness show that they accredit them with important duties and the gifts with which to execute them.

Thus the lament of the elegist suggests a real loss —something more serious than the failure of assistance such as some Roman Catholics try to obtain from St. Anthony in the discovery of lost property. The prophets were regarded as the media of communication between heaven and earth. It was because of the low and narrow habits of the people that their gifts were often put to low and narrow uses which savoured rather of superstition than of devotion. The belief that God did not only reveal His will to great persons and on momentous occasions helped to make Israel a religious nation. That there were humble gifts of prophecy within the reach of the many, and that these gifts were for the helping of men and women in their simplest needs, was one of the articles of the Hebrew faith. The quenching of a host of smaller stars may involve as much loss of life as that of a few brilliant ones. If prophecy fades out from among the people, if the vision of God is no longer perceptible in daily life, if the Church, as a whole, is plunged into gloom, it is of little avail to her that a few choice souls here and there pierce the mists like solitary mountain peaks so as to stand alone in the clear light of heaven. The perfect condition would be that in which "all the Lord's people were prophets." If this is not yet attainable, at all events we may rejoice when the capacity for communion with heaven is widely enjoyed, and we must deplore it as one of the greatest calamities of the Church that the quickening influence of the prophetic spirit should be absent from her assemblies. The Jews had not fallen so low that they could contemplate the cessation of communications with heaven unmoved. They were far from the practical materialism which leads its victims to be perfectly satisfied to remain in a condition of spiritual paralysis —a totally different thing from the theoretical materialism of Priestley and Tyndall. They knew that "man shall not live by bread alone, but by every word that proceedeth out of the mouth of God"; and therefore they understood that a famine of the word of God must result in as real a starvation as a famine of wheat. When we have succeeded in recovering this Hebrew standpoint we shall be prepared to recognise that there are worse calamities than bad harvests and seasons of commercial depression; we shall be brought to acknowledge that it is possible to be starved in the midst of plenty, because the greatest abundance of such food as we have lacks the elements requisite for our complete nourishment. According to reports of sanitary authorities, children in Ireland are suffering from the substitution of the less expensive and sweeter diet of maize for the more wholesome oatmeal on which their parents were brought up. Must it not be confessed that a similar substitution of cheap and savoury soul pabulum—in literature, music, amusements—for the "sincere milk of the word" and the "strong meat" of truth is the reason why so many of us are not growing up to the stature of Christ? The "liberty of prophesying" for which our fathers contended and suffered is ours. But it will be a barren heritage if in cherishing the liberty we lose the prophesying. There is no gift enjoyed by the Church for which she should be more jealous than that of the prophetic spirit.

As we look across the wide field of history we must

perceive that there have been many dreary periods in which the prophets could find no vision from the Lord. At first sight it would even seem that the light of heaven only shone on a few rare luminous spots, leaving the greater part of the world and the longer periods of time in absolute gloom. But this pessimistic view results from our limited capacity to perceive the light that is there. We look for the lightning. But inspiration is not always electric. The prophet's vision is not necessarily startling. It is a vulgar delusion to suppose that revelation must assume a sensational aspect. It was predicted of the Word of God incarnate that He should "not strive, or cry, or lift up His voice";[1] and when He came He was rejected because He would not satisfy the wonder-seekers with a flaring portent—a "sign from heaven." Still it cannot be denied that there have been periods of barrenness. They are found in what might be called the secular regions of the operation of the Spirit of God. A brilliant epoch of scientific discovery, artistic invention, or literary production is followed by a time of torpor, feeble imitation, or meretricious pretence. The Augustan and Elizabethan ages cannot be conjured back at will. Prophets of nature, poets, and artists can none of them command the power of inspiration. This is a gift which may be withheld, and which, when denied, will elude the most earnest pursuit. We may miss the vision of prophecy when the prophets are as numerous as ever, and unfortunately as vocal. The preacher possesses learning and rhetoric. We only miss one thing in him—inspiration. But, alas! that is just the one thing needful.

---

[1] Isa. xlii. 1.

Now the question forces itself upon our attention, what is the explanation of these variations in the distribution of the spirit of prophecy? Why is the fountain of inspiration an intermittent spring, a Bethesda? We cannot trace its failure to any shortness of supply, for this fountain is fed from the infinite ocean of the Divine life. Neither can we attribute caprice to One whose wisdom is infinite, and whose will is constant. It may be right to say that God withholds the vision, withholds it deliberately; but it cannot be correct to assert that this fact is the final explanation of the whole matter. God must be believed to have a reason, a good and sufficient reason, for whatever He does. Can we guess what His reason may be in such a case as this? It may be conjectured that it is necessary for the field to lie fallow for a season in order that it may bring forth a better crop subsequently. Incessant cultivation would exhaust the soil. The eye would be blinded if it had no rest from visions. We may be overfed; and the more nutritious our diet is the greater will be the danger of surfeit. One of our chief needs in the use of revelation is that we should thoroughly digest its contents. What is the use of receiving fresh visions if we have not yet assimilated the truth that we already possess? Sometimes, too, no vision can be found for the simple reason that no vision is needed. We waste ourselves in the pursuit of unprofitable questions when we should be setting about our business. Until we have obeyed the light that has been given us it is foolish to complain that we have not more light. Even our present light will wane if it is not followed up in practice.

But while considerations such as these must be attended to if we are to form a sound judgment on the whole question, they do not end the controversy, and they scarcely apply at all to the particular illustration of it that is now before us. There is no danger of surfeit in a famine; and it is a famine of the word that we are now confronted with. Moreover, the elegist supplies an explanation that sets all conjectures at rest.

The fault was in the prophets themselves. Although the poet does not connect the two statements together, but inserts other matter between them, we cannot fail to see that his next words about the prophets bear very closely on his lament over the denial of visions. He tells us that they had seen visions of vanity and foolishness.[1] This is with reference to an earlier period. Then they had had their visions; but these had been empty and worthless. The meaning cannot be that the prophets had been subject to unavoidable delusions, that they had sought truth, but had been rewarded with deception. The following words show that the blame was attributed entirely to their own conduct. Addressing the daughter of Zion the poet says: " Thy prophets have seen visions *for thee.*" The visions were suited to the people to whom they were declared— manufactured, shall we say?—with the express purpose of pleasing them. Such a degradation of sacred functions in gross unfaithfulness deserved punishment; and the most natural and reasonable punishment was the withholding for the future of true visions from men who in the past had forged false ones. The very possibility of this conduct proves that the influence of inspiration had not the hold upon these Hebrew prophets that it had obtained over the heathen prophet

---

[1] ii. 14.

Balaam, when he exclaimed, in face of the bribes and threats of the infuriated king of Moab: "If Balak would give me his house full of silver and gold, I cannot go beyond the word of the Lord, to do either good or bad of mine own mind; what the Lord speaketh, that will I speak."[1]

It must ever be that unfaithfulness to the light we have already received will bar the door against the advent of more light. There is nothing so blinding as the habit of lying. People who do not speak truth ultimately prevent themselves from perceiving truth, the false tongue leading the eye to see falsely. This is the curse and doom of all insincerity. It is useless to enquire for the views of insincere persons; they can have no distinct views, no certain convictions, because their mental vision is blurred by their long-continued habit of confounding true and false. Then if for once in their lives such people may really desire to find a truth in order to assure themselves in some great emergency, and therefore seek a vision of the Lord, they will have lost the very faculty of receiving it.

The blindness and deadness that characterise so much of the history of thought and literature, art and religion, are to be attributed to the same disgraceful cause. Greek philosophy decayed in the insincerity of professional sophistry. Gothic art degenerated into the florid extravagance of the Tudor period when it had lost its religious motive, and had ceased to be what it pretended. Elizabethan poetry passed through *euphuism* into the uninspired conceits of the sixteenth century. Dryden restored the habit of true speech,

---

[1] Numb. xxiv. 13.

but it required generations of arid eighteenth century sincerity in literature to make the faculty of seeing visions possible to the age of Burns and Shelley and Wordsworth.

In religion this fatal effect of insincerity is terribly apparent. The formalist can never become a prophet. Creeds which were kindled in the fires of passionate conviction will cease to be luminous when the faith that inspired them has perished; and then if they are still repeated as dead words by false lips the unreality of them will not only rob them of all value, it will blind the eyes of the men and women who are guilty of this falsehood before God, so that no new vision of truth can be brought within their reach. Here is one of the snares that attach themselves to the privilege of receiving a heritage of teaching from our ancestors. We can only avoid it by means of searching inquests over the dead beliefs which a foolish fondness has permitted to remain unburied, poisoning the atmosphere of living faith. So long as the fact that they are dead is not honestly admitted it will be impossible to establish sincerity in worship; and the insincerity, while it lasts, will be an impassable barrier to the advent of truth.

The elegist has laid his finger on the particular form of untruth of which the Jerusalem prophets had been guilty. They had not discovered her iniquity to the daughter of Zion.[1] Thus they had hastened her ruin by keeping back the message that would have urged their hearers to repentance. Some interpreters have given quite a new turn to the last clause of the fourteenth verse. Literally this states that the prophets have

---

[1] ii. 14.

seen "drivings away"; and accordingly it has been taken to mean that they pretended to have had visions about the captivity when this was an accomplished fact, although they had been silent on the subject, or had even denied the danger, at the earlier time when alone their words could have been of any use; or, again, the words have been thought to suggest that these prophets were now at the later period predicting fresh calamities, and were blind to the vision of hope which a true prophet like Jeremiah had seen and declared. But such ideas are over-refined, and they give a twist to the course of thought that is foreign to the form of these direct, simple elegies. It seems better to take the final clause of the verse as a repetition of what went before, with a slight variety of form. Thus the poet declares that the burdens, or prophecies, which these unfaithful men have presented to the people have been causes of banishment.

The crying fault of the prophets is their reluctance to preach to people of their sins. Their mission distinctly involves the duty of doing so. They should not shun to declare the whole counsel of God. It is not within the province of the ambassador to make selections from among the despatches with which he has been entrusted in order to suit his own convenience. There is nothing that so paralyses the work of the preacher as the habit of choosing favourite topics and ignoring less attractive subjects. Just in proportion as he commits this sin against his vocation he ceases to be the prophet of God, and descends to the level of one who deals in *obiter dicta*, mere personal opinions to be taken on their own merits. One of the gravest possible omissions is the neglect to give due weight to the tragic fact of sin. All the great prophets have been conspicuous for their fidelity to this painful and sometimes dangerous part of their work. If we would call up a typical picture of a prophet in the discharge of his task, we should present to our minds Elijah confronting Ahab, or John the Baptist before Herod, or Savonarola accusing Lorenzo de Medici, or John Knox preaching at the court of Mary Stuart. He is Isaiah declaring God's abomination of sacrifices and incense when these are offered by blood-stained hands, or Chrysostom seizing the opportunity that followed the mutilation of the imperial statues at Antioch to preach to the dissolute city on the need of repentance, or Latimer denouncing the sins of London to the citizens assembled at Paul's Cross.

The shallow optimism that disregards the shadows of life is trebly faulty when it appears in the pulpit. It falsifies facts in failing to take account of the stern realities of the evil side of them; it misses the grand opportunity of rousing the consciences of men and women by forcing them to attend to unwelcome truths, and thus encourages the heedlessness with which people rush headlong to ruin; and at the same time it even renders the declaration of the gracious truths of the gospel, to which it devotes exclusive attention, ineffectual, because redemption is meaningless to those who do not recognise the present slavery and the future doom from which it brings deliverance. On every account the rose-water preaching that ignores sin and flatters its hearers with pleasant words is thin, insipid, and lifeless. It tries to win popularity by echoing the popular wishes; and it may succeed in lulling the storm of opposition with which the prophet is commonly assailed. But in the end it must be sterile. When, "through fear or favour," the messenger of heaven thus prostitutes his mission to suit the ends of a low, selfish, worldly expediency, the very least punishment with which his offence can be visited is for him to be deprived of the gifts he has so grossly abused. Here, then, we have the most specific explanation of the failure of heavenly visions; it comes from the neglect of earthly sin. This is what breaks the magician's wand, so that he can no longer summon the Ariel of inspiration to his aid.

CHAPTER X

THE CALL TO PRAYER

ii. 18-22

IT is not easy to analyse the complicated construction of the concluding portion of the second elegy. If the text is not corrupt its transitions are very abrupt. The difficulty is to adjust the relations of three sections. First we have the sentence, "Their heart cried unto the Lord." Next comes the address to the wall, "O wall of the daughter of Zion," etc. Lastly, there is the prayer which extends from verse 20 to the end of the poem.

The most simple grammatical arrangement is to take the first clause in connection with the preceding verse. The last substantive was the word "adversaries." Therefore in the rigour of grammar the pronoun should represent that word. Read thus, the sentence relates an action of the enemies of Israel when their horn has been exalted. The word rendered "cried" is one that would designate a loud shout, and that translated "Lord" here is not the sacred name *Jehovah* but *Adonai*, a general term that might very well be used in narrating the behaviour of the heathen towards God. Thus the phrase would seem to describe the insolent shout of triumph which the adversaries of the Jews fling at the God of their victims.

On the other hand, it is to be observed that the general title "Lord" (*Adonai*) is also employed in the very next verse in the direct call to prayer. The heart, too, is mentioned again there as it is here, and that to express the inner being and deepest feelings of the afflicted city. It seems unlikely that the elegist would mention a heart-cry of the enemies and describe this as addressed to "The Lord."

Probably then we should apply this opening clause to the Jews, although they had not been named in the near context, a construction favoured by the abrupt transitions in which the elegist indulges elsewhere. It is the heart of the Jews that cried unto the Lord. Now the question arises, How shall we take this assertion in view of the words that follow? The common reading supposes that it introduces the immediately succeeding sentences. The heart of the Jews calls to the wall of the daughter of Zion, and bids it arise and pray. But with this construction we should look for another word (such as "saying") to introduce the appeal, because the Hebrew word rendered "cried" is usually employed absolutely, and not as the preface to quoted speech. Besides, the ideas would be strangely involved. Some people, indefinitely designated "they," exhort the wall to weep and pray! How can this exhortation to a wall be described as a calling to the Lord? The complication is increased when the prayer follows sharply on the anonymous appeal without a single connecting or explanatory clause.

A simpler interpretation is to follow Calvin in rendering the first clause absolutely, but still applying it to the Jews, who, though they are not named here, are supposed to be always in mind. We may not agree with the stern theologian of Geneva in asserting that the cry thus designated is one of impatient grief flowing not "from a right feeling or from the true fear of God, but from the strong and turbid impulse of nature." The elegist furnishes no excuse for this somewhat ungracious judgment. After his manner, already familiar to us, the poet interjects a thought— viz., that the distressed Jews cried to God. This suggests to him the great value of the refuge of prayer, a topic on which he forthwith proceeds to enlarge first by making an appeal to others, and then by himself breaking out into the direct language of petition.

This is not the first occasion on which the elegist has shown his faith in the efficacy of prayer. But hitherto he has only uttered brief exclamations in the middle of his descriptive passages. Now he gives a solemn call to prayer, and follows this with a deliberate, full petition, addressed to God. We must feel that the elegy is lifted to a higher plane by the new turn that the thought of its author takes at this place. Grief is natural; it is useless to pretend to be impassive; and, although our Teutonic habits of reserve may make it difficult for us to sympathise with the violent outbursts that an Oriental permits himself without any sense of shame, we must admit that a reasonable expression of the emotions is good and wholesome. Tennyson recognises this in the well-known lyric where he says of the dead warrior's wife—

"She must weep or she will die."

Nevertheless, an unchecked rush of feeling, not followed by any action, cannot but evince weakness; it has no lifting power. Although, if the emotion is distressful, such an expression may give relief to its subject, it is certainly very depressing to the spectator.

For this reason the Book of Lamentations strikes us as the most depressing part of the Bible—would it not be just to say, as the *only* part that can be so described? But it would not be fair to this Book to suppose that it did nothing beyond realising the significance of its title. It contains more than a melancholy series of laments. In the passage before us the poet raises his voice to a higher strain.

This new and more elevated turn in the elegy is itself suggestive. The transition from lamentation to prayer is always good for the sufferer. The first action may relieve his pent-up emotions; it cannot destroy the source from which they flow. But prayer is more practical, for it aims at deliverance. That, however, is its least merit. In the very act of seeking help from God the soul is brought into closer relations with Him, and this condition of communion is a better thing than any results that can possibly follow in the form of answers to the prayer, great and helpful as these may be. The trouble that drives us to prayer is a blessing because the state of a praying soul is a blessed state.

Like the *muezzin* on his minaret, the elegist calls to prayer. But his exhortation is addressed to a strange object—to the *wall* of the daughter of Zion. This wall is to let its tears flow like a river. It is so far personified that mention is made of the apple of its eye; it is called upon to arise, to pour out its heart, to lift up its hands. The license of Eastern poetry permits the unflinching application of a metaphor to an extent that would be considered extravagant and even absurd in our own literature. It is only in a travesty of melodrama that Shakespeare permits the Thisbe of *A Midsummer Night's Dream* to address a wall. Browning has an exquisitely beautiful little poem apostrophising an old wall; but this is not done so as to leave out of account the actual form and nature of his subject. Walls can not only be beautiful and even sublime, as Mr. Ruskin has shewn in his *Stones of Venice*; they may also wreathe their severe outlines in a multitude of thrilling associations. This is especially so when, as in the present instance, it is the wall of a city that we are contemplating. Not a new piece of builder's work, neat and clean and bald, bare of all associations, as meaningless as in too many cases it is ugly, but an old wall, worn by the passing to and fro of generations that have turned to dust long years ago, bearing the bruises of war on its battered face, crumbling to powder, or perhaps half buried in weeds—such a wall is eloquent in its wealth of associations, and there is pathos in the thought of its mere age when this is considered in relation to the many men and women and children who have rested beneath its shadow at noon, or sheltered themselves behind its solid masonry amid the terrors of war. The walls that encircle the ancient English city of Chester and keep alive memories of mediæval life, the bits of the old London wall that are left standing among the warehouses and offices of the busy mart of modern commerce, even the remote wall of China for quite different reasons, and many another famous wall, suggest to us multitudinous reflections. But the walls of Jerusalem surpass them all in the pathos of the memories that cling to their old grey stones. It does not require a great stretch of imagination to picture these walls as once glowing and throbbing with an intense life, and now dreaming over the unfathomable depths of age-long memories.

In personifying the wall of Zion, however, the Hebrew poet does not indulge in reflections such as these, which are more in harmony with the mild melancholy of Gray's *Elegy* than with the sadder mood of the mourning patriot. He names the wall to give unity and concreteness to his appeal, and to clothe it in an atmosphere of poetic fancy. But his sober thought in the background is directed towards the citizens whom that historic wall once enclosed. Herein is his justification for carrying his personification so far. This is more than a wild apostrophe, the outburst of an excited poet's fancy. The imaginative conceit wings the arrow of a serious purpose.

Let us look at the appeal in detail. First the elegist encourages a free outflow of grief, that tears should run like a river, literally, like a torrent—the allusion being to one of those steep watercourses which, though dry in summer, become rushing floods in the rainy season. This introduction shews that the call to prayer is not intended in any sense as a rebuke for the natural expression of grief, nor as a denial of its existence. The sufferers cannot say that the poet does not sympathise with them. It might seem needless to give this assurance. But anybody who has attempted to offer exhortation to a person in trouble must have discovered how delicate his task is. Let him approach the subject as carefully as he may, it is almost certain that he will chafe the quivering nerves he desires to soothe, so sensitive is the soul in pain to any interference from without. Under these circumstances, the one method by which it is at all possible to smooth the way of approach is an expression of genuine sympathy.

There may be a deeper reason for this encouragement of the expression of grief as a preliminary to a call to prayer. The helplessness which it so eloquently proclaims is just the condition in which the soul is most ready to cast itself on the mercy of God. Calm fortitude must always be better than an undisciplined abandonment to grief. But before this has been attained there may come an apathy of despair, under the influence of which the feelings are simply benumbed. That apathy is the very opposite to drying up the fountain of grief as it may be dried in the sunshine of love; it is freezing it. The first step towards deliverance will be to melt the glacier. The soul must feel before it can pray. Therefore the tears are encouraged to run like torrents, and the sufferer to give himself no respite, nor let the apple of his eye cease from weeping.

Next the poet exhorts the object of his sympathy—this strange personification of the "wall of the daughter of Zion," under the image of which he is thinking of the Jews—to arise. The weeping is but a preliminary to more promising acts. The sufferer is not to spend the long night in an unbroken flow of grief, like the psalmist "watering his couch with his tears."[1] The very opposite attitude is now suggested. Grief must not be treated as a normal condition, to be acquiesced in or even encouraged. The victim is tempted to cherish his sorrow as a sacred charge, to feel hurt if any mitigation of it is suggested, or ashamed of confessing that relief has been received. When he has reached this condition it is obvious that the substance of grief has passed; the ghost of it that remains is fast becoming a harmless sentiment. If, however, the trouble should be still maintaining the tightness of its grip on

---

[1] Psalm vi. 6.

the heart, there is positive danger in permitting it to be indulged without intermission. The sufferer must be roused if he is to be saved from the disease of *melancholia*.

He must be roused also if he would pray. True prayer is a strenuous effort of the soul, requiring the most wakeful attention and taxing the utmost energy of will. The Jew stood up to pray with hands outstretched to heaven. The relaxed and feeble devotions of a somnolent worshipper must fall flat and fruitless. There is no value in the length of a prayer, but there is much in its depth. It is the weight of its earnestness, not the comprehensiveness of its topics, that gives it efficacy. Therefore we must gird up our loins to pray just as we would to work, or run, or fight.

Now the awakened soul is urged to cry out in the night, and in the beginning of the night watches—that is to say, not only at the commencement of the night, for this would require no rousing, but at the beginning of each of the three watches into which the Hebrews divided the hours of darkness—at sunset, at ten o'clock, and at two in the morning. The sufferer is to keep watch with prayer—observing his vespers, his nocturns, and his matins, not of course to fulfil forms, but because, since his grief is continuous, his prayer also must not cease. This is all assigned to the night, perhaps because that is a quiet, solemn season for undisturbed reflection, when therefore the grief that requires the prayer is most acutely felt; or perhaps because the time of sorrow is naturally pictured as a night, as a season of darkness.

Proceeding with our consideration of the details of this call to prayer, we come upon the exhortation to pour out the heart like water before the face of the

Lord. The image here used is not without parallel in scripture. Thus a psalmist exclaims—

> "I am poured out like water,
> And all my bones are out of joint:
> My heart is like wax;
> It is melted in the midst of my bowels."[1]

But the ideas are not just the same in the two cases. While the psalmist thinks of himself as crushed and shattered, as though his very being were dissolved, the thought of the elegist has more action about it, with a deliberate intention and object in view. His image suggests complete openness before God. Nothing is to be withheld. It is not so much that the secrets of the soul are to be disclosed. The end aimed at is not confession, but confidence. Therefore what the writer would urge is that the sufferer should tell the whole tale of his grief to God, quite freely, without any reserve, trusting absolutely to the Divine sympathy.

This confidence is a primary requisite in prayer. Until we can trust our Father it is useless to petition for His aid; we could not avail ourselves of it if it were offered us. Indeed, the soul must come into relations of sympathy with God before any real prayer is at all possible.

We may go further. The attitude of soul that is here recommended is in itself the very essence of prayer. The devotions that consist in a series of definite petitions are of secondary worth, and superficial in comparison with this outpouring of the heart before God. To enter into relations of sympathy and confidence with God is to pray in the truest, deepest way possible, or even conceivable. Prayer in the heart

---

Psalm xxii. 14.

of it is not petition; that is the beggar's resort. It is communion—the child's privilege. We must often be as beggars, empty of everything before God; yet we may also enjoy the happier relationship of sonship with our Father. Even in the extremity of need perhaps the best thing we can do is to spread out the whole case before God. It will certainly relieve our own minds to do so, and everything will appear changed when viewed in the light of the Divine presence. Perhaps we shall then cease to think ourselves aggrieved and wronged; for what are our deserts before the holiness of God? Passion is allayed in the stillness of the sanctuary, and the indignant protest dies upon our lips as we proceed to lay our case before the eyes of the All-Seeing. We cannot be impatient any longer; He is so patient with us, so fair, so kind, so good. Thus when we cast our burden upon the Lord we may be surprised with the discovery that it is not so heavy as we supposed. There are times when it is not possible for us to go any further. We do not know what relief to ask for, or even whether we should request to be in any way delivered from a load which it may be our duty to bear, or the endurance of which may be a most wholesome discipline for us. These possibilities must always put a restraint upon the utterance of positive petitions. But they do not apply to the prayer that is a simple act of confidence in God. The secret of failure in prayer is not that we do not ask enough; it is that we do not pour out our hearts before God, the restraint of confidence rising from fear or doubt simply paralysing the energies of prayer. Jesus teaches us to pray not only because He gives us a model prayer, but much more because He is in Himself so true and full and winsome a revelation of God, that as we come to know and follow Him our lost confidence in God is restored. Then the heart that knows its own bitterness, and that shrinks from permitting the stranger even to meddle with its joy—how much more then with its sorrow?—can pour itself out quite freely before God, for the simple reason that He is no longer a stranger, but the one perfectly intimate and absolutely trusted Friend.

It is to be noted that the elegist points to a definite occasion for the outpouring of the heart before God. He singles out specifically the sufferings of the starving children—a terrible subject that appears more than once in this elegy, shewing how the horror of it has fastened on the imagination of the poet. This was the most heart-rending and mysterious ingredient in the bitter cup of the woes of Jerusalem. If we may bring any trouble to God we may bring the worst trouble. So this becomes the main topic of the prayer that follows. Here the cases of the principal victims are cited. Priest and prophet, notwithstanding the dignity of office, young man and maiden, old man and little child—all alike have fallen victims. The ghastly incident of a siege, where hunger has reduced human beings to the level of savage beasts, women devouring their own children, is here cited, and its cause, as well as that of all the other scenes of the great tragedy, boldly ascribed to God. It is God who has summoned His Terrors as at other times He had summoned His people to the festivals of the sacred city. But if God mustered the whole army of calamities it seems right to lay the story of the havoc they have wrought before His face; and the prayer reads almost like an accusation, or at least an expostulation, a remonstrance. It is not such, however; for we have seen that elsewhere the elegist makes full confession of the guilt of Jerusalem and admits that the doom of the wretched city was quite merited. Still if the dire chastisement is from the hand of God it is God alone who can bring deliverance. That is the final point to be reached.

CHAPTER XI

THE MAN THAT HATH SEEN AFFLICTION

iii. 1-21

WHETHER we regard it from a literary, a speculative, or a religious point of view, the third and central elegy cannot fail to strike us as by far the best of the five. The workmanship of this poem is most elaborate in conception and most finished in execution, the thought is most fresh and striking, and the spiritual tone most elevated, and, in the best sense of the word, evangelical. Like Tennyson, who is most poetic when he is most artistic, as in his lyrics, and like all the great sonneteers, the author of this exquisite Hebrew melody has not found his ideas to be cramped by the rigorous rules of composition. It would seem that to a master the elaborate regulations that fetter an inferior mind are no hindrances, but rather instruments fitted to his hand, and all the more serviceable for their exactness. Possibly the artistic refinement of form stimulates thought and rouses the poet to exert his best powers; or perhaps—and this is more probable—he selects the richer robe for the purpose of clothing his choicer conceptions. Here we have the acrostics worked up into triplets, so that they now appear at the beginning of every line, each letter occurring three times successively as an initial, and the whole poem falling into sixty-six verses or twenty-two triplets. Yet none of the other four poems have any approach to the wealth of thought or the uplifting inspiration that we meet with in this highly finished product of literary art.

This elegy differs from its sister poems in another respect. It is composed, for the most part, in the first person singular, the writer either speaking of his own experience or dramatically personating another sufferer. Who is this "man that hath seen affliction?" On the understanding that Jeremiah is the author of the whole book, it is commonly assumed that the prophet is here revealing his own feelings under the multitude of troubles with which he has been overwhelmed. But if, as we have seen, this hypothesis is, to say the least, extremely dubious, of course the assumption that has been based upon it loses its warranty. No doubt there is much in the touching picture of the afflicted person that agrees with what we know of the experience of the great prophet. And yet, when we look into it, we do not find anything of so specific a character as to settle us in the conclusion that the words could have been spoken by no one else. There is just the possibility that the poet is not describing himself at all; he may be representing somebody well known to his contemporaries—perhaps even Jeremiah, or just a typical character, in the manner of Browning's *Dramatis Personæ*.

While some mystery hangs over the personality of this man of sorrows the power and pathos of the poem are certainly heightened by the concentration of our attention upon one individual. Few persons are moved by general statements. Necessarily the comprehensive is all outline. It is by the supply of the particular that we fill up the details; and it is only when these details are present that we have a full-bodied picture. If an incident is typical it is illustrative of its kind. To know one such fact is to know all. Thus the science lecturer produces his specimen, and is satisfied to teach from it without adding a number of duplicates. The study of abstract reports is most important to those who are already interested in the subjects of these dreary documents; but it is useless as a means of exciting interest. Philanthropy must visit the office of the statistician if it would act with enlightened judgment, and not permit itself to become the victim of blind enthusiasm; but it was not born there, and the sympathy which is its parent can only be found among individual instances of distress.

In the present case the speaker who recounts his own misfortunes is more than a casual witness, more than a mere specimen picked out at random from the heap of misery accumulated in this age of national ruin. He is not simply *a* man who has seen affliction, one among many similar sufferers; he is *the* man, the well-known victim, one pre-eminent in distress even in the midst of a nation full of misery. Yet he is not isolated on a solitary peak of agony. As the supreme sufferer, he is also the representative sufferer. He is not selfishly absorbed in the morbid occupation of brooding over his private grievances. He has gathered into himself the vast and terrible woes of his people. Thus he foreshadows our Lord in His passion. We cannot but be struck with the aptness of much in this third elegy when it is read in the light of the last scenes of the gospel history. It would be a mistake to say that these outpourings from the heart of the Hebrew patriot were intended to convey a prophetic meaning with reference to another Sufferer in a far-distant future. Nevertheless the application of the poem to the Man of Sorrows is more than a case of literary illustration; for the idea of representative suffering which here emerges, and which becomes more definite in the picture of the servant of Jehovah in Isa. liii., only finds its full realisation and perfection in Jesus Christ. It is repeated, however, with more or less distinctness wherever the Christ spirit is revealed. Thus in a noble interpretation of St. Paul, the Apostle is represented as experiencing—

> "Desperate tides of the whole world's anguish
> Forced through the channel of a single heart."[1]

The portrait of himself drawn by the author of this elegy is the more graphic by reason of the fact that the present is linked to the past. The striking commencement, "I *am* the man," etc., sets the speaker in imagination before our eyes. The addition "who *has* seen" (or rather, experienced) "affliction" connects him with his present sufferings. The unfathomable mystery of personal identity here confronts us. This is more than memory, more than the lingering scar of a previous experience; it is, in a sense, the continuance of that experience, its ghostly presence still haunting the soul that once knew it in the glow of life. Thus we are what we have thought and felt and done, and our present is the perpetuation of our past. The man who has seen affliction does not only keep the history of his distresses in the quiet chamber of memory. His own personality has slowly acquired a depth, a fulness, a ripeness that remove him far from the raw and superficial character he once was. We are silenced into

---

[1] *St. Paul*, by Frederick Myers.

awe before Job, Jeremiah, and Dante, because these men grew great by suffering. Is it not told even of our Lord Jesus Christ that He was made perfect by the things that He suffered?[1] Unhappily it cannot be said that every hero of tragedy climbs to perfection on the rugged steps of his terrible life-drama; some men are shattered by discipline which proves to be too severe for their strength. Christ rose to His highest glory by means of the cruelty of His enemies and the treason of one of His trusted disciples; but cruel wrongs drove Lear to madness, and a confidant's treachery made a murderer of Othello. Still all who pass through the ordeal come out other than they enter, and the change is always a growth in some direction, even though in many cases we must admit with sorrow that this is a downward direction.

It is to be observed that here in his self-portraiture —just as elsewhere when describing the calamities that have befallen his people—the elegist attributes the whole series of disastrous events to God. This characteristic of the Book of Lamentations throughout is nowhere more apparent than in the third chapter. So close is the thought of God to the mind of the writer, he does not even think it necessary to mention the Divine name. He introduces his pronouns without any explanation of their objects, saying "*His* wrath" and "*He* hath led me," and so on through the succeeding verses. This quiet assumption of a recognised reference of all that happens to one source, a source that is taken to be so well known that there is no occasion to name it, speaks volumes for the deep-seated faith of the writer. He is at the antipodes of the too

---

[1] Heb. v. 8, 9.

common position of those people who habitually forget to mention the name of God because He is never in their thoughts. God is always in the thoughts of the elegist, and that is why He is not named. Like Brother Lawrence, this man has learnt to "practise the presence of God."

In amplifying the account of his sufferings, after giving a general description of himself as the man who has experienced affliction, and adding a line in which this experience is connected with its cause—the rod of the wrath of Him who is unnamed, though ever in mind—the stricken patriot proceeds to illustrate and enforce his appeal to sympathy by means of a series of vivid metaphors. This is the most crisp and pointed writing in the book. It hurries us on with a breathless rush of imagery, scene after scene flashing out in bewildering speed like the whirl of objects we look at from the windows of an express train.

Let us first glance at the successive pictures in this rapidly moving panorama of similes, and then at the general import and drift of the whole.

The afflicted man was under the Divine guidance; he was not the victim of blind self-will; it was not when straying from the path of right that he fell into this pit of misery. The strange thing is that God led him straight into it—led him into darkness, not into light as might have been expected with such a Guide.[1] The first image, then, is that of a traveller misled. The perception of the terrible truth that is here suggested prompts the writer at once to draw an inference as to the relation in which God stands to him, and the nature and character of the Divine treatment of him

---

[1] iii. 2.

throughout. God, whom he has trusted implicitly, whom he has followed in the simplicity of ignorance, God proves to be his Opponent! He feels like one duped in the past, and at length undeceived as he makes the amazing discovery that his trusted Guide has been turning His hand against him repeatedly all the day of his woful wanderings.[1] For the moment he drops his metaphors, and reflects on the dreadful consequences of this fatal antagonism. His flesh and skin, his very body is wasted away; he is so crushed and shattered, it is as though God had broken his bones.[2] Now he can see that God has not only acted as an enemy in guiding him into the darkness; God's dealings have shewn more overt antagonism. The helpless sufferer is like a besieged city, and God, who is conducting the assault, has thrown up a wall round him. With that daring mixture of metaphors, or, to be more precise, with that freedom of sudden transition from the symbol to the subject symbolised which we often meet with in this Book, the poet calls the rampart with which he has been girdled "gall and travail,"[3] for he has felt himself beset with bitter grief and weary toil.[4]

Then the scene changes. The victim of Divine wrath is a captive languishing in a dungeon, which is as dark as the abodes of the dead, as the dwellings of those who have been *long* dead.[5] The horror of this metaphor is intensified by the idea of the antiquity of Hades. How dismal is the thought of being plunged into a darkness that is already aged—a stagnant darkness,

---

[1] iii. 3.   [2] iii. 4.
[3] The Authorised Version has "travel," a mere variation in spelling. The word means painful labour, toil.
[4] iii. 4.   iii. 6

the atmosphere of those who long since lost the last rays of the light of life! There the prisoner is bound by a heavy chain.[1] He cries for help; but he is shut down so low that his prayer cannot reach his Captor.[2]

Again we see him still hampered, though in altered circumstances. He appears as a traveller whose way is blocked, and that not by some accidental fall of rock, but of set purpose, for he finds the obstruction to be of carefully prepared masonry, "hewn stones."[3] Therefore he has to turn aside, so that his paths become crooked. Yet more terrible does the Divine enmity grow. When the pilgrim is thus forced to leave the highroad and make his way through the adjoining thickets his Adversary avails Himself of the cover to assume a new form, that of a lion or a bear lying in ambush.[4] The consequence is that the hapless man is torn as by the claws and fangs of beasts of prey.[5] But now these wild regions in which the wretched traveller is wandering at the peril of his life suggest the idea of the chase. The image of the savage animals is defective in this respect, that man is their superior in intelligence, though not in strength. But in the present case the victim is in every way inferior to his Pursuer. So God appears as the Huntsman, and the unhappy sufferer as the poor hunted game. The bow is bent, and the arrow directed straight for its mark.[6] Nay, arrow after arrow has already been let fly, and the dreadful Huntsman, too skilful ever to miss His mark, has been shooting "the sons of His quiver" into the very vitals of the object of His pursuit.[7]

---

[1] iii. 7.   [3] iii. 9.   [5] iii. 11.   [7] iii. 13.
[2] iii. 8.   [4] iii. 10. [6] iii. 12.

Here the poet breaks away from his imagery for a second time to tell us that he has become an object of derision to all his people, and the theme of their mocking songs.[1] This is a striking statement. It shews that the afflicted man is not simply one member of the smitten nation of Israel, sharing the common hardships of the race whose "badge is servitude." He not merely experiences exceptional sufferings. He meets with no sympathy from his fellow-countrymen. On the contrary, these people so far dissociate themselves from his case that they can find amusement in his misery. Thus, while even a misguided Don Quixote is a noble character in the rare chivalry of his soul, and while his very delusions are profoundly pathetic, many people can only find material for laughter in them, and pride themselves in their superior sanity for so doing, although the truth is, their conduct proves them to be incapable of understanding the lofty ideals that inspire the object of their empty derision; thus Jeremiah was mocked by his unthinking contemporaries, when, whether in error, as they supposed, or wisely, as the event shewed, he preached an apparently absurd policy; and thus a greater than Jeremiah, One as supreme in reasonableness as in goodness, was jeered at by men who thought Him at best a Utopian dreamer, because they were grovelling in earthly thoughts far out of reach of the spiritual world in which He moved.

Returning to imagery, the poet pictures himself as a hardly used guest at a feast. He is fed, crammed, sated; but his food is bitterness, the cup has been forced to his lips, and he has been made drunk—not with pleasant wine, however, but with wormwood.[2]

---

[1] iii. 14.   [2] iii. 15

Gravel has been mixed with his bread, or perhaps the thought is that when he has asked for bread stones have been given him. He has been compelled to masticate this unnatural diet, so that his teeth have been broken by it. Even that result he ascribes to God, saying, "He hath broken my teeth."[1] It is difficult to think of the interference with personal liberty being carried farther than this. Here we reach the extremity of crushed misery.

Reviewing the whole course of his wretched sufferings from the climax of misery, the man who has seen all this affliction declares that God has cast him off from peace.[2] The Christian sufferer knows what a profound consolation there is in the possession of the peace of God, even when he is passing through the most acute agonies—a peace which can be maintained both amid the wildest tempests of external adversity and in the presence of the fiercest paroxysms of personal anguish. Is it not the acknowledged secret of the martyrs' serenity? Happily many an obscure sufferer has discovered it for himself, and found it better than any balm of Gilead. This most precious gift of heaven to suffering souls is denied to the man who here bewails his dismal fate. So too it was denied to Jesus in the garden, and again on the cross. It is possible that the dark day will come when it will be denied to one or another of His people. Then the experience of the moment will be terrible indeed. But it will be brief. An angel ministered to the Sufferer in Gethsemane. The joy of the resurrection followed swiftly on the agonies of Calvary. In the elegy we are now studying a burst of praise and glad confidence breaks

---

[1] iii. 16. [2] iii. 17.

out almost immediately after the lowest depths of misery have been sounded, shewing that, as Keats declares in an exquisite line—

"There is a budding morrow in midnight."

It is not surprising, however, that, for the time being, the exceeding blackness of the night keeps the hope of a new day quite out of sight. The elegist exclaims that he has lost the very idea of prosperity. Not only has his strength perished, his hope in God has perished also.[1] Happily God is far too good a Father to deal with His children according to the measure of their despair. He is found by those who are too despondent to seek Him, because He is always seeking His lost children, and not waiting for them to make the first move towards Him.

When we come to look at the series of pictures of affliction as a whole we shall notice that one general idea runs through them. This is that the victim is hindered, hampered, restrained. He is led into darkness, besieged, imprisoned, chained, driven out of his way, seized in ambuscade, hunted, even forced to eat unwelcome food. This must all point to a specific character of personal experience. The troubles of the sufferer have mainly assumed the form of a thwarting of his efforts. He has not been an indolent, weak, cowardly creature, succumbing at the first sign of opposition. To an active man with a strong will resistance is one of the greatest of troubles, although it will be accepted meekly, as a matter of course, by a person of servile habits. If the opposition comes from God, may it not be that the severity of the trouble is

---

[1] iii. 18.

just caused by the obstinacy of self-will? Certainly it does not appear to be so here; but then we must remember the writer is stating his own case.

Two other characteristics of the whole passage may be mentioned. One is the *persistence* of the Divine antagonism. This is what makes the case look so hard. The pursuer seems to be ruthless; He will not let his victim alone for a moment. One device follows sharply on another. There is no escape. The second of these characteristics of the passage is a gradual *aggravation* in the severity of the trials. At first God is only represented as a guide who misleads; then He appears as a besieging enemy; later like a destroyer. And correspondingly the troubles of the sufferer grow in severity, till at last he is flung into the ashes, crushed and helpless.

All this is peculiarly painful reading to us with our Christian thoughts of God. It seems so utterly contrary to the character of our Father revealed in Jesus Christ. But then it is not a part of the Christian revelation, nor was it uttered by a man who had received the benefits of that highest teaching. That, however, is not a complete explanation. The dreadful thoughts about God that are here recorded are almost without parallel even in the Old Testament. How contrary they are to such an idea as that of the pitiful Father in Psalm ciii.! On the other hand, it should be remembered that if ever we have to make allowance for the personal equation we must be ready to do so most liberally when we are listening to the tale of his wrongs as this is recounted by the sufferer himself. The narrator may be perfectly honest and truthful, but it is not in human nature to be impartial under such circumstances. Even when, as in the present instance, we have reason to believe that the speaker is under the influence of a Divine inspiration, we have no right to conclude that this gift would enable him to take an all-round vision of truth. Still, can we deny that the elegist has presented to our minds but one facet of truth? If we do not accept it as intended for a complete picture of God, and if we confine it to an account of the Divine action under certain circumstances as this appears to one who is most painfully affected by it, without any assertion concerning the ultimate motives of God—and this is all we have any justification for doing—it may teach us important lessons which we are too ready to ignore in favour of less unpleasant notions. Finally it would be quite unfair to the elegist, and it would give us a totally false impression of his ideas, if we were to go no further than this. To understand him at all we must hear him out. The contrast between the first part of this poem and the second is startling in the extreme, and we must not forget that the two are set in the closest juxtaposition, for it is plain that the one is intended to balance the other. The harshness of the opening words could be permitted with the more daring, because a perfect corrective to any unsatisfactory inferences that might be drawn from it was about to be immediately supplied.

The triplet of verses 19 to 21 serves as a transition to the picture of the other side of the Divine action. It begins with prayer. Thus a new note is struck. The sufferer knows that God is not at heart his enemy. So he ventures to beseech the very Being concerning whose treatment of him he has been complaining so bitterly, to remember his affliction and the misery it has brought on him, the wormwood, the gall of his hard lot. Hope now dawns on him out of his own recollections. What are these? The Authorised Version would lead us to think that when he uses the expression, "This I recall to my mind,"[1] the poet is referring to the encouraging ideas of the verses that immediately follow in the next section. But it is not probable that the last line of a triplet would thus point forward to another part of the poem. It is more consonant with the method of the composition to take this phrase in connection with what precedes it in the same triplet, and a perfectly permissible change in the translation of the 20th verse gives good sense in that connection. We may read this:

"Thou (O God) wilt surely remember, for my soul is bowed down within me."

Thus the recollection that God too has a memory and that He will remember His suffering servant becomes the spring of a new hope.

---

[1] iii. 21.

CHAPTER XII

THE UNFAILING GOODNESS OF GOD

iii. 22-4

ALTHOUGH the elegist has prepared us for brighter scenes by the more hopeful tone of an intermediate triplet, the transition from the gloom and bitterness of the first part of the poem to the glowing rapture of the second is among the most startling effects in literature. It is scarcely possible to conceive of darker views of Providence, short of a Manichæan repudiation of the God of the physical universe as an evil being, than those which are boldly set forth in the opening verses of the elegy; we shudder at the awful words, and shrink from repeating them, so near to the verge of blasphemy do they seem to come. And now those appalling utterances are followed by the very choicest expression of confidence in the boundless goodness of God! The writer seems to leap in a moment out of the deepest, darkest pit of misery into the radiance of more than summer sunlight. How can we account for this extraordinary change of thought and temper?

It is not enough to ascribe the sharpness of the contrast either to the clumsiness of the author in giving utterance to his teeming fancies just as they occur to him, without any consideration for their bearings one upon another; or to his art in designedly preparing an awakening shock. We have still to answer the question, How could a man entertain two such conflicting currents of thought in closest juxtaposition?

In their very form and structure these touching elegies reflect the mental calibre of their author. A wooden soul could never have-invented their movements. They reveal a most sensitive spirit, a spirit that resembles a finely strung instrument of music, quivering in response to impulses from all directions. People of a mercurial temperament live in a state of perpetual oscillation between the most contrary moods, and the violence of their despair is always ready to give place to the enthusiasm of a new hope. We call them inconsistent; but their inconsistency may spring from a quick-witted capacity to see two sides of a question in the time occupied by slower minds with the contemplation of one. As a matter of fact, however, the revulsion in the mind of the poet may not have been so sudden as it appears in his work. We can scarcely suppose that so elaborate a composition as this elegy was written from beginning to end at a single sitting. Indeed, here we seem to have the mark of a break. The author composes the first part in an exceptionally gloomy mood, and leaves the poem unfinished, perhaps for some time. When he returns to it on a subsequent occasion he is in a totally different frame of mind, and this is reflected in the next stage of his work. Still the point of importance is the possibility of the very diverse views here recorded.

Nor is this wholly a matter of temperament. Is it not more or less the case with all of us, that since absorption with one class of ideas entirely excludes their opposites, when the latter are allowed to enter the mind they will rush in with the force of a pent-up flood? Then we are astonished that we could ever have forgotten them. We build our theories in disregard of whole regions of thought. When these occur to us it is with the shock of a sudden discovery, and in the flash of the new light we begin at once to take very different views of our universe. Possibly we have been oblivious of our own character, until suddenly we are awakened to our true state, to be overwhelmed with shame at an unexpected revelation of sordid meanness, of despicable selfishness. Or perhaps the vision is of the heart of another person, whose quiet, unassuming goodness we have not appreciated, because it has been so unvarying and dependable that we have taken it as a matter of course, like the daily sunrise, never perceiving that this very constancy is the highest merit. We have been more grateful for the occasional lapses into kindness with which habitually churlish people have surprised us. Then there has come the revelation, in which we have been made to see that a saint has been walking by our side all the day. Many of us are very slow in reaching a similar discovery concerning God. But when we begin to take a right view of His relations to us we are amazed to think that we had not perceived them before, so rich and full and abounding are the proofs of His exceeding goodness.

Still it may seem to us a strange thing that this most perfect expression of a joyous assurance of the mercy and compassion of God should be found in the Book of Lamentations of all places. It may well give heart to those who have not sounded the depths of sorrow, as the author of these sad poems had done, to learn that even he had been able to recognise the merciful kindness of God in the largest possible measure. A little reflection, however, should teach us that it is not so unnatural a thing for this gem of grateful appreciation to appear where it is. We do not find, as a rule, that the most prosperous people are the foremost to recognise the love of God. The reverse is very frequently the case. If prosperity is not always accompanied by callous ingratitude—and of course it would be grossly unjust to assert anything so harsh—at all events it is certain that adversity is far from blinding our eyes to the brighter side of the revelation of God. Sometimes it is the very means by which they are opened. In trouble the blessings of the past are best valued, and in trouble the need of God's compassion is most acutely felt. But this is not all. The softening influence of sorrow seems to have a more direct effect upon our sense of Divine goodness. Perhaps, too, it is some compensation for melancholy, that persons who are afflicted with it are most responsive to sympathy. The morbid, despondent poet Cowper has writtten most exquisitely about the love of God. Watts is enthusiastic in his praise of the Divine grace ; but a deeper note is sounded in the Olney hymns, as, for example, in that beginning with the line—

"Hark, my soul, it is the Lord."

While reading this hymn to-day we cannot fail to feel the peculiar thrill of personal emotion that still quivers through its living words, revealing the very soul of their author. This is more than joyous praise ; it is the expression of a personal experience of the compassion of God in times of deepest need. The same sensitive poet has given us a description of the very condition that is illustrated by the passage in the Hebrew elegist we are now considering, in lines which, familiar as they are, acquire a fresh meaning when read in this association—the lines—

> "Sometimes a light surprises
> The Christian while he sings:
> It is the Lord who rises
> With healing in His wings.
> When comforts are declining,
> He grants the soul, again,
> A season of clear shining,
> To cheer it after rain."

We may thank the Calvinistic poet for here touching on another side of the subject. He reminds us that it is God who brings about the unexpected joy of renewed trust in His unfailing mercy. The sorrowful soul is, consciously or unconsciously, visited by the Holy Spirit, and the effect of contact with the Divine is that scales fall from the eyes of the surprised sufferer. If it is right to say that one portion of Scripture is more inspired than another we must feel that there is more Divine light in the second part of this elegy than in the first. It is this surprising light from Heaven that ultimately accounts for the sudden revolution in the feelings of the poet.

In his new consciousness of the love of God the elegist is first struck by its amazing persistence. Probably we should follow the Targum and the Syriac version in rendering the twenty-second verse thus—

> "The Lord's mercies, verily they cease not," etc.

instead of the usual English rendering—

> "It is of the Lord's mercies that we are not consumed," etc.

There are two reasons for this emendation. *First*, the momentary transition to the plural "we" is harsh and improbable. It is true the author makes a somewhat similar change a little later;[1] but there it is in an extended passage, and one in which he evidently wishes to represent his people with ideas that are manifestly appropriate to the community at large. Here, on the other hand, the sentence breaks into the midst of personal reflections. *Second*—and this is the principal consideration—the balance of the phrases, which is so carefully observed throughout this elegy, is upset by the common rendering, but restored by the emendation. The topic of the triplet in which the disputed passage occurs is the amazing persistence of God's goodness to His suffering children. The proposed alteration is in harmony with this.

The thought here presented to us rests on the truth of the eternity and essential changelessness of God. We cannot think of Him as either fickle or failing; to do so would be to cease to think of Him as God. If He is merciful at all He cannot be merciful only spasmodically, erratically, or temporarily. For all that, we need not regard these heart-stirring utterances as the expressions of a self-evident truism. The wonder and glory of the idea they dilate upon are not the less for the fact that we should entertain no doubt of its truth. The certainty that the character of God is good and great does not detract from His goodness or His greatness. When we are assured that His nature is not fallible our contemplation of it does not cease to be an act of adoration. On the contrary, we can worship the immutable perfection of God with fuller praises than we should give to fitful gleams of less abiding qualities.

As a matter of fact, however, our religious ex-

---

[1] iii. 40-8.

perience is never the simple conclusion of bare logic. Our feelings, and not these only, but also our faith, need repeated assurances of the continuance of God's goodness, because it seems as though there were so much to absorb and quench it. Therefore the perception of the fact of its continuance takes the form of a glad wonder that God's mercies do not cease. Thus it is amazing to us that these mercies are not consumed by the multitude of the sufferers who are dependent upon them—the extent of God's family not in any way cramping His means to give the richest inheritance to each of His children; nor by the depth of individual need—no single soul having wants so extreme or so peculiar that His aid cannot avail entirely for them; nor by the shocking ill-desert of the most unworthy of mankind—even sin, while it necessarily excludes the guilty from any present enjoyment of the love of God, not really quenching that love or precluding a future participation in it on condition of repentance; nor by the wearing of time, beneath which even granite rocks crumble to powder.

The elegist declares that the reason why God's mercies are not consumed is that His compassions do not fail. Thus he goes behind the kind actions of God to their originating motives. To a man in the condition of the writer of this poem of personal confidences the Divine sympathy is the one fact in the universe of supreme importance. So will it be to every sufferer who can assure himself of the truth of it. But is this only a consolation for the sorrowing? The pathos, the very tragedy of human life on earth, should make the sympathy of God the most precious fact of existence to all mankind. Portia rightly reminds Shylock that "we all do look for mercy"; but if so, the spring of mercy, the Divine compassion, must be the one source of true hope for every soul of man. Whether we are to attribute it to sin alone, or whether there may be other dark, mysterious ingredients in human sorrow, there can be no doubt that the deepest need is that God should have pity on His children. The worship of heaven among the angels may be one pure song of joy; but here, even though we are privileged to share the gladness of the celestial praises, a plaintive note will mingle with our anthem of adoration, because a pleading cry must ever go up from burdened spirits; and when relief is acknowledged our thanksgiving must single out the compassion of God for deepest gratitude. It is much, then, to know that God not only helps the needy—that is to say, all mankind—but that He feels with His suffering children. The author of the Epistle to the Hebrews has taught us to see this reassuring truth most clearly in the revelation of God in His Son, repeatedly dwelling on the sufferings of Christ as the means by which He was brought into sympathetic, helpful relations to the sufferings of mankind.[1]

Further, the elegist declares that the special form taken by these unceasing mercies of God is daily renewal. The love of God is constant—one changeless Divine attribute; but the manifestations of that love are necessarily successive and various according to the successive and various needs of His children. We have not only to praise God for His eternal, immutable goodness, vast and wonderful as that is; to our perceptions, at all events, His immediate, present actions are even more significant because they

---

[1] Heb. ii. 18, iv. 15.

shew His personal interest in individual men and women, and His living activity at the very crisis of need. There is a certain aloofness, a certain chillness, in the thought of ancient kindness, even though the effects of it may reach to our own day in full and abundant streams. But the living God is an active God, who works in the present as effectually as He worked in the past. There is another side to this truth. It is not sufficient to have received the grace of God once for all. If "He giveth more grace," it is because we need more grace. This is a stream that must be ever flowing into the soul, not the storage of a tank filled once for all and left to serve for a lifetime. Therefore the channel must be kept constantly clear, or the grace will fail to reach us, although in itself it never runs dry.

There is something cheering in the poet's idea of the morning as the time when these mercies of God are renewed. It has been suggested that he is thinking of renewals of brightness after dark seasons of sorrow, such as are suggested by the words of the psalmist—

"Weeping may come in to lodge at even,
But joy cometh in the morning."[1]

This idea, however, would weaken the force of the passage, which goes to shew that God's mercies do not fail, are not interrupted. The emphasis is on the thought that no day is without God's new mercies, not even the day of darkest trouble; and further, there is the suggestion that God is never dilatory in coming to our aid. He does not keep us waiting and wearying while He tarries. He is prompt and

---

[1] Psalm xxx. 5, R.V. Marg.

early with His grace. The idea may be compared with that of the promise to those who seek God *early*, literally, *in the morning*.[1] Or we may think of the night as the time of repose, when we are oblivious of God's goodness, although even through the hours of darkness He who neither slumbers nor sleeps is constantly watching over His unconscious children. Then in the morning there dawns on us a fresh perception of His goodness. If we are to realise the blessing sought in Sir Thomas Browne's prayer, and

"Awake into some holy thought,"

no more holy thought can be desired than a grateful recognition of the new mercies on which our eyes open with the new day. A morning so graciously welcomed is the herald of a day of strength and happy confidence.

To the notion of the morning renewal of the mercies of God the poet appends a recognition of His great faithfulness. This is an additional thought. Faithfulness is more than compassion. There is a strength and a stability about the idea that goes further to insure confidence. It is more than the fact that God is true to His word, that He will certainly perform what He has definitely promised. Fidelity is not confined to compacts—it is not limited to the question of what is "in the bond"; it concerns persons rather than phrases. To be faithful to a friend is more than to keep one's word to him. We may have given him no pledge; and yet we must confess to an obligation to be true—to be true to the man himself. Now while we are called upon to be loyal to God, there is a sense in which we may venture without irreverence to say

---

[1] Prov. viii. 17.

that He may be expected to be faithful to us. He is our Creator, and He has placed us in this world by His own will; His relations with us cannot cease at this point. So Moses pleaded that God, having led His people into the wilderness, could not desert them there; and Jeremiah even ventured on the daring prayer—

"Do not disgrace the throne of Thy glory."[1]

It is because we are sure the just and true God could never do anything so base that His faithfulness becomes the ground of perfect confidence. It may be said, on the other hand, that we cannot claim any good thing from God on the score of merit, because we only deserve wrath and punishment. But this is not a question of merit. Fidelity to a friend is not exhausted when we have treated him according to his deserts. It extends to a treatment of him in accordance with the direct claims of friendship, claims which are to be measured by need rather than by merit.

The conclusion drawn from these considerations is given in an echo from the Psalms—

"The Lord is my portion."[2]

The words are old and well-worn; but they obtain a new meaning when adopted as the expression of a new experience. The lips have often chanted them in the worship of the sanctuary. Now they are the voice of the soul, of the very life. There is no plagiarism in such a quotation as this, although in making it the poet does not turn aside to acknowledge his obligation to the earlier author who coined the immortal phrase. The seizure of the old words

---

[1] Jer. xiv. 21.   [2] Psalm lxxiii. 26.

by the soul of the new writer make them his own in the deepest sense, because under these circumstances it is not their literary form, but their spiritual significance, that gives them their value. This is true of the most frequently quoted words of Scripture. They are new words to every soul that adopts them as the expression of a new experience.

It is to be observed that the experience now reached is something over and above the conscious reception of daily mercies. The Giver is greater than His gifts. God is first known by means of His actions, and then being thus known He is recognised as Himself the portion of His people, so that to possess Him is their one satisfying joy in the present and their one inspiring hope for the future.

CHAPTER XIII

QUIET WAITING

iii. 25-36

HAVING struck a rich vein, our author proceeds to work it with energy. Pursuing the ideas that flow out of the great truth of the endless goodness of God, and the immediate inference that He of whom so wonderful a character can be affirmed is Himself the soul's best possession, the poet enlarges upon their wider relations. He must adjust his views of the whole world to the new situation that is thus opening out before him. All things are new in the light of the splendid vision before which his gloomy meditations have vanished like a dream. He sees that he is not alone in enjoying the supreme blessedness of the Divine love. The revelation that has come to him is applicable to other men if they will but fulfil the conditions to which it is attached.

In the first place, it is necessary to perceive clearly what those conditions are on which the happy experience of God's unfailing mercies may be enjoyed by any man. The primary requisite is affirmed to be *quiet waiting*.[1] The passivity of this attitude is accentuated in a variety of expressions. It is difficult for us of the modern western world to appreciate such teaching.

---

[1] iii. 26.

No doubt if it stood by itself it would be so one-sided as to be positively misleading. But this is no more than must be said of any of the best lessons of life. We require the balancing of separate truths in order to obtain truth, as we want the concurrence of different impulses to produce the resultant of a right direction of life. But in the present case the opposite end of the scale has been so much overweighted that we sorely need a very considerable addition on the side to which the elegist here leans. Carlyle's gospel of work—a most wholesome message as far as it went—fell on congenial Anglo-Saxon soil; and this and the like teaching of kindred minds has brought forth a rich harvest in the social activity of modern English life. The Church has learnt the duty of working—which is well. She does not appear so capable of attaining the blessedness of waiting. Our age is in no danger of the dreaminess of quietism. But we find it hard to cultivate what Wordsworth calls "wise passiveness." And yet in the heart of us we feel the lack of this spirit of quiet. Charles Lamb's essay on the "Quakers' Meeting" charms us, not only on account of its exquisite literary style, but also because it reflects a phase of life which we own to be most beautiful.

The waiting here recommended is more than simple passiveness, however, more than a bare negation of action. It is the very opposite of lethargy and torpor. Although it is quiet, it is not asleep. It is open-eyed, watchful, expectant. It has a definite object of anticipation, for it is a waiting for God and His salvation; and therefore it is hopeful. Nay, it has a certain activity of its own, for it seeks God. Still, this activity is inward and quiet; its immediate aim is not to get at some visible earthly end, however much this may be desired, nor to attain some inward personal experience, some stage in the soul's culture, such as peace, or purity, or power, although this may be the ultimate object of the present anxiety; primarily it seeks God—all else it leaves in His hands. Thus it is rather a change in the tone and direction of the soul's energies than a state of repose. It is the attitude of the watchman on his lonely tower—calm and still, but keen-eyed and alert, while down below in the crowded city some fret themselves with futile toil and others slumber in stupid indifference.

To this waiting for Him and definite seeking of Him God responds in some special manifestation of mercy. Although, as Jesus Christ tells us, our Father in heaven "maketh His sun to rise on the evil and the good, and sendeth rain on the just and the unjust,"[1] the fact here distinctly implied, that the goodness of God is exceptionally enjoyed on the conditions now laid down, is also supported by our Lord's teaching in the exhortations, "Ask, and it shall be given you; seek, and ye shall find; knock, and it shall be opened to you; for every one that asketh receiveth; and he that seeketh findeth; and to him that knocketh it shall be opened."[2] St. James adds, "Ye have not because ye ask not."[3] This, then, is the method of the Divine procedure. God expects His children to wait on Him as well as to wait for Him. We cannot consider such an expectation unreasonable. Of course it would be foolish to imagine God piquing Himself on His own dignity, so as to decline aid until He had been gratified by a due observance of homage. There is a deeper motive for the requirement. God's relations with men and women

---

[1] Matt. v. 45. [2] vii. 7, 8. [3] James iv. 2.

are personal and individual; and when they are most happy and helpful they always involve a certain reciprocity. It may not be necessary or even wise to demand definite things from God whenever we seek His assistance; for He knows what is good, while we often blunder and ask amiss. But the seeking here described is of a different character. It is not seeking things; it is seeking God. This is always good. The attitude of trust and expectancy that it necessitates is just that in which we are brought into a receptive state. It is not a question of God's willingness to help; He is always willing. But it cannot be fitting that He should act towards us when we are distrustful, indifferent, or rebellious, exactly as He would act if He were approached in submission and trustful expectation.

Quiet waiting, then, is the right and fitting condition for the reception of blessing from God. But the elegist holds more than this. In his estimation the state of mind he here commends is itself good for a man. It is certainly good in contrast with the unhappy alternatives—feeble fussiness, wearing anxiety, indolent negligence, or blank despair. It is good also as a positive condition of mind. He has reached a happy inward attainment who has cultivated the faculty of possessing his soul in patience. His eye is clear for visions of the unseen. To him the deep fountains of life are open. Truth is his, and peace and strength also. When we add to this calmness the distinct aim of seeking God we may see how the blessedness of the condition recommended is vastly enhanced. We are all insensibly moulded by our desires and aims. The expectant soul is transformed into the image of the hope it pursues. When its treasure is in heaven its heart is there also, and therefore its very nature becomes heavenly.

To his reflections on the blessedness of quiet waiting the elegist adds a very definite word about another experience, declaring that "it is good for a man that he bear the yoke in his youth."[1] This interesting assertion seems to sound an autobiographical note, especially as the whole poem treats of the writer's personal experience. Some have inferred that the author must have been a young man at the time of writing. But if, as seems probable, he is calling to mind what he has himself passed through, this may be a recollection of a much earlier period of his life. Thus he would seem to be recognising, in the calm of subsequent reflection, what perhaps he may have been far from admitting while bearing the burdens, that the labours and hardships of his youth prove to have been for his own advantage. This truth is often perceived in the meditations of mature life, although it is not so easily acknowledged in the hours of strain and stress.

It is impossible to say what particular yoke the writer is thinking about. The persecutions inflicted on Jeremiah have been cited in illustration of this passage; and although we may not be able to ascribe the poem to the great prophet, his toils and troubles will serve as instances of the truth of the words of the anonymous writer, for undoubtedly his sympathies were quickened while his strength was ripened by what he endured. If we will have a definite meaning the yoke may stand for one of three things—for instruction, for labour, or for trouble. The sentence is true of either of these forms of yoke. We are not

---

[1] iii. 27.

likely to dispute the advantages of youthful education over that which is delayed till adult age ; but even if the acquisition of knowledge is here suggested, we cannot suppose it to be book knowledge, it must be that got in the school of life. Thus we are brought to the other two meanings. Then the connection excludes the notion of pleasant, attractive work, so that the yoke of labour comes near to the burden of trouble. This seems to be the essential idea of the verse. Irksome work, painful toil, forced labour partaking of the nature of servitude—these ideas are most vividly suggested by the image of a yoke. And they are what we most shrink from in youth. Inactivity is then by no means sought or desired. The very exercise of one's energies is a delight at the time of their fresh vigour. But this exercise must be in congenial directions, in harmony with one's tastes and inclinations, or it will be regarded as an intolerable burden. Liberty is sweet in youth ; it is not work that is dreaded, but compulsion. Youth emulates the bounding energies of the war horse, but it has a great aversion to the patient toil of the ox. Hence the yoke is resented as a grievous burden ; for the yoke signifies compulsion and servitude. Now, as a matter of fact, this yoke generally has to be borne in youth. People might be more patient with the young if they would but consider how vexatious it must be to the shoulders that are not yet fitted to wear it, and in the most liberty-loving age. As time passes custom makes the yoke easier to be borne ; and yet then it is usually lightened. In our earlier days we must submit and obey, must yield and serve. This is the rule in business, the drudgery and restraint of which naturally attach themselves to the first stages. If older persons reflected on what this must mean at the very time when the appetite for delight is most keen, and the love of freedom most intense, they would not press the yoke with needless harshness.

But now the poet has been brought to see that it was for his own advantage that he was made to bear the yoke in his youth. How so? Surely not because it prevented him from taking too rosy views of life, and so saved him from subsequent disappointment. Nothing is more fatal to youth than cynicism. The young man who professes to have discovered the hollowness of life generally is in danger of making his own life a hollow and wasted thing. The elegist could never have fallen to this miserable condition, or he would not have written as he has done here. With faith and manly courage the yoke has the very opposite effect. The faculty of cherishing hope in spite of present hardships, which is the peculiar privilege of youth, may stand a man in stead at a later time, when it is not so easy to triumph over circumstances, because the old buoyancy of animal spirits, which means so much in early days, has vanished; and then if he can look back and see how he has been cultivating habits of endurance through years of discipline without his soul having been soured by the process, he may well feel profoundly thankful for those early experiences which were undoubtedly very hard in their rawness.

The poet's reflections on the blessedness of quiet waiting are followed by direct exhortations to the behaviour which is its necessary accompaniment—for such seems to be the meaning of the next triplet, verses 28 to 30. The Revisers have corrected this from the indicative mood, as it stands in the Authorised

Version, to the imperative—" Let him sit alone," etc., " Let him put his mouth in the dust," etc., " Let him give his cheek to him that smiteth him," etc. The exhortations flow naturally out of the preceding statements, but the form they assume may strike us as somewhat singular. Who is the person thus indirectly addressed? The grammar of the sentences would invite our attention to the " man " of the twenty-seventh verse. If it is good for everybody to bear the yoke in his youth, it might be suggested further that it would be well for everybody to act in the manner now indicated —that is to say, the advice would be of universal application. We must suppose, however, that the poet is thinking of a sufferer similar to himself.

Now the point of the exhortation is to be found in the fact that it goes beyond the placid state just described. It points to solitude, silence, submission, humiliation, non-resistance. The principle of calm, trustful expectancy is most beautiful; and if it were regarded by itself it could not but fascinate us, so that we should wonder how it would be possible for anybody to resist its attractions. But immediately we try to put it in practice we come across some harsh and positively repellent features. When it is brought down from the ethereal regions of poetry and set to work among the gritty facts of real life, how soon it seems to lose its glamour! It can never become mean or sordid; and yet its surroundings may be so. Most humiliating things are to be done, most insulting things endured. It is hard to sit in solitude and silence— a Ugolino in his tower of famine, a Bonnivard in his dungeon; there seems to be nothing heroic in this dreary inactivity. It would be much easier to attempt some deed of daring, especially if that were in the heat of battle. Nothing is so depressing as loneliness—the torture of a prisoner in solitary confinement. And yet now there must be no word of complaint because the trouble comes from the very Being who is to be trusted for deliverance. There is a call for action, however, but only to make the submission more complete and the humiliation more abject. The sufferer is to lay his mouth in the dust like a beaten slave.[1] Even this he might brace himself to do, stifling the last remnant of his pride because he is before the Lord of heaven and earth. But it is not enough. A yet more bitter cup must be drunk to the dregs. He must actually turn his cheek to the smiter, and quietly submit to reproach.[2] God's wrath may be accepted as a righteous retribution from above. But it is hard indeed to manifest the same spirit of submission in face of the fierce malignity or the petty spite of men. Yet silent waiting involves even this. Let us count the cost before we venture on the path which looks so beautiful in idea, but which turns out to be so very trying in fact.

We cannot consider this subject without being reminded of the teaching and—a more helpful memory —the example also of our Lord. It is hard to receive even from His lips the command to turn the other cheek to one who has smitten us on the right cheek. But when we see Jesus doing this very thing the whole aspect of it is changed. What before looked weak and cowardly is now seen to be the perfection of true courage and the height of moral sublimity. By His own endurance of insult and ignominy our Lord has completely revolutionised our ideas of humiliation. His

---

[1] iii. 29.   [2] iii. 30.

humiliation was His glorification. What a Roman would despise as shameful weakness He has proved to be the triumph of strength. Thus, though we may not be able to take the words of the Lamentations as a direct prophecy of Jesus Christ, they so perfectly realise themselves in the story of His Passion, that to Christendom they must always be viewed in the light of that supreme wonder of a victory won through submission ; and while they are so viewed they cannot fail to set before us an ideal of conduct for the sufferer under the most trying circumstances.

This advice is not so paradoxical as it appears. We are not called upon to accept it merely on the authority of the speaker. He follows it up by assigning good reasons for it. These are all based on the assumption which runs through the elegies, that the sufferings therein described come from the hand of God. They are most of them the immediate effects of man's enmity. But a Divine purpose is always to be recognised behind the human instrumentality. This fact at once lifts the whole question out of the region of miserable, earthly passions and mutual recriminations. In apparently yielding to a tyrant from among his fellow-men the sufferer is really submitting to his God.

Then the elegist gives us three reasons why the submission should be complete and the waiting quiet. The *first* is that the suffering is but temporary. God seems to have cast off His afflicted servant. If so it is but for a season.[1] This is not a case of absolute desertion. The sufferer is not treated as a reprobate. How could we expect patient submission from a soul that had passed the portals of a hell over which Dante's

---

[1] iii. 31, 32.

awful motto of despair was inscribed? If they who entered were to "forsake all hope" it would be a mockery to bid them "be still." It would be more natural for these lost souls to shriek with the fury of madness. The first ground of quiet waiting is hope. The *second* is to be found in God's unwillingness to afflict.[1] He never takes up the rod, as we might say, *con amore*. Therefore the trial will not be unduly prolonged. Since God Himself grieves to inflict it, the distress can be no more than is absolutely necessary. The *third* and last reason for this patience of submission is the certainty that God cannot commit an injustice. So important is this consideration in the eyes of the elegist that he devotes a complete triplet to it, illustrating it from three different points of view.[2] We have the conqueror with his victims, the magistrate in a case at law, and the private citizen in business. Each of these instances affords an opportunity for injustice. God does not look with approval on the despot who crushes all his prisoners—for Nebuchadnezzar's outrages are by no means condoned, although they are utilised as chastisements; nor on the judge who perverts the solemn process of law, when deciding, according to the Jewish theocratic idea, in place of God, the supreme Arbitrator, and, as the oath testifies, in His presence; nor on the man who in a private capacity circumvents his neighbour. But how can we ascribe to God what He will not sanction in man? "Shall not the Judge of all the earth do right?"[3] exclaims the perplexed patriarch; and we feel that his plea is unanswerable. But if God is just we can afford to be patient. And yet we feel that while there is

---

[1] iii. 33.   [2] iii. 34-6.   [3] Gen. xviii. 25.

something to calm us and allay the agonising terrors of despair in this thought of the unswerving justice of God, we must fall back for our most satisfying assurance on that glorious truth which the poet finds confirmed by his daily experience, and which he expresses with such a glow of hope in the rich phrase, "Yet will He have compassion according to the multitude of His mercies."[1]

---

[1] iii. 32.

CHAPTER XIV

GOD AND EVIL

iii. 37-9

THE eternal problem of the relation of God to evil is here treated with the keenest discrimination. That God is the supreme and irresistible ruler, that no man can succeed with any design in opposition to His will, that whatever happens must be in some way an execution of His decree, and that He, therefore, is to be regarded as the author of evil as well as good—these doctrines are so taken for granted that they are neither proved nor directly affirmed, but thrown into the form of questions that can have but one answer, as though to imply that they are known to everybody, and cannot be doubted for a moment by any one. But the inference drawn from them is strange and startling. It is that not a single living man has any valid excuse for complaining. That, too, is considered to be so undeniable that, like the previous ideas, it is expressed as a self-answering question. But we are not left in this paradoxical position. The evil experienced by the sufferer is treated as the punishment of his sin. What right has he to complain of that? A slightly various rendering has been proposed for the thirty-ninth verse, so as to resolve into a question and its answer. Read in this way, it asks, why should a living man complain? and then suggests the reply, that if he is to complain at all it should not be on account of his sufferings, treated as wrongs. He should complain against himself, his own conduct, his sin. We have seen, however, in other cases, that the breaking of a verse in this way is not in harmony with the smooth style of the elegiac poetry in which the words occur. This requires us to take the three verses of the triplet as continuous, flowing sentences.

Quite a number of considerations arise out of the curious juxtaposition of ideas in this passage. In the first place, it is very evident that by the word "evil" the writer here means trouble and suffering, not wickedness, because he clearly distinguishes it from the sin the mention of which follows. That sin is a man's own deed, for which he is justly punished. The poet, then, does not attribute the causation of sin to God; he does not speculate at all on the origin of moral evil. As far as he goes in the present instance, he would seem to throw back the authorship of it upon the will of man. How that will came to turn astray he does not say. This awful mystery remains unsolved through the whole course of the revelation of the Old Testament, and even through that of the New also. It cannot be maintained that the story of the Fall in Genesis is a solution of the mystery. To trace temptation back to the serpent is not to account for its existence, nor for the facility with which man was found to yield to it. When, at a later period, Satan appears on the stage, it is not to answer the perplexing question of the origin of evil. In the Old Testament he is nowhere connected with the Fall—his identification with the serpent first occurring in the Book of Wisdom,[1] from which

---

[1] Wisdom ii. 23 ff.

apparently it passed into current language, and so was adopted by St. John in the Apocalypse.[1] At first Satan is the adversary and accuser of man, as in Job[2] and Zechariah;[3] then he is recognised as the tempter, in Chronicles, for example.[4] But in no case is he said to be the primary cause of evil. No plummet can sound the depths of that dark pit in which lurks the source of sin.

Meanwhile a very different problem, the problem of suffering, is answered by attributing this form of evil quite unreservedly and even emphatically to God. It is to be remembered that our Lord, accepting the language of His contemporaries, ascribes this to Satan, speaking of the woman afflicted with a spirit of infirmity as one whom Satan had bound;[5] and that similarly St. Paul writes of his thorn in the flesh as a messenger of Satan,[6] to whom he also assigns the hindrance of a projected journey.[7] But in these cases it is not in the least degree suggested that the evil spirit is an irresistible and irresponsible being. The language only points to his immediate agency. The absolute supremacy of God is never called in question. There is no real concession to Persian dualism anywhere in the Bible. In difficult cases the sacred writers seem more anxious to uphold the authority of God than to justify His actions. They are perfectly convinced that those actions are all just and right, and not to be called in question, and so they are quite fearless in attributing to His direct commands occurrences that we should perhaps think more satisfactorily accounted for in some other

---

[1] Rev. xii. 9.
[2] Job i. 6-12, ii. 1-7.
[3] Zech. iii. 1, 2.
[4] 1 Chron. xxi. 1.
[5] Luke xiii. 16.
[6] 2 Cor. xii. 7.
[7] 1 Thess. ii. 18.

way. In such cases theirs is the language of unfailing faith, even when faith is strained almost to breaking.

The unquestionable fact that good and evil both come from the mouth of the Most High is based on the certain conviction that He *is* the Most High. Since it cannot be believed that His decrees should be thwarted, it cannot be supposed that there is any rival to His power. To speak of evil as independent of God is to deny that He is God. This is what a system of pure dualism must come to. If there are two mutually independent principles in the universe neither of them can be God. Dualism is as essentially opposed to the idea we attach to the name "God" as polytheism. The gods of the heathen are no gods, and so also are the imaginary twin divinities that divide the universe between them, or contend in a vain endeavour to suppress one another. "God," as we understand the title, is the name of the Supreme, the Almighty, the King of kings and Lord of lords. The Zend-Avesta escapes the logical conclusion of atheism by regarding its two principles, Ormuzd and Ahriman, as two streams issuing from a common fountain, or as two phases of one existence. But then it saves its theism at the expense of its dualism. In practice, however, this is not done. The dualism, the mutual antagonism of the two powers, is the central idea of the Parsee system; and being so, it stands in glaring contrast to the lofty monism of the Bible.

Nevertheless, it may be said, although it is thus necessary to attribute evil as well as good to God if we would not abandon the thought of His supremacy, a thought that is essential to our conception of His very nature, this is a perplexing necessity, and not one to be accepted with any sense of satisfaction. How then can the elegist welcome it with acclamation and set it before us with an air of triumph? That he does so is undeniable, for the spirit and tone of the poem here become positively exultant.

We may reply that the writer appears as the champion of the Divine cause. No attack on God's supremacy is to be permitted. Nothing of the kind, however, has been suggested. The writer is pursuing another aim, for he is anxious to still the murmurs of discontent. But how can the thought of the supremacy of God have that effect? One would have supposed the ascription to God of the trouble complained of would deepen the sense of distress and turn the complaint against Him. Yet it is just here that the elegist sees the unreasonableness of a complaining spirit.

Of course the uselessness of complaining, or rather the uselessness of attempting resistance, may be impressed upon us in this way. If the source of our trouble is nothing less than the Almighty and Supreme Ruler of all things it is stupid to dream of thwarting His purposes. If a man will run his head like a battering-ram against a granite cliff the most he can effect by his madness will be to bespatter the rock with his brains. It may be necessary to warn the rebel against Providence of this danger by shewing him that what he mistakes for a flimsy veil or a shadowy cloud is an immovable wall. But what will he find to exult over in the information? The hopelessness of resistance is no better than the consolation of pessimism, and its goal is despair. Our author, on the other hand, evidently intends to be reassuring.

Now, is there not something reassuring in the thought that evil and good come to us from one and the same source? For, consider the alternative. Remember, the evil exists as surely as the good. The elegist does not attempt to deny this, or to minimise the fact. He never calls evil good, never explains it away. There it stands before us, in all its ugly actuality, speculations concerning its origin neither aggravating the severity of its symptoms nor alleviating them. Whence, then, did this perplexing fact arise? If we postulate some other source than the Divine origin of good, what is it? A dreadful mystery here yawns at our feet. If evil came from an equally potent origin it would contend with good on even terms, and the issue would always hang in the balance. There could be nothing reassuring in that tantalising situation. The fate of the universe would be always quivering in uncertainty. And meanwhile we should have to conclude, that the most awful conflict with absolutely doubtful issues was raging continually. We could only contemplate the idea of this vast schism with terror and dismay. But now assuredly there is something calming in the thought of the unity of the power that distributes our fortunes; for this means that a man is in no danger of being tossed like a shuttlecock between two gigantic rival forces. There must be a singleness of aim in the whole treatment of us by Providence, since Providence is one. Thus, if only as an escape from an inconceivably appalling alternative, this doctrine of the common source of good and evil is truly reassuring.

We may pursue the thought further. Since good and evil spring from one and the same source, they cannot be so mutually contradictory as we have been accustomed to esteem them. They are two children of a common parent; then they must be brothers. But if they are so closely related a certain family likeness may be traced between them. This does not destroy the actuality of evil. But it robs it of its worst features. The pain may be as acute as ever in spite of all our philosophising. But the significance of it will be wholly changed. We can now no longer treat it as an accursed thing. If it is so closely related to good, we may not have far to go in order to discover that it is even working for good.

Then if evil and good come from the same source it is not just to characterise that source by reference to one only of its effluents. We must not take a rose-coloured view of all things, and relapse into idle complacency, as we might do if we confined our observation to the pleasant facts of existence, for the unpleasant facts—loss, disappointment, pain, death—are equally real, and are equally derived from the very highest Authority. Neither are we justified in denying the existence of the good when overwhelmed with a sense of the evil in life. At worst we live in a very mixed world. It is unscientific, it is unjust to pick out the ills of life and gibbet them as specimens of the way things are going. If we will recite the first part of such an elegy as that we are now studying, at least let us have the honesty to read on to the second part, where the surpassingly lovely vision of the Divine compassion so much more than counterbalances the preceding gloom. Is it only by accident that the poet says "evil and good," and not, as we usually put the phrase, "good and evil"? Good shall have the last word. Evil exists; but the finality and crown of existence is not evil, but good.

The conception of the primary unity of causation which the Hebrew poet reaches through his religion is brought home to us to-day with a vast accumulation of proof by the discoveries of science. The uniformity of law, the co-relation of forces, the analyses of the most diverse and complex organisms into their common chemical elements, the evidence of the spectroscope to the existence of precisely the same elements among the distant stars, as well as the more minute homologies of nature in the animal and vegetable kingdoms, are all irrefutable confirmations of this great truth. Moreover, science has demonstrated the intimate association of what we cannot but regard as good and evil in the physical universe. Thus, while carbon and oxygen are essential elements for the building up of all living things, the effect of perfectly healthy vital functions working upon them is to combine them into carbonic acid, which is a most deadly poison; but then this noxious gas becomes the food of plants, from which the animal life in turn derives its nourishment. Similarly microbes, which we commonly regard as the agents of corruption and disease, are found to be not only nature's scavengers, but also the indispensable ministers of life, when clustering round the roots of plants in vast crowds they convert the organic matter of the soil, such as manure, into those inorganic nitrates which contain nitrogen in the form suitable for absorption by vegetable organisms. The mischief wrought by germs, great as it is, is infinitely outweighed by the necessary service existences of this kind render to all life by preparing some of its indispensable conditions. The inevitable conclusion to be drawn from facts such as these is that health and disease, and life and death, interact, are inextricably blended together, and mutually transformable—what we call disease and death in one place being necessary for life and health in another. The more clearly we understand the processes of nature the more evident is the fact of her unity, and therefore the more impossible is it for us to think of her objectionable characteristics as foreign to her being—alien immigrants from another sphere. Physical evil itself looks less dreadful when it is seen to take its place as an integral part of the complicated movement of the whole system of the universe.

But the chief reason for regarding the prospect with more than satisfaction has yet to be stated. It is derived from the character of Him to whom both the evil and the good are attributed. We can go beyond the assertion that these contrarieties spring from one common origin to the great truth that this origin is to be found in God. All that we know of our Father in heaven comes to our aid in reflecting upon the character of the actions thus attributed to Him. The account of God's goodness that immediately precedes this ascription of the two extreme experiences of life to Him would be in the mind of the writer, and it should be in the mind of the reader also. The poet has just been dwelling very emphatically on the indubitable justice of God. When, therefore, he reminds us that both evil and good come from the Divine Being, it is as though he said that they both originated in justice. A little earlier he was expressing the most fervent appreciation of the mercy and compassion of God. Then these gracious attributes should be in our thoughts while we hear that the mixed experiences of life are to be traced back to Him of whom so cheering a view can be taken.

We know the love of God much more fully since it has been revealed to us in Jesus Christ. Therefore we have a much better reason for building our faith and hope on the fact of the universal Divine origin of events. In itself the evil exists all the same whether we can trace its cause or not, and the discovery of the cause in no way aggravates it. But this discovery may lead us to take a new view of its issues. If it comes from One who is as just and merciful as He is mighty we may certainly conclude that it will lead to the most blessed results. Considered in the light of the assured character of its purpose, the evil itself must assume a totally different character. The child who receives a distasteful draught from the hand of the kindest of parents knows that it cannot be a cup of poison, and has good reason for believing it to be a necessary medicine.

The last verse of the triplet startles the reader with an unexpected thought. The considerations already adduced are all meant to check any complaint against the course of Providence. Now the poet appends a final argument, which is all the more forcible for not being stated as an argument. At the very end of the passage, when we are only expecting the language to sink into a quiet conclusion, a new idea springs out upon us, like a tiger from its lair. This trouble about which a man is so ready to complain, as though it were some unaccountable piece of injustice, is simply *the punishment of his sin*! Like the other ideas of the passage, the notion is not tentatively argued; it is boldly taken for granted. Once again we see that there is no suspicion in the mind of the elegist of the perplexing problem that gives its theme to the Book of Job. But do we not sometimes press that problem too far? Can it be denied that, to a large extent, suffering is the direct consequence and the natural punishment of sin? Are we not often burnt for the simple reason that we have been playing with fire? At all events, the whole course of previous prophecy went to shew that the national sins of Israel must be followed by some dreadful disasters; and when the war-cloud was hovering on the horizon Jeremiah saw in it the herald of approaching doom. Then the thunderbolt fell; and the wreck it caused became the topic of this Book of Lamentations. After such a preparation, what was more natural, and reasonable, and even inevitable, than that the elegist should calmly assume that the trouble complained of was no more than was due to the afflicted people? This is clear enough when we think of the nation as a whole. It is not so obvious when we turn our attention to individual cases; but the bewildering problem of the sufferings of innocent children, which constitutes the most prominent feature in the poet's picture of the miseries of the Jews, is not here revived.

We must suppose that he is thinking of a typical citizen of Jerusalem. If the guilty city merited severe punishment, such a man as this would also merit it; for the deserts of the city are only the deserts of her citizens. It will be for everybody to say for himself how far the solution of the mystery of his own troubles is to be looked for in this direction. A humble conscience will not be eager to repudiate the possibility that its owner has not been punished beyond his deserts, whatever may be thought of other people, innocent children in particular. There is one word that may bring out this aspect of the question with more distinctness—the word "living." The poet asks, "Wherefore doth a *living* man complain?" Why does he attach this attribute to the subject of his question? The only satisfactory explanation that has been offered is that he would remind us that while the sufferer has his life preserved to him he has no valid ground of complaint. He has not been overpaid; he has not even been paid in full; for it is an Old Testament doctrine which the New Testament repeats when it declares that "the wages of sin is death."[1]

---

[1] Rom. vi. 23.

CHAPTER XV

THE RETURN

iii. 40-42

WHEN prophets, speaking in the name of God, promised the exiles a restoration to their land and the homes of their fathers, it was always understood and often expressly affirmed that this reversal of their outward fortunes must be preceded by an inner change, a return to God in penitent submission. Expulsion from Canaan was the chastisement of apostasy from God; it was only right and reasonable that the discipline should be continued as long as the sin that necessitated it remained. It would be a mistake, however, to relegate the treatment of this deadly sin to a secondary place, as only the cause of a more serious trouble. There could be no more serious trouble. The greatest evil from which Israel suffered was not the Babylonian exile; it was her self-inflicted banishment from God. The greatest blessing to be sought for her was not liberty to return to the hills and cities of Palestine; it was permission and power to come back to God. It takes us long to learn that sin is worse than punishment, and that to be brought home to our Father in heaven is a more desirable good than any earthly recovery of prosperity. But the soul that can say with the elegist, "The Lord is my portion," has reached the vantage ground from which the best things can be seen in their true proportions; and to such a soul no advent of temporal prosperity can compare with the gaining of its one prized possession. In the triplet of verses that follows the pointed phrase which rebukes complaint for suffering by attributing it to sin the poet conducts us to those high regions where the more spiritual truth concerning these matters can be appreciated.

The form of the language here passes into the plural. Already we have been made to feel that the man who has seen affliction is a representative sufferer, although he is describing his own personal distresses. The immediately preceding clause seems to point to the sinful Israelite generally, in its vague reference to a "living man."[1] Now there is a transition in the movement of the elegy, and the solitary voice gives place to a chorus, the Jews as a body appearing before God to pour out their confessions in common. According to his usual method the elegist makes the transition quite abruptly, without any explanatory preparation. The style resembles that of an oratorio, in which solo and chorus alternate with close sequence. In the present instance the effect is not that of dramatic variety, because we feel the vital sympathy that the poet cherishes for his people, so that their experience is as his experience. It is a faint shadow of the condition of the great Sin-bearer, of whom it could be said, "In all their affliction He was afflicted."[2]

Before it is possible to return to God, before the desire to return is even awakened, a much less inviting action must be undertaken. The first and greatest

---

[1] iii. 39.   [2] Isa. lxiii. 9.

hindrance to reconciliation with our Father is our failure to recognise that any such reconciliation is necessary. The most deadening effect of sin is seen in the fact that it prevents the sinner from perceiving that he is at enmity with God at all, although by everything he does he proclaims his rebellion. The Pharisee of the parable cannot be justified, cannot really approach God at all, because he will not admit that he needs any justification, or is guilty of any conduct that separates him from God. Just as the most hopeless state of ignorance is that in which there is a serene unconsciousness of any deficiency of knowledge, so the most abandoned condition of guilt is the inability to perceive the very existence of guilt. The sick man who ignores his disease will not resort to a physician for the cure of it. If the soul's quarrel with her Lord is ever to be ended it must be discovered. Therefore the first step will be in the direction of self-examination.

We are led to look in this direction by the startling thought with which the previous triplet closes. If the calamities bewailed are the chastisements of sin it is necessary for this sin to be sought out. The language of the elegist suggests that we are not aware of the nature of our own conduct, and that it is only by some serious effort that we can make ourselves acquainted with it, for this is what he implies when he represents the distressed people resolving to "search and try" their ways. Easy as it may seem in words, experience proves that nothing is more difficult in practice than to fulfil the precept of the philosopher, "Know thyself." The externalism in which most of our lives are spent makes the effort to look within a painful contradiction of habit. When it is attempted pride and prejudice face the inquirer, and too often quite hide the true self from view. If the pursuit is pushed on in spite of these hindrances the result may prove to be a sad surprise. Sometimes we see ourselves unexpectedly revealed, and then the sight of so great a novelty amazes us. The photographer's proof of a portrait dissatisfies the subject, not because it is a bad likeness, but rather because it is too faithful to be pleasing. A wonderful picture of Rossetti's represents a young couple who are suddenly confronted in a lonely forest by the apparition of their two selves as simply petrified with terror at the appalling spectacle.

Even when the effort to acquire self-knowledge is strenuous and persevering, and accompanied by an honest resolution to accept the results, however unwelcome they may be, it often fails for lack of a standard of judgment. We compare ourselves with ourselves—our present with our past, or at best our actual life with our ideals. But this is a most illusory process, and its limits are too narrow. Or we compare ourselves with our neighbours—a possible advance, but still a most unsatisfactory method; for we know so little of them, all of us dwelling more or less like stars apart, and none of us able to sound the abysmal depths of another's personality. Even if we could fix this standard it too would be very illusory, because those people with whom we are making the comparison, quite as much as we ourselves, may be astray, just as a whole planetary system, though perfectly balanced in the mutual relations of its own constituent worlds, may yet be out of its orbit, and rushing on all together towards some awful common destruction.

A more trustworthy standard may be found in the heart-searching words of Scripture, which prove to be as much a revelation of man to himself as one of God to man. This Divine test reaches its perfection in the historical presentation of our Lord. We discover our actual characters most effectually when we compare our conduct with the conduct of Jesus Christ. As the Light of the world, He leads the world to see itself. He is the great touchstone of character. During His earthly life hypocrisy was detected by His searching glance; but that was not admitted by the hypocrite. It is when He comes to us spiritually that His promise is fulfilled, and the Comforter convinces of *sin* as well as of righteousness and judgment. Perhaps it is not so eminently desirable as Burns would have us believe, that we should see ourselves as others see us; but it is supremely important to behold ourselves in the pure, searching light of the Spirit of Christ.

We may be reminded, on the other hand, that too much introspection is not wholesome, that it begets morbid ways of thought, paralyses the energies, and degenerates into insipid sentimentality. No doubt it is best that the general tendency of the mind should be towards the active duties of life. But to admit this is not to deny that there may be occasions when the most ruthless self-examination becomes a duty of first importance. A season of severe chastisement, such as that to which the Book of Lamentations refers, is one that calls most distinctly for the exercise of this rare duty. We cannot make our daily meal of drugs; but drugs may be most necessary in sickness. Possibly if we were in a state of perfectly sound spiritual health it might be well for us never to spare a thought for ourselves from our complete absorption with the happy duties of a full and busy life. But since we are far from being thus healthy, since we err and fail and sin, time devoted to the discovery of our faults may be exceedingly well spent.

Then while a certain kind of self-study is always mischievous—the sickly habit of brooding over one's feelings, it is to be observed that the elegist does not recommend this. His language points in quite another direction. It is not emotion but action that he is concerned with. The searching is to be into our "ways," the course of our conduct. There is an objectivity in this inquiry, though it is turned inward, that contrasts strongly with the investigation of shadowy sentiments. Conduct, too, is the one ground of the judgment of God. Therefore the point of supreme importance to ourselves is to determine whether conduct is right or wrong. With this branch of self-examination we are not in so much danger of falling into complete delusions as when we are considering less tangible questions. Thus this is at once the most wholesome, the most necessary, and the most practicable process of introspection.

The particular form of conduct here referred to should be noted. The word "ways" suggests habit and continuity. These are more characteristic than isolated deeds—short spasms of virtue or sudden falls before temptation. The final judgment will be according to the life, not its exceptional episodes. A man lives his habits. He may be capable of better things, he may be liable to worse; but he is what he does habitually. The world will applaud him for some outburst of heroism in which he rises for the moment above the sordid level of his every-day life, or execrate him for his shameful moment of self-forgetfulness; and the world will have this amount of justice in its action, that the capacity for the occasional is itself a permanent attribute, although the opportunity for the active working of the latent good or evil is rare. The startling outburst may be a revelation of old but hitherto hidden "ways." It must be so to some extent; for no man wholly belies his own nature unless he is mad—beside himself, as we say. Still it may not be so entirely, or even chiefly; the surprised self may not be the normal self, often is not. Meanwhile our main business in self-examination is to trace the course of the unromantic beaten track, the long road on which we travel from morning to evening through the whole day of life.

The result of this search into the character of their ways on the part of the people is that it is found to be necessary to forsake them forthwith; for the next idea is in the form of a resolution to turn out of them, nay, to turn back, retracing the footsteps that have gone astray, in order to come to God again. These ways are discovered, then, to be bad—vicious in themselves, and wrong in their direction. They run downhill, away from the home of the soul, and towards the abodes of everlasting darkness. When this fact is perceived it becomes apparent that some complete change must be made. This is a case of ending our old ways, not mending them. Good paths may be susceptible of improvement. The path of the just should "shine more and more unto the perfect day." But here things are too hopelessly bad for any attempt at amelioration. No engineering skill will ever transform the path that points straight to perdition into one that conducts us up to the heights of heaven. The only chance of coming to walk in the right way is to forsake the wrong way altogether, and make an entirely new start. Here, then, we have the Christian doctrine of conversion—a doctrine which always appears extravagant to people who take superficial views of sin, but one that will be appreciated just in proportion to the depth and seriousness of our ideas of its guilt. Nothing contributes more to unreality in religion than strong language on the nature of repentance apart from a corresponding consciousness of the tremendous need of a most radical change. This deplorable mischief must be brought about when indiscriminate exhortations to the extreme practice of penitence are addressed to mixed congregations. It cannot be right to press the necessity of conversion upon young children and the carefully sheltered and lovingly trained youth of Christian homes in the language that applies to their unhappy brothers and sisters who have already made shipwreck of life. This statement is liable to misapprehension; doubtless to some readers it will savour of the light views of sin deprecated above, and point to the excuses of the Pharisee. Nevertheless it must be considered if we would avoid the characteristic sin of the Pharisee, hypocrisy. It is unreasonable to suppose that the necessity of a complete conversion can be felt by the young and comparatively innocent as it should be felt by abandoned profligates, and the attempt of the preacher to force it on their relatively pure consciences is a direct incentive to cant. The fifty-first Psalm is the confession of his crime by a murderer; Augustine's *Confessions* are the outpourings of a man who feels that he has been dragging his earlier life through the mire; Bunyan's *Grace Abounding* reveals the memories of a rough soldier's shame and folly. No good can come of the unthinking application of such utterances to persons whose history and character are entirely different from those of the authors.

On the other hand, there are one or two further

considerations which should be borne in mind. Thus it must not be forgotten that the greatest sinner is not necessarily the man whose guilt is most glaringly apparent; nor that sins of the heart count with God as equivalent to obviously wicked deeds committed in the full light of day; nor that guilt cannot be estimated absolutely, by the bare evil done, without regard to the opportunities, privileges, and temptations of the offender. Then, the more we meditate upon the true nature of sin, the more deeply must we be impressed with its essential evil even when it is developed only slightly in comparison with the hideous crimes and vices that blacken the pages of history—as, for example, in the careers of a Nero or a Cæsar Borgia. The sensitive conscience does not only feel the exact guilt of its individual offences, but also, and much more, "the exceeding sinfulness of sin." When we consider their times and the state of the society in which they lived, we must feel that neither Augustine nor Bunyan had been so wicked as the intensity of the language of penitence they both employed might lead us to suppose. It is quite foreign to the nature of heartfelt repentance to measure degrees of guilt. In the depth of its shame and humiliation no language of contrition seems to be too strong to give it adequate expression. But this must be entirely spontaneous; it is most unwise to impose it from without in the form of an indiscriminate appeal to abject penitence.

Then it is also to be observed that while the fundamental change described in the New Testament as a new birth cannot well be regarded as a thing of repeated occurrence, we may have occasion for many conversions. Every time we turn into the wrong path we put ourselves under the necessity of turning back if ever we would walk in the right path again. What is that but conversion? It is a pity that we should be hampered by the technicality of a term. This may lead to another kind of error—the error of supposing that if we are once converted we are converted for life, that we have crossed our Rubicon, and cannot recross it. Thus while the necessity of a primary conversion may be exaggerated in addresses to the young, the greater need of subsequent conversions may be neglected in the thoughts of adults. The "converted" person who relies on the one act of his past experience to serve as a talisman for all future time is deluding himself in a most dangerous manner. Can it be asserted that Peter had not been "converted," in the technical sense, when he fell through undue self-confidence, and denied his Master with "oaths and curses?"

Again—a very significant fact—the return is described in positive language. It is a coming back to God, not merely a departure from the old way of sin. The initial impulse towards a better life springs more readily from the attraction of a new hope than from the repulsion of a loathed evil. The hopeful repentance is exhilarating, while that which is only born of the disgust and horror of sin is dismally depressing. Lurid pictures of evil rarely beget penitence. The *Newgate Calendar* is not to be credited with the reformation of criminals. Even Dante's *Inferno* is no gospel. In prosecuting his mission as the prophet of repentance John the Baptist was not content to declare that the axe was laid at the root of the tree; the pith of his exhortation was found in the glad tidings that "the kingdom of heaven is at hand." St. Paul shows that it is the goodness of God that leads us to repentance. Besides, the repentance that is induced by this means is of the best character. It escapes the craven slavishness of fear; it is not a merely selfish shrinking from the lash; it is inspired by the pure love of a worthy end. Only remorse lingers in the dark region of regrets for the past. Genuine repentance always turns a hopeful look towards a better future. It is of little use to exorcise the spirit of evil if the house is not to be tenanted by the spirit of good. Thus the end and purpose of repentance is to be reunited to God.

Following up his general exhortation to return to God, the elegist adds a particular one, in which the process of the new movement is described. It takes the form of a prayer from the heart. The resolution is to lift up the heart with the hands. The erect posture, with the hands stretched out to heaven, which was the Hebrew attitude in prayer, had often been assumed in meaningless acts of formal worship before there was any real approach to God or any true penitence. Now the repentance will be manifested by the reality of the prayer. Let the heart also be lifted up. The true approach to God is an act of the inner life, to which in its entirety—thought, affection, and will—the Jewish metaphor of the heart points.

Lastly, the poet furnishes the returning penitents with the very language of the heart's prayer, which is primarily confession. The doleful fact that God has not pardoned His people is directly stated, but not in the first place. This statement is preceded by a clear and unreserved confession of sin. Repentance must be followed by confession. It is not a private matter concerning the offender alone. Since the offence was directed against another, the amendment must begin with a humble admission of the wrong that has been done. Thus, immediately the prodigal son is met by his father he sobs out his confession;[1] and St. John assigns confession as an essential preliminary to forgiveness, saying: "If we confess our sins, He is faithful and righteous to forgive us our sins, and to cleanse us from all unrighteousness."[2]

---

[1] Luke xv. 21. [2] 1 John i. 9.

CHAPTER XVI

GRIEVING BEFORE GOD

iii. 43-54

AS might have been expected, the mourning patriot quickly forsakes the patch of sunshine which lights up a few verses of this elegy. But the vision of it has not come in vain; for it leaves gracious effects to tone the gloomy ideas upon which the meditations of the poet now return like birds of the night hastening back to their darksome haunts. In the first place, his grief is no longer solitary. It is enlarged in its sympathies so as to take in the sorrows of others. Purely selfish trouble tends to become a mean and sordid thing. If we are not yet freed from our own pain some element of a nobler nature will be imported into it when we can find room for the larger thoughts that the contemplation of the distresses of others arouses. But a greater change than this has taken place. The "man who hath seen affliction" now feels himself to be in the presence of God. Speaking for others as well as for himself he pours out his lamentations before God. In the first part of the elegy he had only mentioned the Divine name as that of his great Antagonist; now it is the name of his close Confidant.

Then the elegist is here giving voice to the people's penitent confession and prayer This is another feature of the changed situation. An unqualified admission of the truth that the sufferings of Israel are just the merited punishment of the people's sin has come between the complaints with which the poem opens, and the renewed expressions of grief.

Still, when all due allowance is made for these improvements, the renewed outburst of grief is sufficiently dismal. The people are supposed to represent themselves as being hunted down like helpless fugitives, and slain without pity by God, who has wrapped Himself in a mantle of anger, which is as a cloud impenetrable to the prayers of His miserable victims.[1] This description of their helpless state follows immediately after an outpouring of prayer. It would seem, therefore, that the poet conceived that this particular utterance was hindered from reaching the ear of God. Now in many cases it may be that a feeling such as is here expressed is purely subjective and imaginary. The soul's cry of agony passes out into the night, and dies away into silence, without eliciting a whisper of response. Yet it is not necessary to conclude that the cry is not heard. The closest attention may be the most silent. But, it may be objected, this possibility only aggravates the evil; for it is better not to hear at all than to hear and not to heed. Will any one attribute such stony indifference to God? God may attend, and yet He may not speak to us—speech not being the usual form of Divine response. He may be helping us most effectually in silence, unperceived by us, at the very moment when we imagine that He has completely deserted us. If we were more keenly alive to the signs of His coming we should be less hasty to

---

[1] iii. 44.

despair at the failure of our prayers. The priests of Baal may scream, "O Baal, hear us!" from morning to night till their phrensy sinks into despair; but that is no reason why men and women who worship a spiritual God should come to the conclusion that their inability to wrest a sign from Heaven is itself a sign of desertion by Him to whom they call. The oracle may be dumb; but the God whom we worship is not limited to the utterance of prophetic voices for the expression of His will. He hears, even if in silence; and, in truth, He also answers, though we are too deaf in our unbelief to discern the still small voice of His Spirit.

But can we say that the idea of the Divine disregard of prayer is always and only imaginary? Are the clouds that come between us and God invariably earth-born? Does He never really wrap Himself in the garment of wrath? Surely we dare not say so much. The anger of God is as real as His love. No being can be perfectly holy and not feel a righteous indignation in the presence of sin. But if God is angry, and while He is so, He cannot at the same time be holding friendly intercourse with the people who are provoking His wrath. Then the Divine anger must be as a thick, impervious curtain between the prayers of the sinful and the gracious hearing of God. The universal confession of the need of an atonement is a witness to the perception of this condition by mankind. Whether we are dealing with the crude notions of ancient sacrifice, or with the high thoughts that circle about Calvary, the same spiritual instinct presses for recognition. We may try to reason it down, but it persistently reasserts itself. Most certainly it is not the teaching of Scripture that the only condition of salvation is prayer. The Gospel is not to the effect that we are to be saved by our own petitions. The penitent is taught to feel that without Christ and the cross his prayers are of no avail for his salvation. Even if they knew no respite—still they would never atone for sin. Is not this an axiom of evangelical doctrine? Then the prayers that are offered in the old unreconciled condition must fall back on the head of the vain petitioner unable to penetrate the awful barrier that he has himself caused to be raised between his cries and the heavens where God dwells.

Turning from the contemplation of the hopeless failure of prayer the lament naturally falls into an almost despairing wail of grief. The state of the Jews is painted in the very darkest colours. God has made them as no better than the refuse people cast out of their houses, or the very sweepings of the streets—not fit even to be trampled under foot of men.[1] This is their position among the nations. The poet seems to be alluding to the exceptional severity with which the obstinate defenders of Jerusalem had been treated by their exasperated conquerors. The neighbouring tribes had been compelled to succumb beneath the devastating wave of the Babylonian invasion; but since none of them had offered so stubborn a resistance to the armies of Nebuchadnezzar none of them had been punished by so severe a scourge of vengeance. So it has been repeatedly with the unhappy people who have encountered unparalled persecutions through the long weary ages of their melancholy history. In the days of Antiochus Epiphanes the Jews were the most insulted and cruelly outraged victims of Syrian tyranny. When their

---

[1] iii. 45.

long tragedy reached a climax at the final siege of Jerusalem by Titus, the more liberal-minded Roman government laid on them harsh punishments of exile, slavery, torture, and death, such as it rarely inflicted on a fallen foe—for with statesmanlike wisdom the Romans preferred, as a rule, conciliation to extermination; but in the case of this one unhappy city of Jerusalem the almost unique fate of the hated and dreaded city of Carthage was repeated. So it was in the Middle Ages, as *Ivanhoe* vividly shows; and so it is to-day in the East of Europe, as the fierce *Juden-hetze* is continually proving. The irony of history is nowhere more apparent than in the fact that the "favoured" people, the "chosen" people of Jehovah, should have been treated so continuously as "the offscouring and refuse in the midst of the peoples." As privilege and responsibility always go hand in hand, so also do blessing and suffering—the Jew hated, the Church persecuted, the Christ crucified. We cannot say that this paradox is simply "a mysterious dispensation of Providence;" because in the case of Israel, at all events in the early ages, the unparalleled misery was traced to the abuse of unparalleled favour. But this does not exhaust the mystery, for in the most striking instances innocence suffers. We can have no satisfaction in our view of these contradictions till we see the glory of the martyr's crown and the even higher glory of the triumph of Christ and His people over failure, agony, insult, and death; but just in proportion as we are able to lift up the eyes of faith to the blessedness of the unseen world, we shall be able also to discover that even here and now there is a pain that is better than pleasure, and a shame that is truest glory.

These truths, however, are not readily perceived at

the time of endurance, when the iron is entering into the soul. The elegist feels the degradations of his people most keenly, and he represents them complaining how their enemies rage at them as with open mouths—belching forth gross insults, shouting curses, like wild beasts ready to devour their hapless victims.[1] There seems to be nothing in store for them but the terrors of death, the pit of destruction.[2]

At the contemplation of this extremity of hopeless misery the poet drops the plural number, in which he has been personating his people, as abruptly as he assumed it a few verses earlier, and bewails the dread calamities in his own person.[3] Then, in truly Jeremiah-like fashion, he describes his incessant weeping for the woes of the wretched citizens of Jerusalem and the surrounding villages. The reference to "the daughters of my city"[4] seems to be best explained as a figurative expression for the neighbouring places, all of which it would seem had shared in the devastation produced by the great wave of conquest which had overwhelmed the capital. But the previous mention of "the daughter of my people,"[5] followed as it is by this phrase about "the daughters of my city," strikes a deeper note of compassion. These places contained many defenceless women, the indescribable cruelty of whose fate when they fell into the hands of the brutal heathen soldiery was one of the worst features of the whole ghastly scene; and the wretchedness of the once proud city and its dependencies when they were completely overthrown is finely represented so as to appeal most effectually to our sympathy by a metaphor that pictures them as hapless maidens, touching us like Spenser's

---

[1] iii. 46.
[2] iii. 47.
[3] iii. 48 ff.
[4] iii. 51.
[5] iii. 48.

piteous picture of the forlorn Una, deserted in the forest and left a prey to its savage denizens. Like Una, too, the daughters in this metaphor claim the chivalry which our English poet has so exquisitely portrayed as awakened even in the breast of a wild animal. The woman of Europe is far removed from her sister in the East, who still follows the ancient type in submitting to the imputation of weakness as a claim for consideration. But this is because Europe has learnt that strength of character—in which woman can be at least the equal of man—is more potent in a community civilised in the Christian way than strength of muscle. Where the more brutal forces are let loose the duties of chivalry are always in requisition. Then it is apparent that deference to the claims of women for protection produces a civilising effect in softening the roughness of men. It is difficult to say it to-day in the teeth of the just claims that women are making, and still more difficult in face of what women are now achieving, in spite of many relics of barbarism in the form of unfair restrictions, but yet it must be asserted that the feebleness of femininity—in the old-fashioned sense of the word—pervades these poems, and is their most touching characteristic, so that much of the pathos and beauty of poetry such as that of these elegies is to be traced to representations of woman wronged and suffering and calling for the sympathy of all beholders.

The poet is moved to tears—quite unselfish tears, tears of patriotic grief, tears of compassion for helpless suffering. Here again the modern Anglo-Saxon habit makes it difficult for us to appreciate his conduct as it deserves. We think it a dreadful thing for a man to be seen weeping; and a feeling of shame accompanies such an outburst of unrestrained distress.

But surely there are holy tears, and tears which it is an honour for any one to be capable of shedding. If mere callousness is the explanation of dry eyes in view of sorrow, there can be no credit for such a condition. This is not the restraint of tears. Nothing is easier than for the unfeeling not to weep. Nor can it be maintained that it is always necessary to restrain the outward expression of sympathy in accordance with its most natural impulses. Our Lord was strong; yet we could never wish that the evangelist had not had occasion to write the ever memorable sentence, " Jesus wept." Sufferers lose much, not only from lack of sympathy, but also from a shy concealment of the fellow-feeling that is truly experienced. There are seasons of keenest agony, when to weep with those who weep is the only possible expression of brotherly kindness; and this may be a very real act of love, appreciably alleviating suffering. A little courage on the part of Englishmen in daring to weep would knit the ties of brotherhood more closely. At present a chill reserve rather than any actual coldness of heart separates people who might be much more helpful to one another if they could but bring themselves to break down this barrier.

But while the poet is thus expressing his large patriotic grief he cannot forget his own private sorrows. They are all parts of one common woe. So he returns to his personal experience, and adds some graphic details that enable us to picture him in the midst of his misery.[1] Though he had never provoked the enemy, he was chased like a bird, flung into a dungeon, where a stone was hurled down upon him, and where

---
[1] iii. 52 ff.

the water was lying so deep that he was completely submerged. There is no reason to question that definite statements such as these represent the exact experience of the writer. At the first glance they call to our minds the persecutions inflicted on Jeremiah by his own people. But the allusion would be peculiarly inappropriate, and the cases do not quite fit together. The poet has been bewailing the sufferings of the Jews at the hands of the Chaldæans, and he seems to identify his own troubles in the closest way with the general flood of calamities that swept over his nation. It would be quite out of place for him to insert here a reminder of earlier troubles which his own people had inflicted upon him. Besides, the particulars do not exactly agree with what we learn of the prophet's hardships from his own pen. The dungeon into which he was flung was very foul, and he sank in the mire, but it is expressly stated that there was no water in it, and there is no mention of stoning.[1] There were many sufferers in that dark time of tumult and outrage whose fate was as hard as that of Jeremiah.

A graphic picture like this helps us to imagine the fearful accompaniments of the destruction of Jerusalem much better than any general summary. As we gaze at this one scene among the many miseries that followed the siege—the poet hunted out and run down, his capture and conveyance to the dungeon, apparently without a shadow of a trial, the danger of drowning and the misery of standing in the water that had gathered in a place so utterly unfit for human habitation, the needless additional cruelty of the stone-throwing—there rises before us a picture which cannot but impress our

---

[1] Jer. xxxviii. 6.

minds with the unutterable wretchedness of the sufferers from such a calamity as the siege of Jerusalem. Of course there must have been some special reason for the exceptionally severe treatment of the poet. What this was we cannot tell. If the same patriotic spirit burned in his soul in the midst of the war as we now find at the time of later reflection, it would be most reasonable to conjecture that the ardent lover of his country had done or said something to irritate the enemy, and possibly that as he devoted his poetic gifts at a subsequent time to lamenting the overthrow of his city, he may have employed them with a more practical purpose among the battle scenes to write some inspiring martial ode in which we may be sure he would not have spared the ruthless invader. But then he says his persecution was without a cause. He may have been undeservedly suspected of acting as a spy. It is only by chance that now and again we get a glimpse of the backwaters of a great flood such as that which was now devastating the land of Judah; most of the dreary scene is shrouded in gloom.

Lastly, we must not fail to remember, in reading these expressions of patriotic and personal grief, that they are the outpourings of the heart of the poet before God. They are all addressed to God's ear; they are all part of a prayer. Thus they illustrate the way in which prayer takes the form of confiding in God. It is a great relief to be able simply to tell Him everything. Perhaps, however, here we may detect a note of complaint; but if so it is not a note of rebellion or of unbelief. Although the evils from which the elegist and his people are suffering so grievously are attributed to God in the most uncompromising manner, the writer does not hesitate to look to God for deliverance. Thus in the very midst of his lamentations he says that his weeping is to continue "till the Lord look down, and behold from heaven."[1] He will not cease weeping until this happens; but he does not expect to have to spend all the remainder of his days in tears. He is assured that God will hear, and answer, and deliver. The time of the Divine response is quite unknown to him; it may be still far off, and there may be much weary waiting to be endured first. But it will come, and if no one can tell how long the interval of trial may be, so also no one can say but that the deliverance may arrive suddenly and with a surprise of mercy. Thus the poet weeps on, but in undying hope.

This is the right attitude of the Christian mourner. We cannot penetrate the mystery of God's times; but that they are in His own hands is not to be denied. Therefore the test of faith is often given in the necessity for indefinite waiting. To the man who trusts God there is always a future. Whatever such a man may have to endure he should find a place in his plaint for the word "until." He is not plunged into everlasting night. He has but to endure until the day dawn.

---

[1] iii. 50.

CHAPTER XVII

DE PROFUNDIS

iii. 55-66

AS this third elegy—the richest and the most elaborate of the five that constitute the Book of Lamentations—draws to a close it retains its curious character of variability, not aiming at any climax, but simply winding on till its threefold acrostics are completed by the limits of the Hebrew alphabet, like a river that is monotonous in the very succession of its changes, now flowing through a dark gorge, then rippling in clear sunlight, and again plunging into gloomy caverns. The beauty and brightness of this very variegated poem is found at its centre. Sadder thoughts follow. But these are not so wholly complaining as the opening passages had been. There is one thread of continuity that may be traced right through the series of changes which occupy the latter part of the poem. The poet having once turned to the refuge of prayer never altogether forsakes it. The meditations as much as the petitions that here occur are all directed to God.

A peculiarity of the last portion of the elegy that claims special attention is the interesting reminiscence with which the poet finds encouragement for his present prayers. He is recalling the scenes of that most distressing period of his life, the time when he had been cast into a flooded dungeon. If ever he had come near to death it must have been then; though his life was spared the misery of his condition had been extreme. While in this most wretched situation the persecuted patriot cried to God for help, and as he now recollects for his present encouragement, he received a distinct and unmistakable answer. The scene is most impressive. As it shapes itself to his memory, the victim of tyranny is in *the lowest dungeon*. This phrase suggests the thought of the awful Hebrew Sheol. So dark was his experience, and so near was the sufferer to death, it seems to him as though he had been indeed plunged down into the very abode of the dead. Yet here he found utterance for prayer. It was the prayer of utter extremity, almost the last wild cry of a despairing soul, yet not quite, for that is no prayer at all, all prayer requiring some real faith, if only as a grain of mustard seed. Moreover, the poet states that he called upon the *name* of God. Now in the Bible the name always stands for the attributes which it connotes. To call on God's name is to make mention of some of His known and revealed characteristics. The man who will do this is more than one "feeling after God;" he has a definite conception of the nature and disposition of the Being to whom he is addressing himself. Thus it happens that old, familiar ideas of God, as He had been known in the days of light and joy, rise up in the heart of the miserable man, and awaken a longing desire to seek the help of One so great and good and merciful. Just in proportion to the fulness of the meaning of the name of God as it is conceived by us, will our prayers win definiteness of aim and strength of wing. The altar to "an unknown god" can excite but the feeblest and vaguest devotion. Inasmuch as our Lord has greatly enriched the contents of the name of God by His full revelation of the Divine Father, to us Christians there has come a more definite direction and a more powerful impulse for prayer. Even though this is a prayer *de profundis* it is an enlightened prayer. We may believe that, like a star seen from the depths of a well which excludes the glare of day, the significance of the sacred Name shone out to the sufferer with a beauty never before perceived when he looked up to heaven from the darkness of his pit of misery.

It has been suggested that in this passage the elegist is following the sixty-ninth psalm, and that perhaps that psalm is his own composition and the expression of the very prayer to which he is here referring. At all events, the psalm exactly fits the situation; and therefore it may be taken as a perfect illustration of the kind of prayer alluded to. The psalmist is "in deep mire, where there is no standing;" he has "come into deep waters, where the floods overthrow" him; he is persecuted by enemies who hate him "without a cause;" he has been weeping till his eyes have failed. Meanwhile he has been waiting for God, in prayers mingled with confessions. It is his zeal for God's house that has brought him so near to death. He beseeches God that the flood may not be allowed to overwhelm him, nor "the pit shut her mouth upon him." He concludes with an invocation of curses upon the heads of his enemies. All these as well as some minor points agree very closely with our poet's picture of his persecutions and the prayer he here records.

Read in the light of the elegist's experience, such a

prayer as that of the psalm cannot be taken as a model for daily devotion. It is a pity that our habitual use of the Psalter should encourage this application of it. The result is mischievous in several ways. It tends to make our worship unreal, because the experience of the psalmist, even when read metaphorically, as it was probably intended to be read, is by no means a type of the normal condition of human life. Besides, in so far as we bring ourselves to sympathise with this piteous outcry of a distressed soul, we reduce our worship to a melancholy plaint, when it should be a joyous anthem of praise. At the same time, we unconsciously temper the language we quote with the less painful feelings of our own experience, so that its force is lost upon us.

Yet the psalm is of value as a revelation of a soul's agony relieved by prayer; and there are occasions when its very words can be repeated by men and women who are indeed overwhelmed by trouble. If we do not spoil the occasional by attempting to make it habitual it is wonderful to see how rich the Bible is in utterances to suit all cases and all conditions. Such an outpouring of a distressed heart as the elegist hints at and the psalmist illustrates, is itself full of profound significance. The stirring of a soul to its depths is a revelation of its depths. This revelation prevents us from taking petty views of human nature. No one can contemplate the Titanic struggle of Laocoon or the immeasurable grief of Niobe without a sense of the tragic greatness of which human life is capable. We live so much on the surface that we are in danger of forgetting that life is not always a superficial thing. But when a volcano bursts out of the quiet plain of everyday existence, we are startled into the perception that there must be hidden fires which we may not have suspected before. And, further, when the soul in its extremity is seen to be turning for refuge to God, the revelation of its Gethsemane gives a new meaning to the very idea of prayer. Here is prayer indeed, and at the sight of such a profound reality we are shamed into doubting whether we have ever begun to pray at all, so stiff and chill do our utterances to the Unseen now appear to be in comparison with this Jacob-like wrestling.

Immediately after mentioning the fact of his prayer the elegist adds that this was heard by God. His cry rose up from "the lowest dungeon" and reached the heights of heaven. And yet we cannot credit this to the inherent vigour of prayer. If a petition can thus wing its way to heaven, that is because it is of heavenly origin. There is no difficulty in making air to rise above water; the difficulty is to sink it; and if any could be taken to the bottom of the sea, the greater the depth descended the swifter would it shoot up. Since all true prayer is an inspiration it cannot spend itself until it has, so to speak, restored the equilibrium by returning to its natural sphere. But the elegist puts the case another way. In His great condescension God stoops to the very lowest depths to find one of His distressed children. It is not hard to make the prayer of the dungeon reach the ear of God, because God is in the dungeon. He is most near when He is most needed.

The prayer was more than heard; it was answered —there was a Divine voice in response to this cry to God, a voice that reached the ear of the desolate prisoner in the silence of his dungeon. It consisted of but two words, but those two words were clear and unmistakable, and quite sufficient to satisfy the listener. The voice said, "Fear not."[1] That was enough.

Shall we doubt the reality of the remarkable experience that the elegist here records? Or can we explain it away by reference to the morbid condition of the mind of a prisoner enduring the punishment of solitary confinement? It is said that this unnatural punishment tends to develop insanity in its miserable victims. But the poet is now reviewing the occurrence, which made so deep an impression on his mind at the time, in the calm of later reflection; and evidently *he* has no doubt of its reality. It has nothing in it of the wild fancy of a disordered brain. Lunacy raves; this simple message is calm. And it is just such a message as God might be expected to give if He spoke at all—just like Him, we may say. To this remark some doubting critic may reply, "Exactly; and therefore the more likely to have been imagined by the expectant worshipper." But such an inference is not psychologically correct. The reply is not in harmony with the tone of the prayer, but directly opposed to it. Agony and terror cannot generate an assurance of peace and safety. The poison does not secrete its own antidote. Here is an indication of the presence of another voice, because the words breathe another spirit. Besides, this is not an unparalleled experience.

Most frequently, no doubt, the answer to prayer is not vocal, and yet the reality of it may not be any the less certain to the seeking soul. It may be most definite, although it comes in a deed rather than in a word. Then the grateful recipient can exclaim with the psalmist—

---

[1] iii. 57.

"This poor man cried, and the Lord heard him,
And saved him out of all his troubles."[1]

Here is an answer, but not a spoken one, only an action, in saving from trouble. In other cases, however, the reply approaches nearer the form of a message from heaven. When we remember that God is our Father the wonder is not that at rare intervals these voices have been heard, but rather that they are so infrequent. It is so easy to become the victim of delusions that some caution is requisite to assure ourselves of the existene of Divine utterances. The very idea of the occurrence of such phenomena is discredited by the fact that those persons who profess most eagerly to have heard supernatural voices are commonly the subjects of hysteria; and when the voices become frequent this fact is taken by physicians as a symptom of approaching insanity. Among semi-civilised people madness is supposed to be closely allied to inspiration. The *mantis* is not far from the mad man. Such a man is not the better off for the march of civilisation. The ancients would have honoured him as a prophet; we shut him up in a lunatic asylum. But these discouraging considerations do not exhaust the question. Delusions are not in themselves disproofs of the existence of the occurrences they emulate. Each case must be taken on its own merits; and when, as in that which is now under our consideration, the character of the incident points to a conviction of its solid reality, it is only a mark of narrowness of thought to refuse to lift it out of the category of idle fancies.

But, quite apart from the question of the sounding of Divine voices in the bodily ear, the more important

---

[1] Psalm xx 6.

truth to be considered is that in some way, if only by spiritual impression, God does most really speak to His children, and that He speaks now as surely as He spoke in the days of Israel. We have no new prophets and apostles who can give us fresh revelations in the form of additions to our Bible. But that is not what is meant. The elegist did not receive a statement of doctrine in answer to his prayer, nor, on this occasion, even help for the writing of his inspired poetry. The voice to which he here alludes was of quite a different character.

This was in the olden times; but if then, why not also now? Evidently the elegist regarded it as a rare and wonderful occurrence—a single experience to which he looked back in after years with the interest one feels in a vivid recollection which rises like a mountain, clean cut against the sky, above the mists that so quickly gather on the low plains of the uneventful past. Perhaps it is only in one of the crises of life that such an indubitable message is sent—when the soul is in the lowest dungeon, *in extremis*, crying out of the darkness, helpless if not yet hopeless, overwhelmed, almost extinguished. But if we listened for it, who can tell but that the voice might not be so rare? We do not believe in it; therefore we do not hear it. Or the noise of the world's great loom and the busy thoughts of our own hearts drown the music that still floats down from heaven to ears that are tuned to catch its notes; for it does not come in thunder, and we must ourselves be still if we would hear the still small voice, inwardly still, still in soul, stifling the chatter of self, stopping our ears to the din of the world. There are those to-day who tell us with calm assurance, not at all in the visionary's falsetto notes, that they have known just what is here described by the poet—in the silence of a mountain valley, in the quiet of a sick chamber, even in the noisy crowd at a railway station.

When this is granted it is still well for us to remember that we are not dependent for Divine consolation on voices which to many must ever be as dubious as they are rare. This short message of two words is in effect the essence of teachings that can be gathered as freely from almost every page of the Bible as flowers from a meadow in May. We have the "more sure word of prophecy," and the burden of it is the same as the message of the voice that comforted the poet in his dungeon.

That message is wholly reassuring—"Fear not." So said God to the patriarch: "Fear not, Abram; I am thy shield, and thy exceeding great reward;"[1] and to His people through the prophet of the restoration: "Fear not, thou worm Jacob;"[2] and Jesus to His disciples in the storm: "Be of good cheer: it is I: be not afraid";[3] and our Lord again in His parting address: "Let not your heart be troubled, neither let it be fearful";[4] and the glorified Christ to His terrified friend John, when He laid His right hand on him with the words: "Fear not; I am the first and the last, and the Living One; and I was dead, and behold, I am alive for ever more, and I have the keys of death and of Hades."[5] This is the word that God is continually speaking to His faint-hearted children. When "the burthen of the mystery," and

> "the heavy and the weary weight
> Of all this unintelligible world"

---

[1] Gen. xv. 1.   [3] Mark vi. 50.   [5] Rev. i. 17, 18.
[2] Isa. xli. 14.   [4] John xiv. 27.

oppress, when the greater sorrows threaten to crush outright, listening for the voice of God, we may hear the message of love from a Father's heart as though spoken afresh to each of us; for we have but to acquaint ourselves with Him to be at peace.

The elegist does not recall this scene from his past life merely in order to indulge in the pleasures of memory—generally rather melancholy pleasures, and even mocking if they are in sharp contrast to the present. His object is to find encouragement for renewed hope in the efficacy of prayer. In the complaint that he has put into the mouth of His people He has just been depicting the failure of prayer. But now he feels that if for a time God has wrapped Himself in a mantle of wrath this cannot be for ever, for He who was so gracious to the cry of His servant on that ever-memorable occasion will surely attend again to the appeal of distress. This is always the greatest encouragement for seeking help from God. It is difficult to find much satisfaction in what is called with an awkward inconsequence of diction the "philosophy of prayer"; the spirit of philosophy is so wholly different from the spirit of prayer. The great justification for prayer is the experience of prayer. It is only the prayerless man who is wholly sceptical on this subject. The man of prayer cannot but believe in prayer; and the more he prays and the oftener he turns to this refuge in all times of need the fuller is his assurance that God hears and answers him.

Considering how God acted as his advocate when he was in danger in the earlier crisis, and then redeemed his life, the poet points to this fact as a plea in his new necessity.[1] God will not desert the cause He has

---
[1] iii. 58.

adopted. Men feel a peculiar interest in those whom they have already helped, an interest that is stronger than the sense of gratitude, for we are more attracted to our dependants than to our benefactors. If God shares this feeling, how strongly must He be drawn to us by His many former favours! The language of the elegist gains a great enrichment of meaning when read in the light of the Christian Gospel. In a deep sense, of which he could have had but the least glimmering of apprehension, we can appeal to God as the Redeemer of our life, for we can take the Cross of Christ as our plea. St. Paul makes use of this strongest of all arguments when He urges that if God gave His Son, and if Christ died for us, all other needful blessings, since they cannot involve so great a sacrifice, will surely follow. Accordingly, we can pray in the language of the *Dies Iræ*—

> "Wearily for me Thou soughtest,
> On the Cross my life Thou boughtest,
> Lose not all for which Thou wroughtest."

Rising from the image of the advocate to that of the magistrate the distressed man begs God to judge his cause.[1] He would have God look at his enemies—how they wrong him, insult him, make him the theme of their jesting songs.[2]

It would have been more to our taste if the poem had ended here, if there had been no remaining letters in the Hebrew alphabet to permit the extension of the acrostics beyond the point we have now reached. We cannot but feel that its tone is lowered at the close. The writer here proceeds to heap imprecations on the heads of his enemies. It is vain for some com-

---

[1] iii. 59. [2] iii. 60-3.

mentators to plead the weak excuse that the language is "prophetic." This is certainly more than the utterance of a prediction. No unprejudiced reader can deny that it reveals a desire that the oppressors may be blighted and blasted with ruin, and even if the words were only a foretelling of a divinely-decreed fate they would imply a keen sense of satisfaction in the prospect, which they describe as something to be gloated over. We cannot expect this Jewish patriot to anticipate our Lord's intercession and excuse for His enemies. Even St. Paul so far forgot himself as to treat the High Priest in a very different manner from his Master's behaviour. But we may see here one of the worst effects of tyranny—the dark passion of revenge that it rouses in its victims. The provocation was maddening, and not only of a private nature. Think of the situation—the beloved city sacked and destroyed, the sacred temple a heap of smouldering ruins, village homesteads all over the hills of Judah wrecked and deserted; slaughter, outrage, unspeakable wrongs endured by wives and maidens, little children starved to death. Is it wonderful that the patriot's temper was not the sweetest when he thought of the authors of such atrocities? There is no possibility of denying the fact —the fierce fires of Hebrew hatred for the oppressors of the much-suffering race here burst into a flame, and towards the end of this finest of elegies we read the dark imprecation, "Thy curse upon them!"[1]

---

[1] iii. 65.

CHAPTER XVIII

CONTRASTS

iv. 1-12

IN form the fourth elegy is slightly different from each of its predecessors. Following the characteristic plan of the Book of Lamentations, it is an acrostic of twenty-two verses arranged in the order of the Hebrew alphabet. In it we meet with the same curious transposition of two letters that is found in the second and third elegies; it has also the peculiar metre of Hebrew elegiac poetry—the very lengthy line, broken into two unequal parts. But, like the first and second, it differs from the third elegy, which repeats the acrostic letters in three successive lines, in only using each acrostic once—at the beginning of a fresh verse; and it differs from all the three first elegies, which are arranged in triplets, in having only two lines in each verse.

This poem is very artistically constructed in the balancing of its ideas and phrases. The opening section of it, from the beginning to the twelfth verse, consists of a pair of duplicate passages—the first from verse one to verse six, the second from verse seven to verse eleven, the twelfth verse bringing this part of the poem to a close by adding a reflection on the common subject of the twin passages. Thus the parallelism which we usually meet with in individual verses is here extended to two series of verses, we might perhaps say, two *stanzas*, except that there is no such formal division.

In each of these elaborately-wrought sections the elegist brings out a rich array of similes to enforce the tremendous contrast between the original condition of the people of Jerusalem and their subsequent wretchedness. The details of the two descriptions follow closely parallel lines, with sufficient diversity, both in idea and in illustration, though chiefly in illustration, to avoid tautology and to serve to heighten the general effect by mutual comparisons. Both passages open with images of beautiful and costly natural objects to which the *élite* of Jerusalem are compared. Next comes the violent contrast of their state after the overthrow of the city. Then turning aside to more distant scenes, each of which is more or less repellent—the lair of wild beasts in the first case, in the second the battle-field—the poet describes the much more degraded and miserable condition of his people. Both passages direct especial attention to the fate of children—the first to their starvation, the second to a perfectly ghastly scene. At this point in each part the previous daintiness of the upbringing of the more refined classes is contrasted with the condition of degradation worse than that of savages to which they have been reduced. Each passage concludes with a reference to those deeper facts of the case which make it a sign of the wrath of heaven against exceptionally guilty sinners.

The elegist begins with an evident allusion to the consequences of the burning of the temple, which we learn from the history was effected by the Babylonian general Nebuzar-adan.[1] The costly splendour with

---
[1] 2 Kings xxv. 9.

which this temple at Jerusalem was decorated allowed of a rare glitter of gold, such as Josephus describes when writing of the later temple; gold not like that of the domes of St. Mark's, mellowed by the climate of Venice to a sober depth of hue, but all ablaze with dazzling radiance. The first effect of the smoke of a great conflagration would be to cloud and soil this somewhat raw magnificence, so that the choice gold became dull. That the precious stones stolen from the temple treasury would be flung carelessly about the streets, as our Authorised Version would seem to suggest, is not to be supposed in the case of the sack of a city by a civilised army, whatever might happen if a Vandal host swept through it. "The stones of the sanctuary,"[1] however, might be the stones with which the building had been constructed. Still, even with this interpretation the statement seems very improbable that the invaders would take the trouble to cart these huge blocks about the city in order to distribute them in heaps at all the street corners. We are driven to the conclusion that the poet is speaking metaphorically, that he is meaning the Jews themselves, or perhaps the more favoured classes, "the noble sons of Zion" of whom he writes openly in the next verse.[2] This interpretation is confirmed when we consider the comparison with the parallel passage, which starts at once with a reference to the "princes."[3] It seems likely then that the gold that has been so sullied also represents the choicer part of the people. The writer deplores the destruction of his beloved sanctuary, and the image of that calamity is in his mind at the present time; and yet it is not this that he is most deeply

---

[1] iv. 1. [2] iv. 2. [3] iv. 7

lamenting. He is more concerned with the fate of his people. The patriot loves the very soil of his native land, the loyal citizen the very streets and stones of his city. But if such a man is more than a dreamer or a sentimentalist, flesh and blood must mean infinitely more to him than earth and stones. The ruin of a city is something else than the destruction of its buildings; an earthquake or a fire may effect this, and yet, like Chicago, the city may rise again in greater splendour. The ruin that is most deplorable is the ruin of human lives.

This somewhat aristocratic poet, the mouthpiece of an aristocratic age, compares the sons of the Jewish nobility to purest gold. Yet he tells us that they are treated as common earthen vessels, perhaps meaning in contrast to the vessels of precious metal used in the palaces of the great. They are regarded as of no more value than potter's work, though formerly they had been prized as the dainty art of a goldsmith. This first statement only treats of insult and humiliation. But the evil is worse. The jackals that he knows must be prowling about the deserted ruins of Jerusalem even while he writes suggests a strange, wild image to the poet's mind.[1] These fierce creatures suckle their young, though not in the tame manner of domestic animals. It is singular that the nurture of princes amid the refinements of wealth and luxury should be compared to the feeding of their cubs by scavengers of the wilderness. But our thoughts are thus directed to the wide extent, the universal exercise of maternal instincts throughout the animal world, even among the most savage and homeless creatures. Startling indeed

---

[1] iv. 3.

is it to think that such instincts should ever fail among men, or even that circumstances should ever hinder the natural performance of the functions to which they point with imperious urgency. Although the second passage tells of the violent reversal of the natural feelings of maternity under the maddening influence of famine, here we read how starvation has simply stopped the tender ministry which mothers render to their infants, with a vague hint at some cruelty on the part of the Jewish mothers. A comparison with the supposed conduct of ostriches in leaving their eggs suggests that this is negative cruelty; their hearts being frozen with agony, the wretched mothers lose all interest in their children. But then there is not food for them. The calamities of the times have staunched the mother's milk; and there is no bread for the older children.[1] It is the extreme reversal of their fortunes that makes the misery of the children of princely homes most acute; even those who do not suffer the pangs of hunger are flung down to the lowest depths of wretchedness. The members of the aristocracy have been accustomed to live luxuriously; now they wander about the streets devouring whatever they can pick up. In the old days of luxury they used to recline on scarlet couches; now they have no better bed than the filthy dunghill.[2]

The passage concludes with a reflection on the general character of this dreadful condition of Israel.[3] It must be closely connected with the sins of the people. The drift of the context would lead us to judge that the poet does not mean to compare the guilt of Jerusalem with that of Sodom, but rather the

---

[1] iv. 4.   [2] iv. 5.   [3] iv. 6.

fate of the two cities. The punishment of Israel is greater than that of Sodom. But this is punishment; and the odious comparison would not be made unless the sin had been of the blackest dye. Thus in this elegy the calamities of Jerusalem are again traced back to the ill-doings of her people. The awful fate of the cities of the plain stands out in the ancient narrative as the exceptional punishment of exceptional wickedness. But now in the race for a first place in the history of doom Jerusalem has broken the record. Even Sodom has been eclipsed in the headlong course by the city once most favoured by heaven. It seems well nigh impossible. What could be worse than total destruction by fire from heaven? The elegist considers that there are two points in the fate of Jerusalem that confer a gloomy pre-eminence in misery. The doom of Sodom was sudden, and man had no hand in it but Jerusalem fell into the hands of man—a calamity which David judged to be worse than falling into the hands of God; and she had to endure a long, lingering agony.

Passing on to the consideration of the parallel section, we see that the author follows the same lines, though with considerable freshness of treatment. Still directing especial attention to the tremendous change in the fortunes of the aristocracy, he begins again by describing the splendour of their earlier state. This had been advertised to all eyes by the very complexion of their countenances. Unlike the toilers who were necessarily bronzed by working under a southern sun, these delicately nurtured persons had been able to preserve fair skins in the shady seclusion of their cool palaces, so that in the hyperbole of the poem they could be described as " purer than snow " and " whiter than milk."[1] Yet they had no sickly pallor. Their health had been well attended to; so that they were also ruddy as "corals," while their dark hair[2] glistened "like sapphires." But now see them! Their faces are "darker than blackness."[3] We need not enquire after a literal explanation of an expression which is in harmony with the extravagance of Oriental language, although doubtless exposure to the weather, and the grime and smoke of the scenes these children of luxury had passed through, must have had a considerable effect on their effeminate countenances. The language here is evidently figurative. So it is throughout the passage. The whole aspect of the lives and fortunes of these delicately nurtured lordlings has been reversed. They tell their story by the gloom of their countenances and by the shrivelled appearance of their bodies. They can no longer be recognised in the streets, so piteous a change has their misfortunes wrought in them. Withered and wizen, they are reduced to skin and bone by sheer famine. Sufferers from such continuous calamities as these fallen princes are passing through are treated to a worse fate than that which overtook their brethren who fell in the war. The sword is better than hunger. The victims of war, stricken down in the heat of battle but in the midst of plenty, so that they leave the fruits of the field behind them untouched because no longer needed,[4] are to be counted happy in being taken from the evil to come.

---

[1] iv. 7.
[2] iv. 7. "Hair." According to a slight emendation of the text recommended by recent criticism.
[3] iv. 8.
[4] So perhaps we should understand ver. 9, applying the last clause to the fallen warriors. In the Revised Version, however this is

The gruesome horror of the next scene is beyond description.[1] More than once history has had to record the absolute extinction, nay, we must say the insane reversal, of maternal instincts under the influence of hunger. We could not believe it possible if we did not know that it had occurred. It is a degradation of what we hold to be most sacred in human nature; perhaps it is only possible where human nature has been degraded already, for we must not forget that in the present case the women who are driven below the level of she-wolves are not children of nature, but the daughters of an effete civilisation who have been nursed in the lap of luxury. This is the climax. Imagination itself could scarcely go further. And yet according to his custom throughout, the elegist attributes these calamities of his people to the anger of God. Such things seem to indicate a very "fury" of Divine wrath; the anger must be fierce indeed to kindle such "a fire in Zion."[2] But now the very foundations of the city are destroyed even that terrible thirst for retribution must be satisfied.

These are thoughts which we as Christians do not care to entertain; and yet it is in the New Testament that we read that "our God is a consuming fire;"[3] and it is of our Lord that John the Baptist declares: "He will throughly purge His threshing-floor."[4] If God is angry at all His anger cannot be light; for no action of His is feeble or ineffectual. The subsequent restoration of Israel shows that the fires to which the elegist here calls our attention were purgatorial. This

---

rendered so as to refer to the famished people who pine away for lack of the fruits of the earth. Yet another rendering is "fade away ... like the growth of the fields."

[1] iv. 10.   [2] iv. 11.   [3] Heb. xii. 29.   [4] Matt. iii. 12.

fact must profoundly affect our view of their character. Still they are very real, or the Book of Lamentations would not have been written.

In view of the whole situation so graphically portrayed by means of the double line of illustrations the poet concludes this part of his elegy with a device that reminds us of the function of the chorus in the Greek drama. We see the kings of all other nations in amazement at the fate of Jerusalem.[1] The mountain city had the reputation of being an impregnable fortress, at least so her fond citizens imagined. But now she has fallen. It is incredible! The news of this wholly unexpected disaster is supposed to send a shock through foreign courts. We are reminded of the blow that stunned St. Jerome when a rumour of the fall of Rome reached the studious monk in his quiet retreat at Bethlehem. Men can tell that a severe storm has been raging out in the Atlantic if they see unusually great rollers breaking on the Cornish crags. How huge a calamity must that be the mere echo of which can produce a startling effect in far countries! But could these kings really be so astonished seeing that Jerusalem had been captured twice before? The poet's language rather points to the overweening pride and confidence of the Jews, and it shows how great the shock to them must have been since they could not but regard it as a wonder to the world. Such then is the picture drawn by our poet with the aid of the utmost artistic skill in bringing out its striking effects. Now before we turn away from it let us ask ourselves wherein its true significance may be said to lie. This is a study in black and white. The very language is such; and

---

[1] iv. 12.

when we come to consider the lessons that language sets forth with so much sharpness and vigour, we shall see that they too partake of the same character.

The force of contrasts—that is the first and most obvious characteristic of the scene. We are very familiar with the heightening of effects by this means, and it is needless to repeat the trite lessons that have been derived from the application of it to life. We know that none suffer so keenly from adversity as those who were once very prosperous. Marius in the Mamertine dungeon, Napoleon at St. Helena, Nebuchadnezzar among the beasts, Dives in Hell, are but notorious illustrations of what we may all see on the smaller canvas of every-day life. Great as are the hardships of the children of the "slums," it is not to them, but to the unhappy victims of a violent change of circumstances, that the burden of poverty is most heavy. We have seen this principle illustrated repeatedly in the Book of Lamentations. But now may we not go behind it, and lay hold of something more than an indubitable psychological law? While looking only at the reversals of fortune which may be witnessed on every hand, we are tempted to hold life to be little better than a gambling bout with high stakes and desperate play. Further consideration, however, should teach us that the stakes are not so high as they appear; that is to say, that the chances of the world do not so profoundly affect our fate as surface views would lead us to suppose. Such things as the pursuit of mere sensation, the life of external aims, the surrender to the excitement of the moment, are doubtless subject to the vicissitudes of contrast; but it is the teaching of our Lord that the higher pursuits are free from these evils. If the treasure is in heaven no thief can steal it, no moth or rust can corrupt it; and therefore since where the treasure is there will the heart be also, it is possible to keep the heart in peace even among the changes that upset a purely superficial life with earthquake shocks. Sincere as is the lament of the elegist over the fate of his people, a subtle thread of irony seems to run through his language. Possibly it is quite unconscious; but if so it is the more significant, for it is the irony of fact which cannot be excluded by the simplest method of statement. It suggests that the grandeur which could be so easily turned to humiliation must have been somewhat tawdry at best.

But unhappily the fall of the pampered youth of Jerusalem was not confined to a reversal of external fortune. The elegist has been careful to point out that the miseries they endured were the punishments of their sins. Then there had been an earlier and much greater collapse. Before any foreign enemy had appeared at her gates the city had succumbed to a fatal foe bred within her own walls. Luxury had undermined the vigour of the wealthy; vice had blackened the beauty of the young. There is a fine gold of character which will be sullied beyond recognition when the foul vapours of the pit are permitted to break out upon it. The magnificence of Solomon's temple is poor and superficial in comparison with the beauty of young souls endowed with intellectual and moral gifts, like jewels of rarest worth. Man is not treated in the Bible as a paltry creature. Was he not made in the image of God? Jesus would not have us despise our own native worth. Hope and faith come from a lofty view of human nature and its possibilities. Souls are not swine; and therefore by all the measure of their superiority to swine souls are worth saving. The shame and sorrow of sin lie just in this fact, that it is so foul a degradation of so fair a thing as human nature. Here is the contrast that heightens the tragedy of lost souls. But then we may add, in its reversal this same contrast magnifies the glory of redemption—from so deep a pit does Christ bring back His ransomed, to so great a height does He raise them!

CHAPTER XIX

LEPERS

iv. 13-16

PASSING from the fate of the princes to that of the prophets and priests, we come upon a vividly dramatic scene in the streets of Jerusalem amid the terror and confusion that precede the final act of the national tragedy. The doom of the city is attributed to the crimes of her religious leaders, whose true characters are now laid bare. The citizens shrink from the guilty men with the loathing felt for lepers, and shriek to them to depart, calling them unclean, and warning them not to touch any one by the way, because there is blood upon them. Dreading the awful treatment measured out to the victims of lynch-law, they stagger through the streets in a state of bewilderment, and stumble like blind men. Fugitives and vagabonds, with the mark of Cain upon them, driven out at the gates by the impatient mob, they can find no refuge even in foreign lands, for none of the nations will receive them.

We do not know whether the poet is here describing actual events, or whether this is an imaginary picture designed to express his own feelings with regard to the persons concerned. The situation is perfectly natural, and what is narrated may very well have happened just as it is described. But if it is not history it is still a revelation of character, a representation of what the writer knows to be the conduct of the moral lepers, and their deserts; and as such it is most suggestive.

In the first place there is much significance in the fact that the overthrow of Jerusalem is unhesitatingly charged to the account of the sins of her prophets and priests. These once venerated men are not merely no longer protected by the sanctity of their offices from the accusations that are brought against the laity; they are singled out for a charge of exceptionally heinous wickedness which is regarded as the root cause of all the troubles that have fallen upon the Jews. The second elegy had affirmed the failure of the prophets and the vanity of their visions.[1] This new and stronger accusation reads like a reminiscence of Jeremiah, who repeatedly speaks of the sins of the clerical class and the mischief resulting therefrom.[2] Evidently the terrible truth the prophet dwelt upon so much was felt by a disciple of his school to be of the most serious consequence.

The accusation is of the very gravest character. These religious leaders are charged with murder. If the elegist is recording historical occurrences he may be alluding to riots in which the feuds of rival factions had issued in bloodshed; or he may have had information of private acts of assassination. His language points to a condition in Jerusalem similar to that which was found in Rome at the Fifteenth Century, when popes and cardinals were the greatest criminals. The crimes were aggravated by the fact that the victims selected were the "righteous," perhaps men of the Jeremiah party, who had been persecuted by the officials

---

[1] ii. 9, 14. [2] Jer. vi. 13; viii. 10; xxiii. 11, 14; xxvi. 7 ff.

of the State religion. But quite apart from these dark and tragic events, the record of which has not been preserved, if the wicked policy of their clergy had brought down on the heads of the citizens of Jerusalem the mass of calamities that accompanied the siege of the city by the Babylonians, this policy was in itself a cause of great bloodshed. The men who invited the ruin of their city were in reality the murderers of all who perished in that calamity. We know from Jeremiah's statements on the subject that the false, time-serving, popular prophets were deceivers of the people, who allayed alarm by means of lies, saying "peace, peace; when there was no peace."[1] When the deception was discovered their angry dupes would naturally hold them responsible for the results of their wickedness.

The sin of these religious leaders of Israel consists essentially in betraying a sacred trust. The priest is in charge of the *Torah*—traditional or written; he must have been unfaithful to his law or he could not have led his people astray. If the prophet's claims are valid this man is the messenger of Jehovah, and therefore he must have falsified his message in order to delude his audience; if, however, he has not himself heard the Divine voice he is no better than a dervish, and in pretending to speak with the authority of an ambassador from heaven he is behaving as a miserable charlatan. In the case now before us the motive for the practice of deceit is very evident. It is thirst for popularity. Truth, right, God's will—these imperial authorities count for nothing, because the favour of the people is reckoned as everything. No doubt there are times when the temptation to descend to untruthfulness

---

[1] Jer. vi. 14; viii. 11.

in the discharge of a public function is peculiarly pressing. When party feeling is roused, or when a mad panic has taken possession of a community, it is exceedingly difficult to resist the current and maintain what one knows to be right in conflict with the popular movement. But in its more common occurrence this treachery cannot plead any such excuse. That truth should be trampled under foot and souls endangered merely to enable a public speaker to refresh his vanity with the music of applause is about the most despicable exhibition of selfishness imaginable. If a man who has been set in a place of trust prostitutes his privileges simply to win admiration for his oratory, or at most in order to avoid the discomfort of unpopularity or the disappointment of neglect, his sin is unpardonable.

The one form of unfaithfulness on the part of these religious leaders of Israel of which we are specially informed is their refusal to warn their reckless fellow-citizens of the approach of danger, or to bring home to their hearers' consciences the guilt of the sin for which the impending doom was the just punishment. They are the prototypes of those writers and preachers who smooth over the unpleasant facts of life. It is not easy for any one to wear the mantle of Elijah, or echo the stern desert voice of John the Baptist. Men who covet popularity do not care to be reckoned pessimists; and when the gloomy truth is not flattering to their hearers they are sorely tempted to pass on to more congenial topics. This was apparent in the Deistic optimism that almost stifled spiritual life during the Eighteenth Century. Our age is far from being optimistic; and yet the same temptation threatens to smother religion to-day. In an aristocratic age the sycophant flatters the great; in a democratic age he flatters the people—who are then in fact the great. The peculiar danger of our own day is that the preacher should simply echo popular cries, and voice the demands of the majority irrespective of the question of their justice. Thrust into the position of a social leader with more urgency than his predecessors of any time since the age of the Hebrew prophets, it is expected that he will lead whither the people wish to go, and if he declines to do so he is denounced as retrograde. And yet as the messenger of Heaven he should consider it his supreme duty to reveal the whole counsel of God, to speak for truth and righteousness, and therefore to condemn the sins of the democracy equally with the sins of the aristocracy. Brave labour-leaders have fallen into disfavour for telling working-men that their worst enemies were their own vices—such as intemperance. The wickedness of a responsible teacher who treasonably neglects thus to warn his brethren of danger is powerfully expressed by Ezekiel's clear, antithetical statements concerning the respective guilt of the watchman and his fellow-citizen, which show conclusively that the greatest burden of blame must rest on the unfaithful watchman.[1]

In the hour of their exposure these wretched prophets and priests lose all sense of dignity, even lose their self-possession, and stumble about like blind men, helpless and bewildered. Their behaviour suggests the idea that they must be drunk with the blood they have shed, or overcome by the intoxication of their thirst for blood; but the explanation is that they cannot lift up their heads to look a neighbour in the face, because all their little devices have been torn to shreds,

---

[1] Ezek. iii. 16-21.

all their specious lies detected, all their empty promises falsified. This shame of dethroned popularity is the greatest humiliation. The unhappy man who has brought himself to live on the breath of fame cannot hide his fall in oblivion and obscurity as a private person may do. Standing in the full blaze of the world's observation which he has so eagerly focussed on himself, he has no alternative but to exchange the glory of popularity for the ignominy of notoriety.

Possibly the confusion consequent on their exposure is all that the poet is thinking of when he depicts the blind staggering of the prophets and priests. But it is not unreasonable to take this picture as an illustration of their moral condition, especially after the references to the faults of the prophets in the second elegy have directed our attention to their spiritual darkness and the vanity of their visions. When the refuge of lies in which they had trusted was swept away they would necessarily find themselves lost and helpless. They had so long worshipped falsehood, it had become so much their god that we might say, in it they had lived, and moved, and had their being. But now they have lost the very atmosphere of their lives. This is the penalty of deceit. The man who begins by using it as his tool becomes in time its victim. At first he lies with his eyes open; but the sure effect of this conduct is that his sight becomes dim and blurred, till, if he persist in the fatal course long enough, he is ultimately reduced to a condition of blindness. By continually mixing truth and falsehood together he loses the power of distinguishing between them. It may be supposed that at an earlier stage of their decline, if the religious leaders of Israel had been honest with regard to their own convictions they must have admitted the possible genuineness of those prophets of ruin whom they had persecuted in deference to popular clamour. But they had rejected all such unwelcome thoughts so persistently that in course of time they had lost the perception of them. Therefore when the truth was flashed upon their unwilling minds by the unquestionable revelation of events they were as helpless as bats and owls suddenly driven out into the daylight by an earthquake that has flung down the crumbling ruins in which they had been sheltering themselves.

The discovery of the true character of these men was the signal for a yell of execration on the part of the people by flattering whom they had obtained their livelihood, or at least all that they most valued in life. This too must have been another shock of surprise to them. Had they believed in the essential fickleness of popular favour, they would never have built their hopes upon so precarious a foundation, for they might as well have set up their dwelling on the strand that would be flooded at the next turn of the tide. History is strewn with the wreckage of fallen popular reputations of all degrees of merit, from that of the conscientious martyr who had always looked to higher ends than the applause which once encircled him, to that of the frivolous child of fortune who had known of nothing better than the world's empty admiration. We see this both in Savonarola martyred at the stake and in Beau Nash starved in a garret. There is no more pathetic scene to be gathered from the story of religion in the present century than that of Edward Irving, once the idol of society, subsequently deserted by fashion, stationing himself at a street corner to proclaim his message to a chance congregation of idlers; and his mistake was that of an honest man who had been misled by a delusion. Incomparably worse is the fate of the fallen favourite who has no honesty of conviction with which to comfort himself when frowned at by the heartless world that had recently fawned upon him.

The Jews show their disgust and horror for their former leaders by pelting them with the leper call. According to the law the leper must go with rent clothes and flowing hair, and his face partly covered, crying, "Unclean, unclean."[1] It is evident that the poet has this familiar mournful cry in his mind when he describes the treatment of the prophets and priests. And yet there is a difference. The leper is to utter the humiliating word himself; but in the case now before us it is flung after the outcast leaders by their pitiless fellow-citizens. The alteration is not without significance. The miserable victim of bodily disease could not hope to disguise his condition. "White as snow," his well-known complaint was patent to every eye. But it is otherwise with the spiritual leprosy, sin. For a time it may be disguised, a hidden fire in the breast. When it is evident to others, too often the last man to perceive it is the offender himself; and when he himself is inwardly conscious of guilt he is tempted to wear a cloak of denial before the world. More especially is this the case with one who has been accustomed to make a profession of religion, and most of all with a religious leader. While the publican who has no character to sustain will smite his breast with self-reproaches and cry for mercy, the professional saint is blind to his own sins, partly no doubt because to admit their existence would be to shatter his profession.

---

[1] Lev. xiii. 45.

But if the religious leader is slow to confess or even perceive his guilt, the world is keen to detect it and swift to cast it in his teeth. There is nothing that excites so much loathing; and justly so, for there is nothing that does so much harm. Such conduct is the chief provocative of practical scepticism. It matters not that the logic is unsound; men will draw rough and ready conclusions. If the leaders are corrupt the hasty inference is that the cause which is identified with their names must also be corrupt. Religion suffers more from the hypocrisy of some of her avowed champions than from the attacks of all the hosts of her pronounced foes. Accordingly a righteous indignation assails those who work such deadly mischief. But less commendable motives urge men in the same direction. Evil itself steals a triumph over good in the downfall of its counterfeit. If they knew themselves there must have been some hypocrisy on the side of the persecutors in the demonstrative zeal with which they hounded to death the once pampered children of fortune the moment they had fallen from the pedestal of respectability; for could these indignant champions of virtue deny that they had been willing accomplices in the deeds they so loudly denounced? or at least that they had not been reluctant to be pleasantly deceived, had not enquired too nicely into the credentials of the flatterers who had spoken smooth things to them? Considering what their own conduct had been, their eagerness in execrating the wickedness of their leaders was almost indecent. There is a Pecksniffian air about it. It suggests a sly hope that by thus placing themselves on the side of outraged virtue they were putting their own characters beyond the suspicion of criticism. They seem to have been too eager to make scapegoats of their clergy. Their action appears to show that they had some idea that even at the eleventh hour the city might be spared if it were rid of this plague of the blood-stained prophets and priests. And yet however various and questionable the motives of the assailants may have been, there is no escape from the conclusion that the wickedness they denounced so eagerly richly deserved the most severe condemnation. Wherever we meet with it, this is the leprosy of society. Disguised for a time, a secret canker in the breast of unsuspected men, it is certain to break out at length; and when it is discovered it merits a measure of indignation proportionate to the previous deception.

Exile is the doom of these guilty prophets and priests. But even in their banishment they can find no place of rest. They wander from one foreign nation to another; they are permitted to stay with none of them. Unlike our English pretenders who were allowed to take up their abode among the enemies of their country, these Jews were suspected and disliked wherever they went. They had been unfaithful to Jehovah; yet they could not proclaim themselves devotees of Baal. The heathen were not prepared to draw fine distinctions between the various factions in the Israelite camp. The world only scoffs at the quarrels of the sects. Moreover, these false, worthless leaders had been the zealots of national feeling in the old boastful days when Jeremiah had been denounced by their party as a traitor. Then they had been the most exclusive of the Jews. As they had made their bed so must they lie on it. The poet suggests no term to this melancholy fate. Perhaps while he was writing his elegy the wretched men were to his own knowledge still journeying wearily from place to place. Thus like the fratricide Cain, like the wandering Jew of mediæval legend, the fallen leaders of the religion of Israel find their punishment in a doom of perpetual homelessness. Is it too severe a penalty for the fatal deceit that wrought death, and so was equivalent to murder of the worst sort, cold-blooded, deliberate murder? There is a perfectly Dantesque appropriateness in it. The Inferno of the popularity-mongers is a homeless desert of unpopularity. Quiet, retiring souls and dreamy lovers of nature might derive rest and refreshment from a hermit life in the wilderness. Not so these slaves of society. Deprived of the support of their surrounding element—like jelly-fish flung on to the beach to shrivel up and perish—in banishment from city life such men must experience a total collapse. Just in proportion to the hollowness and unreality with which a man has made the pursuit of the world's applause the chief object of his life, is the dismal fate he will have to endure when, having sown the wind of vanity, he reaps the whirlwind of indignation. The ill-will of his fellow-men is hard to bear; but behind it is the far more terrible wrath of God, whose judgment the miserable time-server has totally ignored while sedulously cultivating the favour of the world.

CHAPTER XX

VAIN HOPES

iv. 17-20

THE first part of the fourth elegy was specially concerned with the fate of the gilded youth of Jerusalem; the second and closely parallel part with that of the princes; the third introduced us to the dramatic scene in which the fallen priests and prophets were portrayed; now in the fourth part of the elegy the king and his courtiers are the prominent figures. While all the rest of the poem is written in the third person, this short section is composed in the first person plural. The arrangement is not exactly like that of the third elegy, in which, after speaking in his own person, the poet appears as the representative and spokesman of his people. The more simple form of the composition now under consideration would lead us to suppose that the pronoun "we" comes in for the most natural reason—viz., because the writer was himself an actor in the scene which he here describes. We must conclude, then, that he was one of the group of Zedekiah's personal attendants, or at least a member of a company of Jews which escaped at the time of the royal flight and took the same road when the citizens were scattered by the sack of the city.

The picture, however, is somewhat idealised. Events that could only have taken place in succession are described as though they were all occurring in the present. We have first the anxious watching of the besieged for the advent of an army of relief; then the chase of their victims through the streets by the invaders—which must have been after they had broken into the city; next the flight and pursuit over the mountains; and lastly, the capture of the king. This setting of a succession of events in one scene as though they were contemporaneous is so far an imaginary arrangement that we must be on our guard against a too literal interpretation of the details. Evidently we have here a poetic picture, not the bare deposition of a witness.

The burden of the passage is the grievous disappointment of the court party at the failure of their fond hopes. But Jeremiah was directly opposed to that party, and though our author was not the great prophet himself we have abundant evidence that he was a faithful disciple who echoed the very thoughts and shared the deepest convictions of his master. How then can he now appear as one of the court party? It is just possible that he was no friend of Jeremiah at the time he is now describing. He may have been converted subsequently by the logic of facts, or by the more potent influence of the discipline of adversity, a possibility which would give peculiar significance to the personal confessions contained in the previous elegy, with its account of "the man who had seen affliction." But the poetic form of the section dealing with the court, and the fact that all it describes is expressed in the present tense, prevent us from pressing this conjecture to a definite conclusion. It would be enough if we could suppose, as there is no difficulty in doing, that in the general confusion our poet found himself in unexpected companionship with the flying court. Thus he would witness their experiences.

We have, then, in this place an expression of the attitude of the court party in the midst of the great calamities that have overtaken them. It is emphatically one of profound disappointment. These deluded people had been sanguine to the last, and proudly sceptical of danger, with an infatuation almost amounting to insanity which had blinded them to the palpable lessons of defeats already endured—for we must not forget that Jerusalem had been taken twice before this. Naturally their disappointment was proportionate to their previous elation.

The hopes that had been thus rudely dashed to the ground had been based on a feeling of the sacred inviolability of Jerusalem. This feeling had been sedulously nurtured by a bastard form of religion. Like the worship of Rome in Virgil's day, a sort of cult of Jerusalem had now grown up. Men who had no faith in Jehovah put their trust in Jerusalem. The starting-point and excuse of this singular creed are to be traced to the deep-rooted conviction of the Jews that their city was the chosen favourite of Jehovah, and that therefore her God would certainly protect her. But this idea was treated most inconsistently when people coolly ignored the Divine will while boldly claiming Divine favour. In course of time even that position was abandoned, and Jerusalem became practically a fetich. Then, while faith in the destiny of the city was cherished as a superstition, prophets such as Jeremiah, who directed men's thoughts to God, were silenced and persecuted. This folly of the Jews has its counterpart in the exaltation of the papacy during the Middle Ages. The Pope claimed to be seated on his throne by the authority of Christ; but the papacy was really put in the place of Christ. Similarly people who trust in the Church, their City of God, rather than in her Lord, have fallen into an error like that of the Jews, who put confidence in their city rather than in their God. So have those who confide in their own election instead of looking to the Divine Sovereign who, they declare, has named them in His eternal decrees; and those again who set reliance on their religion, its rites and creeds; and lastly, those who trust in their very faith as itself a saving power. In all these cases, the city, the Pope, the election, the Church, the religion, the faith are simply idols, no more able to protect the superstitious people who put them in the place of God than the ark that was captured in battle when the Jews tried to use it as a talisman, or even the fish-god Dagon that lay shattered before it in the Philistine temple.

But now we find the old-established faith in Jerusalem so far undermined that it has to be supplemented by other grounds of hope. In particular there are two of these—the king and a foreign ally. The ally is mentioned first because the poet starts from the time when men still hoped that the Egyptians would espouse the cause of Israel, and come to the help of the little kingdom against the hosts of Babylon. There was much to be said in favour of this expectation. In the past Egypt had been in alliance with the people now threatened. The two great kingdoms of the Nile and the Euphrates were rivals; and the aggressive policy of Babylon had brought her into conflict with Egypt. The Pharaohs might be glad to have Israel preserved as a "buffer state." Indeed, negotiations had been carried on with that end in view,

Nevertheless the dreams of deliverance built on this foundation were doomed to disappointment. The poet shows us the anxious Jews on their city towers straining their eyes till they are weary in watching for the relief that never comes. They could look down through the gap in the hills towards Bethlehem and the south country, and the dust of an army would be visible from afar in the clear Syrian atmosphere; but, alas! no distant cloud promises the approach of the deliverer. We are reminded of the siege of Lucknow; but in the hour of the Jews' great need there is no sign corresponding to the welcome music of the Scotch air that ravished the ears of the British garrison.

Faithful prophets had repeatedly warned the Jews against this false ground of hope. In a former generation Isaiah had cautioned his contemporaries not to lean on "this broken reed"[1] Egypt; and at the present crisis Jeremiah had followed with similar advice, predicting the failure of the Egyptian alliance, and replying to the messengers of Zedekiah who had come to solicit the prophet's prayers: "Thus saith the Lord, the God of Israel: Thus shall ye say to the king of Judah, that sent you unto me to enquire of me; Behold, Pharaoh's army, which is come forth to help you, shall return to Egypt into their own land. And the Chaldæans shall come again, and fight against this city; and they shall take it, and burn it with fire."[2] Though regarded at the time as unpatriotic and even treasonable, this advice proved to be sound, and the predictions of the messenger of Jehovah correct. Now that we can read the events in the light of history we have no difficulty in perceiving that even as a matter

---

[1] Isa. xxxvi. 6.   [2] Jer. xxxvii. 7, 8.

of state policy the counsel of Isaiah and Jeremiah was wise and statesmanlike. Babylon was quite irresistible. Even Egypt could not stand against the powerful empire that was making itself master of the world. Besides, alliance with Egypt involved the loss of liberty, for it had to be paid for, and the weak ally of a great kingdom was no better than a tributary state. Meanwhile Israel was embroiled in quarrels from which she should have tried, as far as possible, to keep herself aloof.

But the prophets shewed that deeper questions than such as concern political diplomacy were at stake. In happier days the arm of Providence had been laid bare, and Jerusalem saved without a blow, when the destroying angel of pestilence swept through the Assyrian host. It is true Jerusalem had to submit soon after this; but the lesson was being taught that her safety really consisted in submission. This was the kernel of Jeremiah's unpopular message. Historically and politically that too was justified. It was useless to attempt to stem the tide of one of the awful marches of a world-conquering army. Only the obstinacy of a fanatical patriotism could have led the Jews of this period to hold out so long against the might of Babylon, just as the very same obstinacy encouraged their mad descendants in the days of Titus to resist the arms of Rome. But then the prophets were constantly preaching to heedless ears that there was real safety in submission, that a humble measure of escape was to be had by simply complying with the demands of the irresistible conquerors. Proud patriots might despise this consolation, preferring to die fighting. But that was scarcely the case with the fugitives; these people had neither the relief that is the reward of a quiet surrender, nor the glory that accompanies death on the battle-field.

To those who could hear the deeper notes of prophetic teaching the safety of surrender meant a much more valuable boon. The submission recommended was not merely to be directed to King Nebuchadnezzar; primarily it consisted in yielding to the will of God. People who will not turn to this one true refuge from all danger and trouble are tempted to substitute a variety of vain hopes. Most of us have our Egypt to which we look when the vision of God has become dim in the soul. The worldly cynicism that echoes and degrades the words of the Preacher, "Vanity of vanities; all is vanity," is really the product of the decay of dead hopes. It would not be so sour if it had not been disappointed. Yet so persistent is the habit of castle-building, that the cloudland in which many previous structures of fancy have melted away is resorted to again and again by an eager throng of fresh aerial architects. After experience has confirmed the warning that riches take to themselves wings and flee away, and in face of our Lord's advice not to lay up treasures where thieves break through and steal, and where moth and rust consume, we see men as eager as ever to scrape wealth together, as ready to put all their trust in it when it has come to them, as astonished and dismayed when it has failed them. Ambition was long ago proved to be a frail bubble; yet ambition never wants for slaves. The cup of pleasure has been drained so often that the world should know by this time how very nauseous its dregs are; and still feverish hands are held out to grasp it.

Now this obstinate disregard of the repeated lessons of experience is too remarkable a habit of life to be reckoned as a mere accident. There must be some adequate causes to account for it. In the first place, it testifies with singular force to the vitality of what we may call the faculty of hope itself. Disappointment does not kill the tendency to reach forth to the future, because this tendency comes from within, and is not a mere response to impressions. In persons of a sanguine temperament this may be taken to be a constitutional peculiarity; but it is too widespread to be disposed of as nothing more than a freak of nature. It is rather to be considered an instinct, and as such a part of the original constitution of man. How then has it come to be? Must we not attribute the native hopefulness of mankind to the deliberate will and purpose of the Creator? But in that case must we not say of this, as we can say with certainty of most natural instincts: He who has given the hunger will also supply the food with which to satisfy it? To reject that conclusion is to land ourselves in a form of pessimism that is next door to atheism. Schopenhauer rests the argument by means of which he thinks to establish a pessimistic view of the universe largely on the delusiveness of natural instincts which promise a satisfaction never attained; but in reasoning in this way he is compelled to describe the supreme Will that he believes to be the ultimate principle of all things as a non-moral power. The mockery of human existence to which his philosophy reduces us is impossible in view of the Fatherhood of God revealed to us in Jesus Christ. Shelley, contrasting our fears and disappointments with the "clear keen joyance" of the skylark, bewails the fact that

> "We look before and after,
> And pine for what is not."

If this is the end of the matter, evolution is a mocking

progress, for it leads to the pit of despair. If the large vision that takes in past and future only brings sorrow, it would have been better for us to have retained the limited range of animal perceptions. But faith sees in the very experience of disappointment a ground for fresh hope. The discovery that the height already attained is not the summit of the mountain, although it appeared to be when viewed from the plain, is a proof that the summit is higher than we had supposed. Meanwhile, the awakening of desires for further climbing is a sign that the disappointments we have experienced hitherto are not occasions for despair. If, as Shelley goes on to say—

"Our sweetest songs are those that tell of saddest thought,"

the sadness cannot be without mitigation, for there must be an element of sweetness in it from the first; and if so this must point to a future when this sadness itself shall pass away. The author of the Epistle to the Hebrews argues on these lines when he draws the conclusion from the repeated disappointments of the hopes of Israel in conjunction with the repeated promises of God that "there remaineth therefore a rest for the people of God."[1] Instincts are God's promises written in the Book of Nature. Seeing that our deepest instincts are not satisfied by any of the common experiences of life, they must point to some higher satisfaction.

Here we are brought to the explanation of the disappointment itself. We must confess, in the first instance, that it arises from the perverse habit of looking for satisfaction in objects that are too low, objects that are unworthy of human nature. This is one of the

[1] Heb. iv. 9.

strongest evidences of a fall. The more mind and heart are corrupted by sin the more will hope be dragged down to inferior things. But the story does not end at this point. God is educating us through illusions. If all our aspirations were fulfilled on earth we should cease to hope for what was higher than earth. Hope is purged and elevated by the discovery of the vanity of its pursuits.

These considerations will be confirmed when we follow the elegist in his treatment of the disappointment of the second ground of hope, that which was found in the royalist's confidence in his sovereign. The poetic account of the events which ended in the capture of Zedekiah seems to consist in a blending of metaphor with history. The image of the chase underlies the whole description. It has been pointed out that with the narrowness of eastern streets and the simplicity of the weapons of ancient warfare, it would be impossible for the Chaldæans to pick out their victims and shoot them down from outside the walls. But when they had effected an entrance they would not simply make the streets dangerous, for then they would be breaking into the houses where the people are here supposed to be hiding. The language seems more fit for the description of a faction fight, such as often occurred in Paris at the time of the French Revolution, than an account of the sack of a city by a foreign enemy. But the hunting image is in the poet's mind, and the whole picture is coloured by it. After the siege the fugitives are pursued over the mountains. Taking the route across the Mount of Olives and so down to the Jordan, that which David had followed in his flight from Absalom, they would soon find themselves in a difficult wilderness country. They had despaired of their lives in the city, exclaiming: "Our end is near, our days are fulfilled; for our end is come."[1] Now they are in sore extremities. The swift pursuit suggests Jeremiah's image of the eagles on the wing overtaking their quarry. "Behold, he shall come up as clouds," said the prophet, "and his chariots shall be as the whirlwind; his horses are swifter than eagles."[2] There was no possibility of escape from such persistent foes. At the same time, ambuscades were in waiting among the many caves that honeycomb these limestone mountains—in the district where the traveller in the parable of "The good Samaritan" fell among thieves. The king himself was taken like a hunted animal caught in a trap, though, as we learn from the history, not till he had reached Jericho.[3]

The language in which Zedekiah is described is singularly strong. He is "the breath of our nostrils, the anointed of the Lord." The hope of the fugitives had been "to live under his shadow among the nations."[4] It is startling to find such words applied to so weak and worthless a ruler. It cannot be the expression of sycophancy; for the king and his kingdom had disappeared before the elegy was written. Zedekiah was not so bad as some of his predecessors. Like Louis XVI., he reaped the long accumulating retribution of the sins of his ancestors. Yet after making due allowance for the exuberance of the Oriental style, we must feel that the language is out of proportion to the possibilities of the most courtly devotion of the time. Evidently the kingly idea means more than the prosaic personality of any particular monarch. The romantic enthusiasm of Cavaliers and Nonjurors for

---

[1] iv. 18.
[2] Jer. iv. 13.
[3] 2 Kings xxv. 4, 5; Jer. xxxix. 4, 5.
[4] iv. 20.

the Stuarts was not to be accounted for by the merits and attractions of the various successive sovereigns and pretenders towards whom it was directed. The doctrine of the Divine right of kings is always associated with vague thoughts of power and glory that are never realised in history. This is most strikingly evident in the Hebrew conception of the status and destiny of the line of David. But in that one supreme case of devotion to royalty the dream of the ages ultimately came to be fulfilled, and more than fulfilled, though in a very different manner from the anticipation of the Jews. There is something pathetic in the last shred of hope to which the fugitives were clinging. They had lost their homes, their city, their land ; yet even in exile they |clung to the idea that they might keep together under the protection of their fallen king. It was a delusion. But the strange faith in the destiny of the Davidic line that here passes into fanaticism is the seed-bed of the Messianic ideas which constitute the most wonderful part of Old Testament prophecy. By a blind but divinely guided instinct the Jews were led to look through the failure of their hopes on to the appointed time when One should come who only could give them satisfaction.

CHAPTER XXI

THE DEBT OF GUILT EXTINGUISHED

iv. 21, 22

ONE after another the vain hopes of the Jews melt in mists of sorrow. But just as the last of these flickering lights is disappearing a gleam of consolation breaks out from another quarter, like the pale yellow streak that may sometimes be seen low on the western sky of a stormy day just before nightfall, indicating that the setting sun is behind the clouds, although its dying rays are too feeble to penetrate them. Hope is scarcely the word for so faint a sign of comfort as this melancholy fourth elegy affords in lifting the curtain of gloom for one brief moment; but the bare, negative relief which the prospect of an end to the accumulation of new calamities offers is a welcome change in itself, besides being a hint that the tide may be on the turn.

It is quite characteristic of our poet's sombre tones that even in an attempt to touch on brighter ideas than usually occupy his thoughts, he should illustrate the improving prospects of Israel by setting them in contrast to a sardonic description of the fate of Edom. This neighbouring nation is addressed in the time of her elation over the fall of Jerusalem. The extension of her territory to the land of Uz in Arabia—Job's country—is mentioned to show that she is in a position of exceptional prosperity. The poet mockingly encourages the jealous people to "rejoice and be glad" at the fate of their rival. The irony of his language is evident from the fact that he immediately proceeds to pronounce the doom of Edom. The cup of God's wrath that Israel has been made to drink shall pass to her also; and she shall drink deeply of it till she is intoxicated and, like Noah, makes herself an object of shame. Thus will God visit the daughter of Edom with the punishment of her sins. The writer says that God will *discover* them. He does not mean by this phrase that God will find them out. They were never hidden from God; there are no discoveries for Him to make concerning any of us, because He knows all about us every moment of our lives. The phrase stands in opposition to the common Hebrew expression for the forgiveness of sins. When sins are forgiven they are said to be covered; therefore when they are said to be uncovered it is as though we were told that God does the reverse of forgiving them—strips them of every rag of apology, lays them bare. That is their condemnation. Nothing is more ugly than a naked sin.

The selection of this one neighbour of the Jews for special attention is accounted for by what contemporary prophets tell us concerning the behaviour of the Edomites when Jerusalem fell. They flew like vultures to a carcass. Ezekiel writes: "Thus saith the Lord God, Because that Edom hath dealt against the house of Judah by taking vengeance, and hath greatly offended, and revenged himself upon them; therefore thus saith the Lord God, I will stretch out Mine hand upon Edom, and will cut off man and beast from it, and I will make it desolate from Teman; even unto Dedan shall they fall by the sword. And I will lay My vengeance upon Edom by the hand of My people Israel, and they shall do in Edom according to Mine anger and according to My fury, and they shall know My vengeance, saith the Lord God."[1] Isaiah xxxiv. is devoted to a vivid description of the coming punishment of Edom. This race of rough mountaineers had seldom been on friendly terms with their Hebrew neighbours. Nations, like individuals, do not always find it easy to avoid quarrels with those who are closest to them. Neither blood relationship nor commerce prevents the outbreak of hostilities in a situation that gives many occasions for mutual jealousy. For centuries France and England, which should be the best friends if proximity generated friendship, regarded one another as natural enemies. Germany is even a nearer neighbour to France than England is, and the frontiers of the two great nations are studded with forts. It does not appear that the extension of the means of communication among the different countries is likely to close the doors of the temple of Janus. The greatest problem of sociology is to discover the secret of living in crowded communities among a variety of conflicting interests without any injustice, or any friction arising from the juxtaposition of different classes. It is far easier to keep the peace among backwoodsmen who live fifty miles apart in lonely forests. Therefore it is not a surprising thing that there were bitter feuds between Israel and Edom. But at the time of the Babylonian invasion these had taken a peculiarly odious turn on the side of the southern people, one that was doubly offensive. The various tribes whom the huge

---

[1] Ezek. xxv. 12—14.

Babylonian empire was swallowing up with insatiable greed should have forgotten their mutual differences in face of their common danger. Besides, it was a cowardly thing for Edom to follow the example of the Bedouin robbers, who hovered on the rear of the great armies of conquest like scavengers. To settle old debts by wreaking vengeance on a fallen rival in the hour of her humiliation was not the way to win the honours of war. Even to a calm student of history in later ages this long-past event shews an ugly aspect. How maddening must it have been to the victims! Accordingly we are not astonished to see that the doom of the Edomites is pronounced by Hebrew prophets with undisguised satisfaction. The proud inhabitants of the rock cities, the wonderful remains of which amaze the traveller in the present day, had earned the severe humiliation so exultingly described.

In all this it is very plain that the author of the Lamentations, like the Hebrew prophets generally, had an unhesitating belief in a supremacy of God over foreign nations that was quite as effective as His supremacy over Israel. On the other hand, iniquity is ascribed to Israel in exactly the same terms that are applied to foreign nations. Jehovah is not imagined to be a mere tribal divinity like the Moabite Chemosh; and the Jews are not held to be so much His favourites that the treatment measured out to them in punishment of sin is essentially different from that accorded to their neighbours.

To Israel, however, the doom of Edom is a sign of the return of mercy. It is not merely that the passion of revenge is thereby satisfied—a poor consolation, even if allowable. But in the overthrow of their most annoying tormentor the oppressed people are at once liberated from a very appreciable part of their troubles. At the same time, they see in this event a clear sign that they are not selected for a solitary example of the vengeance of heaven against sin; that would have been indeed a hard destiny. But above all, this occurrence affords a reassuring sign that God who is thus punishing their enemies is ending the severe discipline of the Jews. In the very middle of the description of the coming doom of Edom we meet with an announcement of the conclusion of the long penance of Israel. This singular arrangement cannot be accidental; nor can it have been resorted to only to obtain the accentuation of contrast which we have seen is highly valued by the elegist. Since it is while contemplating the Divine treatment of the most spiteful of the enemies of Israel that we are led to see the termination of the chastisement of the Jews, we may infer that possibly the process in the mind of the poet took the same course. If so, the genesis of prophecy which is usually hidden from view here seems to come nearer the surface.

The language in which the improving prospect of the Jews is announced is somewhat obscure; but the drift of its meaning is not difficult to trace. The word rendered "punishment of iniquity" in our English versions—Revised as well as Authorised—at the beginning of the twenty-second verse, is one which in its original sense means simply "iniquity"; and in fact it is so translated further down in the same verse, where it occurs a second time, and where the parallel word "sins" seems to settle the meaning. But if it has this meaning when applied to Edom in the later part of the verse is it not reasonable to suppose that it must also have it when applied to the daughter of Zion in an immediately preceding clause? The Septuagint and

Vulgate Versions give it as "iniquity" in both cases. And so does a suggestion in the margin of the Revised Version. But if we accept this rendering, which commends itself to us as verbally most correct, we cannot reconcile it with the evident intention of the writer. The promise that God will no more carry His people away into captivity, which follows as an echo of the opening thought of the verse, certainly points to a cessation of punishment. Then the very idea that the iniquity of the Jews is accomplished is quite out of place here. What could we take it to mean? To say that the Jews had sinned to the full, had carried out all their evil intentions, had put no restraint on their wickedness, is to give a verdict which should carry the heaviest condemnation; it would be absurd to bring this forward as an introduction to a promise of a reprieve. It would be less incongruous to suppose the phrase to mean, as is suggested in the margin of the Revised Version, that the sin has come to an end, has ceased. That might be taken as a ground for the punishment to be stayed also. But it would introduce a refinement of theology out of keeping with the extreme simplicity of the ideas of these elegies. Moreover, in another place, as we have seen already,[1] the word "sins" seems to be used for the *punishment of sins*.[2] We have also met with the idea of the *fulfilment*, literally the *finishing*, of God's word of warning, with the necessary suggestion that there is to be no more infliction of the evil threatened.[3] Therefore, if it were not for the reappearance of the word in dispute where the primary meaning of it seems to be necessitated by the context, we should have no hesitation in

---

[1] Page 269. [2] iii. 39. [3] ii. 17.

taking it here in its secondary sense, as the punishment of iniquity. The German word *schuld*, with its double signification—*debt* and *guilt*—has been suggested as a happy rendering of the Hebrew original in both places; and perhaps this is the best that can be proposed. The debt of the Jews is paid; that of the Edomites has yet to be exacted.

We are brought then to the conclusion that the elegist here announces the extinction of the Jews' debt of guilt. Accordingly they are told that God will no more carry them away into captivity. This promise has occasioned much perplexity to people concerned for the literal exactness of Scripture. Some have tried to get it applied to the time subsequent to the destruction of Jerusalem by the Romans, after which, it is said, the Jews were never again removed from their land. That is about the most extravagant instance of all the subterfuges to which literalists are driven when in a sore strait to save their theory. Certainly the Jews have not been exiled again—not since the last time. They could not be carried away from their land once more, for the simple reason that they have never been restored to it. Strictly speaking, it may be said indeed, something of the kind occurred on the suppression of the revolt under *Bar-cochba* in the second century of the Christian era. But all theories apart, it is contrary to the discovered facts of prophecy to ascribe to the inspired messengers of God the purpose of supplying exact predictions concerning the events of history in far-distant ages. Their immediate message was for their own day, although we have found that the lessons it contains are suitable for all times. What consolation would it be for the fugitives from the ravaging hosts of Nebuchadnezzar to know that six hundred years later an end would come to the successive acts of conquerors in driving the Jews from Jerusalem, even if they were not told that this would be because at that far-off time there would commence one long exile lasting for two thousand years? But if the words of the elegist are for immediate use as a consolation to his contemporaries, it is unreasonable to press their negative statement in an absolute sense, so as to make it serve as a prediction concerning all future ages. It is enough for these sufferers to learn that the last of the series of successive banishments of Jews from their land by the Babylonian government has at length taken place.

But with this information there comes a deeper truth. The debt is paid. Yet this is only at the commencement of the Captivity. Two generations must live in exile before the restoration will be possible. There is no reference to that event, which did not take place till the Babylonian power had been utterly destroyed by Cyrus. Still the deliverance into exile following the terrible sufferings of the siege and the subsequent flight is taken as the final act in the drama of doom. The long years of the captivity, though they constituted an invaluable period of discipline, did not bring any fresh kind of punishment at all comparable with the chastisements already inflicted.

Thus we are brought face to face with the question of the satisfaction of punishment. We have no right to look to a single line of a poem for a final settlement of the abstract problem itself. Whether, as St. Augustine maintained, every sin is of infinite guilt because it is an offence against an infinite Being; whether, therefore, it would take eternity to pay the debts contracted during one short life on earth, and other questions of the same character, cannot be answered one way or the other from the words before us. Still there are certain aspects of the problem of human guilt to which our attention is here drawn.

In the first place, we must make a distinction between the national punishment of national wickedness and the personal consequences of personal wrongdoing. The nation only exists on earth, and it can only be punished on earth. Then the nation outlasts generations of individual lives, and so remains on earth long enough for the harvest of its actions to be reaped. Thus national guilt may be wiped out while the separate accounts of individual men and women still remain unsettled. Next we must remember that the exaction of the uttermost farthing is not the supreme end of the Divine government of the world. To suggest any such idea is to assimilate this perfect government to that of corrupt Oriental monarchies, the chief object of which in dealing with their provinces seems to have been to drain them of tribute. The payment of the debt of guilt in punishment, though just and necessary, cannot be a matter of any satisfaction to God. Again, when, as in the case now before us, the punishment of sin is a chastisement for the reformation of the corrupt nation on whom it is inflicted, it may not be necessary to make it exactly equivalent to the guilt for which it is the remedy rather than the payment. Lastly, even when we think of the punishment as direct retribution, we cannot say what means God may provide for the satisfaction of the due claims of justice. The second Isaiah saw in the miseries inflicted upon the innocent at this very time, a vicarious suffering by the endurance of which pardon was extended to the guilty;[1] and from the days of the

---

[1] Isa. liii. 4–6.

Apostles, Christians have recognised in his language on this subject the most striking prophecy the Bible contains concerning the atonement wrought by our Lord in His sufferings and death. When we put all these considerations together, and also call to our assistance the New Testament teachings about the character of God and the object of the work of Jesus Christ, we shall see that there are various possibilities lying behind the thought of the end of chastisement which no bare statement of the abstract relations of sin, guilt, and doom would indicate.

It may be objected that all such ideas as those just expressed tend to generate superficial views of sin. Possibly they may be employed so as to encourage this tendency. But if so, it will only be by misinterpreting and abusing them. Certainly the elegist does not belittle the rigour of the Divine chastisement. It must not be forgotten that the phrase which gives rise to these ideas concerning the debt of guilt occurs in the doleful Book of Lamentations, and at the close of an elegy that bewails the awful fate of Jerusalem in the strongest language. But in point of fact it is not the severity of punishment, beyond a certain degree, but the certainty of it that most affects the mind when contemplating the prospect of doom. Not only does the imagination fail to grasp that which is immeasurably vast in the pictures presented to it, but even the reason rises in revolt and questions the possibility of such torments, or the conscience ventures to protest against what appears to be unjust. In any of these cases the effect of the menace is neutralised by its very extravagance.

On the other hand, we have St. Paul's teaching about the goodness of God that leads us to repentance.[1] Thus we understand how it can be said that Christ—who is the most perfect revelation of God's goodness—was raised up to give "*repentance* to Israel" as well as "remission of sins."[2] It is at Calvary, not at Sinai, that sin looks most black. When a man sees his guilt in the light of his Saviour's love he is in no mood to apologise for it or to minimise his ill desert. If he then contemplates the prospect of the full payment of the debt it is with a feeling of the impossibility of ever achieving so stupendous a task. The punishment from which he would revolt as an injustice if it were held over him in a threat now presents itself to him of its own accord as something quite right and reasonable. He cannot find words strong enough to characterise his guilt, as he lies at the foot of the cross in absolute self-abasement. There is no occasion to fear that such a man will become careless about sin if he is comforted by a vision of hope. This is just what he needs to enable him to rise up and accept the forgiveness in the strength of which he may begin the toilsome ascent towards a better life.

---

[1] Rom. ii. 4.   [2] Acts v. 31.

CHAPTER XXII

AN APPEAL FOR GOD'S COMPASSION

v. 1-10

UNLIKE its predecessors, the fifth and last elegy is not an acrostic. There is little to be gained by a discussion of the various conjectures that have been put forth to account for this change of style: as that the *crescendo* movement which reached its climax in the third elegy was followed by a *decrescendo* movement, the conclusion of which became more prosaic; that the feelings of the poet having been calmed down during the composition of the main part of his work, he did not require the restraints of an exceptionally artificial method any longer; that such a method was not so becoming in a prayer to God as it had been in the utterance of a lament. In answer to these suggestions, it may be remarked that some of the choicest poetry in the book occurs at the close of this last chapter, that the acrostic was taken before as a sign that the writer had his feelings well under command, and that prayers appear repeatedly in the alphabetical poems. Is it not enough to say that in all probability the elegies were composed on different occasions, and that when they were put together it was natural that one in which the author had not chosen to bind himself down to the peculiarly rigorous method employed in the rest of the book should have been placed at the end? Even here we have a reminiscence of the acrostic; for the poem consists of twenty-two verses—the number of the letters in the Hebrew alphabet.

It is to be observed, further, as regards the form of this elegy, that the author now adopts the parallelism which is the characteristic note of most Hebrew poetry. The Revisers break up the poem into two-line verses. But, more strictly considered, each verse consists of one long line divided into two mutually balancing parts. Thus, while the third elegy consists of triplets, and the fourth of couplets, the fifth is still more brief, with its single line verses. In fact, while the ideas and sentiments are still elegiac and very like those found in the rest of the book, in structure this poem is more assimilated to the poetry contained in other parts of the Bible.

From beginning to end the fifth elegy is directly addressed to God. Brief ejaculatory prayers are frequent in the earlier poems, and the third elegy contains two longer appeals to God; but this last poem differs from the others in being entirely a prayer. And yet it does not consist of a string of petitions. It is a meditation in the presence of God, or, more accurately described, an account of the condition of the Jews spread out before God in order to secure His compassion. In the freedom and fulness of his utterance the poet reveals himself as a man who is not unfamiliar with the habit of prayer. It is of course only the delusion of the Pharisees to suppose that a prayer is valuable in proportion to its length. But on the other hand, it is clear that a person who is unaccustomed to prayer halts and stumbles because he does not feel at home in addressing

God. It is only with a friend that we can converse in perfect freedom. One who has treated God as a stranger will be necessarily stiff and constrained in the Divine presence. It is not enough to assure such a person that God is His Father. A son may feel peculiarly uncomfortable with his own father if he has lived long in separation and alienation from his home. Freedom in the expression of confidences is a sure measure of the extent to which friendship is carried. Of course some people are more reserved than others; but still as in the same person his different degrees of openness or reserve with different people will mark his relative intimacy of friendship with them, so when a man has long accustomed himself to believe in the presence and sympathy of God, and has cultivated the habit of communing with his Father in heaven, his prayers will not be confined to set petitions; he will tell his Father whatever is in his heart. This we have already seen was what the elegist had learnt to do. But in the last of his poems he expresses more explicit and continuous confidences. He will have God know everything.

The prayer opens with a striking phrase—" Remember, O Lord," etc. The miserable condition of the Jews suggests to the imagination, if not to the reason, that God must have forgotten His people. It cannot be supposed that the elegist conceived of his God as Elijah mockingly described their silent, unresponsive divinity to the frantic priests of Baal, or that he imagined that Jehovah was really indifferent, after the manner of the denizens of the Epicurean Olympus. Nevertheless, neither philosophy nor even theology wholly determines the form of an earnest man's prayers. In practice it is impossible not to speak according to appearances. The aspect of affairs is sometimes such as to force home the feeling that God must have deserted the sufferer, or how could He have permitted the misery to continue unchecked? A dogmatic statement of the Divine omniscience, although it may not be disputed, will not remove the painful impression, nor will the most absolute demonstration of the goodness of God, of His love and faithfulness; because the overwhelming influence of things visible and tangible so fully occupies the mind that it has not room to receive unseen, spiritual realities. Therefore, though not to the reason still to the feelings, it is as though God had indeed forgotten His children in their deep distress.

Under such circumstances the first requisite is the assurance that God should remember the sufferers whom He appears to be neglecting. He never really neglects any of His creatures, and His attention is the all-sufficient security that deliverance must be at hand. But this is a truth that does not satisfy us in the bare statement of it. It must be absorbed, and permitted to permeate wide regions of consciousness, in order that it may be an actual power in the life. That, however, is only the subjective effect of the thought of the Divine remembrance. The poet is thinking of external actions. Evidently the aim of his prayer is to secure the attention of God as a sure preliminary to a Divine interposition. But even with this end in view the fact that God remembers is enough.

In appealing for God's attention the elegist first makes mention of the *reproach* that has come upon Israel. This reference to humiliation rather than to suffering as the primary ground of complaint may be accounted for by the fact that the glory of God is frequently taken as a reason for the blessing of His people. That is done for His "name's sake."[1] Then the ruin of the Jews is derogatory to the honour of their Divine Protector. The peculiar relation of Israel to God also underlies the complaint of the second verse, in which the land is described as "our inheritance," with an evident allusion to the idea that it was received as a donation from God, not acquired in any ordinary human fashion. A great wrong has been done, apparently in contravention of the ordinance of Heaven. The Divine inheritance has been turned over to strangers. The very homes of the Jews are in the hands of aliens. From their property the poet passes on to the condition of the persons of the sufferers. The Jews are orphans; they have lost their fathers, and their mothers are widows. This seems to indicate that the writer considered himself to belong to the younger generation of the Jews,—that, at all events, he was not an elderly man. But it is not easy to determine how far his words are to be read literally. No doubt the slaughter of the war had carried off many heads of families, and left a number of women and children in the condition here described. But the language of poetry would allow of a more general interpretation. All the Jews felt desolate as orphans and widows. Perhaps there is some thought of the loss of God, the supreme Father of Israel. Whether this was in the mind of the poet or not, the cry to God to remember His people plainly implies that His sheltering presence was not now consciously experienced. Our Lord foresaw that His departure would smite His disciples with orphanage if He did not return to them.[2] Men who have hardened themselves in a

---

[1] For example, Jer. xiv. 7.   [2] John xiv. 18.

state of separation from God fail to recognise their forlorn condition; but that is no occasion for congratulation, for the family that never misses its father can never have known the joys of true home life. Children of God's house can have no greater sorrow than to lose their heavenly Father's presence.

A peculiarly annoying injustice to which the Jews were subjected by their harsh masters consisted in the fact that they were compelled to buy permission to collect firewood from their own land and to draw water from their own wells.[1] The elegist deplores this grievance as part of the reproach of his people. The mere pecuniary fine of a series of petty exactions is not the chief part of the evil. It is not the pain of flesh that rouses a man's indignation on receiving a slap in the face; it is the insult that stings. There was more than insult in this grinding down of the conquered nation; and the indignities to which the Jews were subjected were only too much in accord with the facts of their fallen state. This particular exaction was an unmistakable symptom of the abject servitude into which they had been reduced.

The series of illustrations of the degradation of Israel seems to be arranged somewhat in the order of time and in accordance with the movements of the people. Thus, after describing the state of the Jews in their own land, the poet next follows the fortunes of his people in exile. There is no mercy for them in their flight. The words in which the miseries of this time are referred to are somewhat obscure. The phrase in the Authorised Version, "Our necks are under persecution,"[2] is rendered by the Revisers, "Our pursuers

---

[1] v. 4.   [2] v. 5.

are upon our necks." It would seem to mean that the hunt is so close that fugitives are on the point of being captured; or perhaps that they are made to bow their heads in defeat as their captors seize them. But a proposed emendation substitutes the word "yoke" for "pursuers." If we may venture to accept this as a conjectural improvement—and later critics indulge themselves in more freedom in the handling of the text than was formerly permitted—the line points to the burden of captivity. The next line favours this idea, since it dwells on the utter weariness of the miserable fugitives. There is no rest for them. Palestine is a difficult country to travel in, and the wilderness south and east of Jerusalem is especially trying. The hills are steep and the roads rocky; for a multitude of famine-stricken men, women, and children, driven out over this homeless waste, a country that taxes the strength of the traveller for pleasure could not but be most exhausting. But the worst weariness is not muscular. Tired souls are more weary than tired bodies. The yoke of shame and servitude is more crushing than any amount of physical labour. On the other hand the yoke of Jesus is easy not because little work is expected of Christians, but for the more satisfactory reason that, being given in exchange for the fearful burden of sin, it is borne willingly and even joyously as a badge of honour.

Finally, in their exile the Jews are not free from molestation. In order to obtain bread they must abase themselves before the people of the land. The fugitives in the south must do homage to the Egyptians; the captives in the east to the Assyrians.[1] Here, then, at

---

[1] v. 6.

the very last stage of the series of miseries, shame and humiliation are the principal grievances deplored. At every point there is a reproach, and to this feature of the whole situation God's attention is especially directed.

Now the elegist turns aside to a reflection on the cause of all this evil. It is attributed to the sins of previous generations. The present sufferers are bearing the iniquities of their fathers. Here several points call for a brief notice. In the first place, the very form of the language is significant. What is meant by the phrase to *bear iniquity*? Strange mystical meanings are sometimes imported into it, such as an actual transference of sin, or at least a taking over of guilt. This is asserted of the sin-offering in the law, and then of the sin-bearing of Jesus Christ on the cross. It would indicate shallow ways of thinking to say that the simple and obvious meaning of an expression in one place is the only signification it is ever capable of conveying. A common process in the development of language is for words and phrases that originally contained only plain physical meanings to acquire in course of time deeper and more spiritual associations. We can never fathom all that is meant by the statement that Christ "His own self bare our sins in His body upon the tree."[1] Still it is well to observe that there is a plain sense in which the Hebrew phrase was used. It is clear in the case now before us, at all events, that the poet had no mystical ideas in mind. When he said that the children bore the sins of their fathers he simply meant that they reaped the consequences of those sins. The expression can mean nothing else here. It would be well, then, to remember this very simple explanation

---

[1] 1 Peter ii. 24.

of it when we are engaged with the discussion of other and more difficult passages in which it occurs.

But if the language is perfectly unambiguous the doctrine it implies is far from being easy to accept. On the face of it, it seems to be glaringly unjust. And yet whether we can reconcile it with our ideas of what is equitable or not there can be no doubt that it states a terrible truth; we gain nothing by blinking the fact. It was perfectly clear to people of the time of the captivity that they were suffering for the persistent misconduct of their ancestors during a succession of generations. Long before this the Jews had been warned of the danger of continued rebellion against the will of God. Thus the nation had been treasuring up wrath for the day of wrath. The forbearance which permitted the first offenders to die in peace before the day of reckoning would assume another character for he unhappy generation on whose head the long-pent-up flood at length descended. It is not enough to urge in reply that the threat of the second commandment to visit the sins of the fathers upon the children to the third and fourth generation was for *them that hate God;* because it is not primarily their own conduct, but the sins of their ancestors, in which the reason for punishing the later generations is found. If these sins were exactly repeated the influence of their parents would make the personal guilt of the later offenders less, not more, than that of the originators of the evil line. Besides, in the case of the Jews there had been some amendment. Josiah's reformation had been very disappointing; and yet the awful wickedness of the reign of Manasseh had not been repeated. The gross idolatry of the earlier times and the cruelties of Moloch worship had disappeared. At least, it must be admitted, they were no longer common practices of court and people. The publication of so great an inspired work as the Book of Deuteronomy had wrought a marked effect on the religion and morals of the Jews. The age which was called upon to receive the payment for the national sins was not really so wicked as some of the ages that had earned it. The same thing is seen in private life. There is nothing that more distresses the author of these poems than the sufferings of innocent children in the siege of Jerusalem. We are frequently confronted with evidences of the fact that the vices of parents inflict poverty, dishonour, and disease on their families. This is just what the elegist means when he writes of children bearing the iniquities of their fathers. The fact cannot be disputed.

Often as the problem that here starts up afresh has been discussed, no really satisfactory solution of it has ever been forthcoming. We must admit that we are face to face with one of the most profound mysteries of providence. But we may detect some glints of light in the darkness. Thus, as we have seen on the occasion of a previous reference to this question,[1] the fundamental principle in accordance with which these perplexing results are brought about is clearly one which on the whole makes for the highest welfare of mankind. That one generation should hand on the fruit of its activity to another is essential to the very idea of progress. The law of heredity and the various influences that go to make up the evil results in the case before us work powerfully for good under other circumstances; and that the balance is certainly on the side of good, is proved by the fact

---

[1] Page 151.

that the world is moving forward, not backward, as would be the case if the balance of hereditary influence was on the side of evil. Therefore it would be disastrous in the extreme for the laws that pass on the punishment of sin to successive generations to be abolished; the abolition of them would stop the chariot of progress. Then we have seen that the solidarity of the race necessitates both mutual influences in the present and the continuance of influence from one age to another. The great unit *Man* is far more than the sum of the little units *men*. We must endure the disadvantages of a system which is so essential to the good of man. This, however, is but to fall back on the Leibnitzian theory of the best of all *possible* worlds. It is not an absolute vindication of the justice of whatever happens—an attainment quite beyond our reach.

But another consideration may shed a ray of light on the problem. The bearing of the sins of others is for the highest advantage of the sufferers. It is difficult to think of any more truly elevating sorrows. They resemble our Lord's passion; and of Him it was said that He was made perfect through suffering.[1] Without doubt Israel benefited immensely from the discipline of the Captivity, and we may be sure that the better "remnant" was most blessed by this experience although it was primarily designed to be the chastisement of the more guilty. The Jews were regenerated by the baptism of fire. Then they could not ultimately complain of the ordeal that issued in so much good.

It is to be observed, however, that there were two currents of thought with regard to this problem.

---

[1] Heb. ii. 10.

While most men held to the ancient orthodoxy, some rose in revolt against the dogma expressed in the proverb, "The fathers have eaten sour grapes, and the children's teeth are set on edge." Just at this time the prophet Ezekiel was inspired to lead the Jews to a more just conception, with the declaration: "As I live, saith the Lord God, ye shall not have occasion any more to use this proverb in Israel. Behold, all souls are mine; as the soul of the father, so also the soul of the son is mine: *the soul that sinneth, it shall die.*"[1] This was the new doctrine. But how could it be made to square with the facts? By strong faith in it the disciples of the advanced school might bring themselves to believe that the course of events which had given rise to the old idea would be arrested. But if so they would be disappointed; for the world goes on in its unvarying way. Happily, as Christians, we may look for the final solution in a future life, when all wrongs shall be righted. It is much to know that in the great hereafter each soul will be judged simply according to its own character.

In conclusion, as we follow out the course of the elegy, we find the same views maintained that were presented earlier. The idea of ignominy is still harped upon. The Jews complain that they are under the rule of servants.[2] Satraps were really the Great King's slaves, often simply household favourites promoted to posts of honour. Possibly the Jews were put in the power of inferior servants. The petty tyranny of such persons would be all the more persistently annoying, if, as often happens, servility to superiors had bred insolence in bullying the weak; and there was no appeal from the

---

[1] Ezek. xviii. 3, 4.   [2] v. 8.

vexatious tyranny. This complaint would seem to apply to the people left in the land, for it is the method of the elegist to bring together scenes from different places as well as scenes from different times in one picture of concentrated misery. The next point is that food is only procured at the risk of life "because of the sword of the wilderness;"[1] which seems to mean that the country is so disorganised that hordes of Bedouins hover about and attack the peasants when they venture abroad to gather in their harvest. The fever of famine is seen on these wretched people; their faces burn as though they had been scorched at an oven.[2] Such is the general condition of the Jews, Such is the scene on which God is begged to look down!

---

[1] v. 9.   [2] v. 10.

CHAPTER XXIII

SIN AND SHAME

v. 11-18

THE keynote of the fifth elegy is struck in its opening verse when the poet calls upon God to remember the *reproach* that has been cast upon His people. The preceding poems dwelt on the sufferings of the Jews; here the predominant thought is that of the humiliations to which they have been subjected. The shame of Israel and the sin which had brought it on are now set forth with point and force. If, as some think, the literary grace of the earlier compositions is not fully sustained in the last chapter of Lamentations —although in parts of it the feeling and imagination and art all touch the high-water mark—it cannot be disputed that the spiritual tone of this elegy indicates an advance on the four earlier poems. We have sometimes met with wild complaints, fierce recriminations, deep and terrible curses that seem to require some apology if they are to be justified. Nothing of the kind ruffles the course of this faultless meditation. There is not a single jarring note from beginning to end, not one phrase calling for explanation by reference to the limited ideas of Old Testament times or to the passion excited by cruelty, insult, and tyranny, not a line that reads painfully even in the clear light of the teachings of Jesus Christ. The vilest outrages are deplored; and yet, strange to say, no word of vindictiveness towards the perpetrators escapes the lips of the mourning patriot! How is this? The sin of the people has been confessed before as the source of all their misery; but since with it shame is now associated as the principal item in their affliction, we can see in this fresh development a decided advance towards higher views of the whole position.

May we not take this characteristic of the concluding chapter of the Book of Lamentations to be an indication of progress in the spiritual experience of its author? Perhaps it is to be partially explained by the fact that the poem throughout consists of a prayer addressed directly to God. The wildest, darkest passions of the soul cannot live in the atmosphere of prayer. When men say of the persecutor, "Behold he prayeth," it is certain that he cannot any longer be "breathing threatening and slaughter." Even the feelings of the persecuted must be calmed in the presence of God. The serenity of the surroundings of the mercy-seat cannot but communicate itself to the feverish soul of the suppliant. To draw near to God is to escape from the tumults of earth and breathe the still, pure air of heaven. He is Himself so calm and strong, so completely sufficient for every emergency, that we begin to enter into His rest as soon as we approach His presence. All unawares, perhaps unsought, the peace of God steals into the heart of the man who brings his troubles to his Father in prayer.

Then the reflections that accompany prayer tend in the same direction. In the light of God things begin to assume their true proportions. We discover that our first fierce outcries were unreasonable, that we had been simply maddened by pain so that our judgment had been confused. A psalmist tells us how he understood the course of events which had previously perplexed him by taking his part in the worship of the sanctuary, when referring to his persecutors, the prosperous wicked, he exclaims, "Then understood I their end."[1] In drawing near to God we learn that vengeance is God's prerogative, that He will repay; therefore we can venture to be still and leave the vindication of our cause in His unerring hands. But, further, the very thirst for revenge is extinguished in the presence of God, and that in several ways: we see that the passion is wrong in itself; we begin to make some allowance for the offender; we learn to own kinship with the man while condemning his wickedness; above all, we awake to a keen consciousness of our own guilt.

This, however, is not a sufficient explanation of the remarkable change in tone that we have observed in the fifth elegy. The earlier poems contain prayers, one of which degenerates into a direct imprecation.[2] If the poet had wholly given himself to prayer in that case as he has done here very possibly his tone would have been mollified. Still, we must look to other factors for a complete explanation. The writer is himself one of the suffering people. In describing their wrongs he is narrating his own, for he is "the man who has seen affliction." Thus he has long been a pupil in the school of adversity. There is no school at which a docile pupil learns so much. This man has graduated in sorrow. It is not surprising that he is not just what he was when he matriculated. We must not press the analogy too far, because, as we have seen, there is good

---

[1] Psalm lxxiii. 17.   [2] Lam. iii. 65.

reason to believe that none of the elegies were written until some time after the occurrence of the calamities to which they refer, that therefore they all represent the fruit of long brooding over their theme. And yet we may allow an interval to have elapsed between the composition of the earlier ones and that of the poem with which the book closes. This period of longer continued reflection may have been utilised in the process of clearing and refining the ideas of the poet. It is not merely that the lessons of adversity impart fresh knowledge or a truer way of looking at life and its fortunes. They do the higher work of education—they develop culture. This, indeed, is the greatest advantage to be gained by the stern discipline of sorrow. The soul that has the grace to use it aright is purged and pruned, chastened and softened, lifted to higher views, and at the same time brought down from self-esteem to deep humiliation. Here we have a partial explanation of the mystery of suffering. This poem throws light on the terrible problem by its very existence, by the spirit and character which it exhibits. The calmness and self-restraint of the elegy, while it deepens the pathos of the whole scene, helps us to see as no direct statement would do, that the chastisement of Israel has not been inflicted in vain. There must be good even in the awful miseries here described in such patient language.

The connection of shame with sin in this poem is indirect and along a line which is the reverse of the normal course of experience. The poet does not pass from sin to shame; he proceeds from the thought of shame to that of sin. It is the humiliating condition in which the Jews are found that awakens the idea of the shocking guilt of which this is the consequence. We often have occasion to acknowledge the fatal hindrance of pride to the right working of conscience. A lofty conception of one's own dignity is absolutely inconsistent with a due feeling of guilt. A man cannot be both elated and cast down at the same moment. If his elation is sufficiently sustained from within it will effectually bar the door to the entrance of those humbling thoughts which cannot but accompany an admission of sin. Therefore when this barrier is first removed, and the man is thoroughly humbled, he is open to receive the accusations of conscience. All his fortifications have been flung down. There is nothing to prevent the invading army of accusing thoughts from marching straight in and taking possession of the citadel of his heart.

The elegy takes a turn at the eleventh verse. Up to this point it describes the state of the people generally in their sufferings from the siege and its consequences. But now the poet directs attention to separate classes of people and the different forms of cruelty to which they are severally subjected in a series of intensely vivid pictures. We see the awful fate of matrons and maidens, princes and elders, young men and children. Women are subjected to the vilest abuse, neither reverence for motherhood nor pity for innocence affording the least protection. Men of royal blood and noble birth are killed and their corpses hung up in ignominy—perhaps impaled or crucified in accordance with the vile Babylonian custom. There is no respect for age or office. Neither is there any mercy for youth. In the East grinding is women's work; but, like Samson among the Philistines, the young men of the Jews are put in charge of the mills. The poet seems to indicate that they have to carry the heavy mill-stones in the march of the returning army with the spoils of the sacked city. The children are set to the slave task of Gibeonites. The Hebrew word here translated *children* might stand for young people who had reached adult years.[1] But in the present case the condition is that of immature strength, for the burden of wood they are required to bear is too heavy for them and they stumble under it. This is the scene—outrage for the girls and women, slaughter for the leading men, harsh slavery for the children.

Next, passing from these exact details, the poet again describes the condition of the people more generally, and this time under the image of an interrupted feast, which is introduced by one more reference to the changes that have come upon certain classes. The elders are no longer to be seen at the gate administering the primitive forms of law entrusted to them. The young men are no longer to be heard performing on their musical instruments.[2] Still speaking for the people, the poet declares that the joy of their heart has ceased. Then the aspect of all life must be changed to them. Instead of the gay pictures of dancers in their revelry we have the waiting of mourners. The guest at a feast would be crowned with a garland of flowers. Such was once the appearance of Jerusalem in her merry festivities. But now the garland has fallen from her head.[3]

This imagery is a relief after the terrible realism of the immediately preceding pictures. We cannot bear to look continuously at scenes of agony, nor is it well that we should attempt to do so, because if we

---

[1] v. 13.   [2] v. 14.   [3] v. 15, 16.

could succeed it would only be by becoming callous. Then the final result would be not to excite deeper sympathy, but the very reverse, and at the same time a distinctly lowering and coarsening effect would be produced in us. And yet we may not smother up abuses in order to spare our own feelings. There are evils that must be dragged out to the light in order that they may be execrated, punished, and destroyed. *Uncle Tom's Cabin* broke the back of American slavery before President Lincoln attacked it. Where, then, shall we find the middle position between repulsive realism and guilty negligence? We have the model for this in the Biblical treatment of painful subjects. Scripture never gloats over the details of crimes and vices; yet Scripture never flinches from describing such things in the plainest possible terms. If these subjects are ever to become the theme of art —and art claims the whole of life for her domain— imagination must carry us away to the secondary effects rather than vivify the hideous occurrences themselves. The passage before us affords an excellent illustration of this method. With a few keen, clear strokes the poet sketches in the exact situation. But he shows no disposition to linger on ghastly details. Though he does not shrink from setting them before us in unmistakable truth of form and colour, he hastens to a more ideal treatment of the subject, and relieves us with the imaginary picture of the spoiled banquet. Even Spenser sometimes excites a feeling of positive nausea when he enlarges on some most loathsome picture. It would be unendurable except that the great Elizabethan poet has woven the witchery of his dainty fancy into the fabric of his verse. Thus things can be said in poetry which would be unbearable in prose, because poetry refines with the aid of imagination the tale that it does not shrink from telling quite truly and most forcibly.

The change in the poet's style prepares for another effect. While we are contemplating the exact details of the sufferings of the different classes of outraged citizens, the insult and cruelty and utter abomination of these scenes rouse our indignation against the perpetrators of the foulest crimes, and leave nothing but pity for their victims. It is not in the presence of such events that the sins of Israel can be brought home to the people or even called to mind. The attempt to introduce the thought of them there would seem to be a piece of heartless officiousness. And yet it is most important to perceive the connection between all this misery and the previous misconduct of the Jews which was its real cause. Accordingly intermediate reflections, while they let the scenes of blood and terror recede, touch on the general character of the whole in a way that permits of more heart-searching self-examination. Thus out of the brooding melancholy of this secondary grief we are led to a distinct confession of sin on the part of the people.[1]

This is the main result aimed at throughout the whole course of chastisement. Until it has been reached little good can be effected. When it is attained the discipline has already wrought its greatest work. As we saw at the outset, it is the shame of the situation that awakens a consciousness of guilt. Humbled and penitent, the chastened people are just in the position at which God can meet them in gracious pardon. Strictly speaking, perhaps we should say that this is

---

[1] v. 16.

the position to which the elegist desires to lead them by thus appearing as their spokesman. And yet we should not make too sharp a distinction between the poet and his people. The elegy is not a didactic work; the flavour of its gentle lines would be lost directly they lent themselves to pedagogic ends. It is only just to take the words before us quite directly, as they are written in the first person plural, for a description of the thoughts of at least the group of Jews with whom their author was associated.

The confession of sin implies in the first place a recognition of its existence. This is more than a bare, undeniable recollection that the deed was done. It is possible by a kind of intellectual jugglery even to come to a virtual denial of this fact in one's own consciousness. But to admit the deed is not to admit the sin. The casuistry of self-defence before the court of self-judgment is more subtle than sound, as every one who has found out his own heart must be aware. In this matter "the heart is deceitful above all things."[1] Now it is not difficult to take part in a decorous service where all the congregation are expected to denominate themselves miserable offenders, but it is an entirely different thing to retreat into the silent chamber of our own thought, and there calmly and deliberately, with full consciousness of what the words mean, confess to ourselves, "We have sinned." The sinking of heart, the stinging humiliation, the sense of self-loathing which such an admission produces, are the most miserable experiences in life. The wretchedness of it all is that there is no possibility of escaping the accuser when he is self. We can do nothing but let the shame of the

---

[1] Jer. xvii. 9.

deed burn in the conscience without any mollifying salve—until the healing of Divine forgiveness is received.

But, in the second place, confession of sin goes beyond the secret admission of it by the conscience, as in a case heard *in camerâ*. Chiefly it is a frank avowal of guilt before God. This is treated by St. John as an essential condition of forgiveness by God, when He says, " If we confess our sins, He is faithful and righteous to forgive us our sins, and to cleanse us from all unrighteousness."[1] How far confession should also be made to our fellow-men is a difficult question. In bidding us confess our " faults one to another,"[2] St. James may be simply requiring that when we have done anybody a wrong we should own it to the injured person. The harsh discipline of the white sheet is not found in apostolic times, the brotherly spirit of which is seen in the charity which " covereth a multitude of sins."[3] And yet, on the other hand, the true penitent will always shrink from sailing under false colours. Certainly public offences call for public acknowledgment, and all sin should be so far owned that whether the details are known or not there is no actual deception, no hypocritical pretence at a virtue that is not possessed, no willingness to accept honours that are quite unmerited. Let a man never pretend to be sinless, nay, let him distinctly own himself a sinner, and, in particular, let him not deny or excuse any specific wickedness with which he is justly accused; and then for the rest, " to his own lord he standeth or falleth."[4]

When the elegist follows his confession of sin with

---

[1] 1 John i. 9.
[2] James v. 16.
[3] 1 Peter iv. 8.
[4] Rom. xiv. 4.

the words, "For this our heart is faint," etc.,[1] it is plain that he attributes the sense of failure and impotence to the guilt that has led to the chastisement. This faintness of heart and the dimness of sight that accompanies it, like the condition of a swooning person, suggest a very different situation from that of the hero struggling against a mountain of difficulties, or that of the martyr triumphing over torture and death. The humiliation is now accounted for, and the explanation of it tears to shreds the last rag of pride with which the fallen people might have attempted to hide it. The abject wretchedness of the Jews is admitted to be the effect of their own sins. No thought can be more depressing. The desolation of Mount Zion, where jackals prowl undisturbed as though it were the wilderness,[2] is a standing testimony to the sin of Israel. Such is the degradation to which the people whom the elegist here represents are reduced. It is a condition of utter helplessness; and yet in it will rise the dawn of hope; for when man is most empty of self he is most ready to receive God. Thus it is that from the deepest pit of humiliation there springs the prayer of trust and hope with which the Book of Lamentations closes.

---

[1] v. 17. [2] ver. 18.

CHAPTER XXIV

THE EVERLASTING THRONE

v. 19-22

WE have lingered long in the valley of humiliation. At the eleventh hour we are directed to look up from this scene of weary gloom to heavenly heights, radiant in sunlight. It is not by accident that the new attitude is suggested only at the very end of the last elegy. The course of the thought and the course of experience that underlies it have been preparing for the change. On entering the valley the traveller must look well to his feet; it is not till he has been a denizen of it for some time that he is able to lift up his eyes to other and brighter realms.

Thus at last our attention is turned from earth to heaven, from man to God. In this change of vision the mood which gave rise to the Lamentations disappears. Since earthly things lose their value in view of the treasures in heaven, the ruin of them also becomes of less account. Thus we read in the *Imitatio*:

> "The life of man is always looking on the things of time,
> Pleased with the pelf of earth,
> Gloomy at loss,
> Pricked by the least injurious word;
> Life touched by God looks on the eternal,—
> With it no cleaving unto time,
> No frown when property is lost,

No sneer when words are harsh,—
Because it puts its treasure and its joy in heaven,
Where nothing fades."

The explanation of this sudden turn is to be found in the fact that for the moment the poet forgets himself and his surroundings in a rapt contemplation of God. This is the glory of adoration, the very highest form of prayer, that prayer in which a man comes nearest to the condition ascribed to angels and the spirits of the blessed who surround the throne and gaze on the eternal light. It is not to be thought of as an idle dreaming like the dreary abstraction of the Indian fanatic who has drilled himself to forget the outside world by reducing his mind to a state of vacancy while he repeats the meaningless syllable *Om*, or the senseless ecstasy of the monk of Mount Athos, who has attained the highest object of his ambition when he thinks he has beheld the sacred light within his own body. It is self-forgetful, not self-centred; and it is occupied with the contemplation of those great truths of the being of God, absorption in which is an inspiration. Here the worshipper is at the river of the water of life, from which if he drinks he will go away refreshed for the battle like the Red-cross knight restored at the healing fountain. It is the misfortune of our own age that it is impractical in the excess of its practicalness when it has not patience for those quiet, calm experiences of pure worship which are the very food of the soul.

The continuance of the throne of God is the idea that now lays hold of the elegist as he turns his thoughts from the miserable scenes of the ruined city to the glory above. This is brought home to his consciousness by the fleeting nature of all things earthly.

He has experienced what the author of the Epistle to the Hebrews describes as "the removing of those things that are shaken, as of things that have been made, that those things which are not shaken may remain."[1] The throne of David has been swept away; but above the earthly wreck the throne of God stands firm, all the more clearly visible now that the distracting influence of the lower object has vanished, all the more valuable now that no other refuge can be found. Men fall like leaves in autumn; one generation follows another in the swift march to death; dynasties which outlive many generations have their day, to be succeeded by others of an equally temporary character; kingdoms reach their zenith, decline and fall. God only remains, eternal, unchangeable. His is the only throne that stands secure above every revolution.

The unwavering faith of our poet is apparent at this point after it has been tried by the most severe tests. Jerusalem has been destroyed, her king has fallen into the hands of the enemy, her people have been scattered; and yet the elegist has not the faintest doubt that her God remains and that His throne is steadfast, immovable, everlasting. This faith reveals a conviction far in advance of that of the surrounding heathen. The common idea was that the defeat of a people was also the defeat of their gods. If the national divinities were not exterminated they were flung down from their thrones, and reduced to the condition of *jins*—demons who avenged themselves on their conquerors by annoying them whenever an opportunity for doing so arose, but with greatly crippled resources. No such notion is ever entertained by the author of these poems

---

[1] Heb. xii. 27.

nor by any of the Hebrew prophets. The fall of Israel in no way affects the throne of God; it is even brought about by His will; it could not have occurred if He had been pleased to hinder it.

Thus the poet was led to find his hope and refuge in the throne of God, the circumstances of his time concurring to turn his thoughts in this direction, since the disappearance of the national throne, the chaos of the sacked city, and the establishment of a new government under the galling yoke of slaves from Babylon, invited the man of faith to look above the shifting powers of earth to the everlasting supremacy of heaven.

This idea of the elegist is in line with a familiar stream of Hebrew thought, and his very words have many an echo in the language of prophet and psalmist, as, for example, in the forty-fifth psalm, where we read, "Thy throne, O God, is for ever and ever."

The grand Messianic hope is founded on the conviction that the ultimate establishment of God's reign throughout the world will be the best blessing imaginable for all mankind. Sometimes this is associated with the advent of a Divinely anointed earthly monarch of the line of David. At other times God's direct sovereignty is expected to be manifested in the "Day of the Lord." The failure of the feeble Zedekiah seems to have discredited the national hopes centred in the royal family. For two generations they slumbered, to be awakened in connection with another disappointing descendant of David, Zerubbabel, the leader of the return. No king was ever equal to the satisfaction of these hopes until the Promised One appeared in the fulness of the times, until Jesus was born into the world to come forth as the Lord's Christ. Meanwhile, since the royal house is under a cloud, the essential Messianic hope turns to God alone. He can deliver His people, and He only. Even apart from personal hopes of rescue, the very idea of the eternal, just reign of God above the transitory thrones of men is a calming, reassuring thought.

It is strange that this idea should ever have lost its fascination among Christian people, who have so much more gracious a revelation of God than was given to the Jews under the old covenant; and yet our Lord's teachings concerning the Fatherhood of God have been set forth as the direct antithesis of the Divine sovereignty, while the latter has been treated as a stern and dreadful function from which it was natural to shrink with fear and trembling. But the truth is the two attributes are mutually illustrative; for he is a very imperfect father who does not rule his own house, and he is a very inadequate sovereign who does not seek to exercise parental functions towards his people. Accordingly, the gospel of Christ is the gospel of the kingdom. Thus the good news declared by the first evangelists was to the effect that the kingdom of God was at hand, and our Lord taught us to pray, "Thy kingdom come." For Christians, at least as much as for Jews, the eternal sovereignty of God should be a source of profound confidence, inspiring hope and joy.

Now the elegist ventures to expostulate with God on the ground of the eternity of His throne. God had not abdicated, though the earthly monarch had been driven from his kingdom. The overthrow of Zedekiah had left the throne of God untouched. Then it was not owing to inability to come to the aid of the suffering people that the eternal King did not intervene to put an end to their miseries. A long time had passed since the siege, and still the Jews were in distress.

It was as though God had forgotten them or voluntarily forsaken them. This is a dilemma to which we are often driven. If God is almighty can He be also all-merciful? If what we knew furnished all the possible data of the problem this would be indeed a serious position. But our ignorance silences us.

Some hint of an explanation is given in the next phrase of the poet's prayer. God is besought to turn the people to Himself. Then they had been moving away from Him. It is like the old popular ideas of sunset. People thought the sun had forsaken the earth, when, in fact, their part of the earth had forsaken the sun. But if the wrong is on man's side on man's side must be the amendment. Under these circumstances it is needless and unjust to speculate as to the cause of God's supposed neglect or forgetfulness.

There can be no reasonable doubt that the language of the elegy here points to a personal and spiritual change. We cannot water it down to the expression of a desire to be restored to Palestine. Nor is it enough to take it as a prayer to be restored to God's favour. The double expression,

"Turn Thou us unto Thee, O Lord, *and we shall be turned*,"

points to a deeper longing, a longing for real conversion, the turning round of the heart and life to God, the return of the prodigal to his Father. We think of the education of the race, the development of mankind, the culture of the soul; and in so thinking we direct our attention to important truths which were not so well within the reach of our forefathers. On the other hand, are we not in danger of overlooking another series of reflections on which they dwelt more persistently? It is not the fact that the world is marching straight on to perfection in an unbroken line of evolution. There are breaks in the progress and long halts, deviations from the course and retrograde movements. We err and go astray, and then continuance in an evil way does not bring us out to any position of advance; it only plunges us down deeper falls of ruin. Under such circumstances, a more radical change than anything progress or education can produce is called for if ever we are even to recover our lost ground, not to speak of advancing to higher attainments. In the case of Israel it was clear that there could be no hope until the nation made a complete moral and religious revolution. The same necessity lies before every soul that has drifted into the wrong way. This subject has been discredited by being treated too much in the abstract, with too little regard for the actual condition of men and women. The first question is, What is the tendency of the life? If that is away from God, it is needless to discuss theories of conversion; the fact is plain that in the present instance some conversion is needed. There is no reason to retain a technical term, and perhaps it would be as well to abandon it if it were found to be degenerating into a mere cant phrase. This is not a question of words. The urgent necessity is concerned with the actual turning round of the leading pursuits of life.

In the next place, it is to be observed that the turning here contemplated is positive in its aims, not merely a flight from the wrong way. It is not enough to cast out the evil spirit, and leave the house swept and garnished, but without a tenant to take care of it. Evil can only be overcome by good. To turn from sin to blank vacancy and nothingness is an impossibility. The great motive must be the attraction of a better course rather than revulsion from the old life. This is the reason why the preaching of the gospel of Christ succeeds where pure appeals to conscience fail.

By his *Serious Call to the Unconverted* William Law started a few earnest men thinking; but he could not anticipate the Methodist revival although he prepared the way for it. The reason seems to be that appeals to conscience are depressing, necessarily and rightly so; but some cheering encouragement is called for if energy is to be found for the tremendous effort of turning the whole life upon its axle. Therefore it is not the threat of wrath but the gospel of mercy that leads to what may be truly called conversion.

Then we may notice, further, that the particular aim of the change here indicated is to turn back to God. As sin is forsaking God, so the commencement of a better life must consist in a return to Him. But this is not to be regarded as a means towards some other end. We must not have the home-coming made use of as a mere convenience. It must be an end in itself, and the chief end of the prayer and effort of the soul, or it can be nothing at all. It appears as such in the passage now under consideration. The elegist writes as though he and the people whom he represents had arrived at the conviction that their supreme need was to be brought back into near and happy relations with God. The hunger for God breathes through these words. This is the truest, deepest, most Divine longing of the soul. When once it is awakened we may be sure that it will be satisfied. The hopelessness of the condition of so many people is not only that they are estranged from God, but that they have no desire to be reconciled to Him. Then the kindling of this desire is itself a great step towards the reconciliation.

And yet the good wish is not enough by itself to attain its object. The prayer is for God to turn the people back to Himself. We see here the mutual relations of the human and the Divine in the process of the recovery of souls. So long as there is no willingness to return to God nothing can be done to force that action on the wanderer. The first necessity, therefore, is to awaken the prayer which seeks restoration. But this prayer must be for the action of God. The poet knows that it is useless simply to resolve to turn. Such a resolution may be repeated a thousand times without any result following, because the fatal poison of sin is like a snake bite that paralyses its victims. Thus we read in the *Theologia Germanica*, "And in this bringing back and healing, I can, or may, or shall do nothing of myself, but simply yield to God, so that He alone may do all things in me and work, and I may suffer Him and all His work and His Divine will." The real difficulty is not to change our own hearts and lives; that is impossible. And it is not expected of us. The real difficulty is rather to reach a consciousness of our own disability. It takes the form of unwillingness to trust ourselves entirely to God for Him to do for us and in us just whatever He will.

The poet is perfectly confident that when God takes His people in hand to lead them round to Himself He will surely do so. If He turns them they will be turned. The words suggest that previous efforts had been made from other quarters, and had failed. The prophets, speaking from God, had urged repentance, but their words had been ineffectual. It is only when God undertakes the work that there is any chance of success. But then success is certain. This truth was illustrated in the preaching of the cross by St. Paul at Corinth, where it was found to be the *power* of God. It is seen repeatedly in the fact that the worst, the oldest, the most hardened are brought round to a new life by the miracle of redeeming power. Herein we have the root principle of Calvinism, the secret of the marvellous vigour of a system which, at the first blush of it, would seem to be depressing rather than encouraging. Calvinism directed the thoughts of its disciples away from self, and man, and the world, for the inspiration of all life and energy. It bade them confess their own impotence and God's almightiness. All who could trust themselves to such a faith would find the secret of victory.

Next, we see that the return is to be a renewal of a previous condition. The poet prays, "Renew our days as of old"—a phrase which suggests the recovery of apostates. Possibly here we have some reference to more external conditions. There is a hope that the prosperity of the former times may be brought back. And yet the previous line, which is concerned with the spiritual return to God, should lead us to take this one also in a spiritual sense. We think of Cowper's melancholy regret—

> "Where is the blessedness I knew
> When first I saw the Lord?"

The memory of a lost blessing makes the prayer for restoration the more intense. It is of God's exceeding lovingkindness that His compassions fail not, so that He does not refuse another opportunity to those who have proved faithless in the past. In some respects restoration is more difficult than a new beginning. The past will not come back. The innocence of childhood, when once it is lost, can never be restored. That first, fresh bloom of youth is irrecoverable. On the other hand, what the restoration lacks in one respect may be more than made up in other directions. Though the old paradise will not be regained, though it has withered long since, and the site of it has become a desert, God will create new heavens and a new earth which shall be better than the lost past. And this new state will be a real redemption, a genuine recovery of what was essential to the old condition. The vision of God had been enjoyed in the old, simple days, and though to weary watchers sobered by a sad experience, the vision of God will be restored in the more blessed future.

In our English Bible the last verse of the chapter reads like a final outburst of the language of despair. It seems to say that the prayer is all in vain, for God has utterly forsaken His people. So it was understood by the Jewish critics who arranged to repeat the previous verse at the end of the chapter to save the omen, that the Book should not conclude with so gloomy a thought. But another rendering is now generally accepted, though our Revisers have only placed it in the margin. According to this we read, "*Unless* Thou hast utterly rejected us," etc. There is still a melancholy tone in the sentence, as there is throughout the Book that it concludes; but this is softened, and now it by no means breathes the spirit of despair. Turn it round, and the phrase will even contain an encouragement. If God has not utterly rejected His people assuredly He will attend to their prayer to be restored to Him. But it cannot be that He has quite cast them off. Then it must be that He will respond and turn them back to Himself. If our hope is only conditioned by the question whether God has utterly forsaken us it is perfectly safe, because the one imaginable cause of shipwreck can never arise. There is but one thing that might make our trust in God vain and fruitless; and that one thing is impossible, nay, inconceivable. So wide and deep is our Father's love, so firm is the adamantine strength of His eternal fidelity, we may be absolutely confident that, though the mountains be removed and cast into the sea, and though the solid earth melt away beneath our feet, He will still abide as the Eternal Refuge of His children, and therefore that He will never fail to welcome all who seek His grace to help them return to Him in true penitence and filial trust. Thus we are led even by this most melancholy book in the Bible to see, as with eyes purged by tears, that the love of God is greater than the sorrow of man, and His redeeming power more mighty than the sin which lies at the root of the worst of that sorrow, the eternity of His throne, in spite of the present havoc of evil in the universe, assuring us that the end of all will be not a mournful elegy, but a pæan of victory.

www.ingramcontent.com/pod-product-compliance
Lightning Source LLC
Chambersburg PA
CBHW032352230426
43672CB00007B/672